Lawyers at Midlife

Laying the Groundwork
for the Road Ahead

D0911809

CAREER RESOURCES FOR A LIFE IN THE LAW

Solo By Choice
How to Be the Lawyer You Always Wanted to Be

By Carolyn Elefant • $45 / 300 pages. (January 2008)

Lawyers at Midlife
A Personal & Financial Retirement Planner for Boomer Attorneys

By Michael Long & John Clyde • $35 / 228 pages. (October 2008)

Should You Really Be a Lawyer?
A Decision-Making Guide to Law School and Beyond

By Deborah Schneider & Gary Belsky • $25 / 248 pages

What Can You Do With a Law Degree?
Career Alternatives Inside, Outside & Around the Law

By Cheryl Heisler • $30 / 300 pages (6th edition, March 2009)

Running From the Law
Why Good Lawyers Are Getting Out of the Legal Profession

By Deborah Arron • $17 / 192 pages (3rd edition)

The Complete Guide to Contract Lawyering
What Every Lawyer & Law Firm Should Know About Temporary Legal Services

By Deborah Arron & Deborah Guyol • $30 / 288 pages (3rd edition)

Should You Marry a Lawyer?
A Couple's Guide to Balancing Work, Love & Ambition

By Fiona Travis, Ph.D. • $19/ 168 pages

Order individual copies and boxed sets at Books@LawyerAvenue.com

Lawyers at Midlife

Laying the Groundwork for the Road Ahead

MICHAEL LONG

JOHN CLYDE, PAT FUNK

A Personal & Financial Retirement Planner for Lawyers

DecisionBooks
Seattle, Washington

Published by DecisionBooks
DecisionBooks is an imprint of LawyerAvenue Press,
A division of Avenue Productions, Inc.

Cover concept by Sandra Imre
Cover and interior design by Rose Michelle Taverniti

DecisionBooks are available at special discounts for bulk purchases. For
information, write to LawyerAvenue Press, 4701 SW Admiral Way #278,
Seattle WA 98116, or e-mail us at *books@LawyerAvenue.com.*

Library of Congress Cataloging-in-Publication Data

Long, Michael P., 1953-
   Lawyers at midlife : laying the groundwork for the road ahead / Mike
Long, John Clyde, Pat Funk.
      p. cm.
   Includes bibliographical references.
   ISBN 978-0-940675-60-5
   1. Lawyers—United States—Retirement. 2. Retirement—United States—
Planning. I. Clyde, John, 1936- II. Funk, Pat, 1952- III. Title.
   KF297.L66 2008
   332.024′0140883400973—dc22
                              2008027107

Why We Wrote This Book

If there is a script for laying the groundwork for retirement, I certainly didn't follow it. My 20's were spent on travel, college, marriage, law school, and two state bar exams. My 30's were about starting a family and launching my law career. When I hit my 40's, I assumed primary care-giving responsibilities for my aging parents. Now in my 50's, I've got one daughter starting college, and my youngest is still in high school.

Through it all—husband, parent, care-giver, lawyer, and lawyer assistance professional—there have been many conflicting priorities and interests along the way, all of them competing for a limited amount of discretionary income that otherwise might be invested for the future. Of course, this is a common refrain; so common these days that those of us coping with the needs of our children and our aging parents are often referred to as "the sandwich generation". This was not the script for the generation of lawyers preceding us. Which is why Boomer lawyers will need all the creativity and ingenuity we can muster to navigate midlife.

In my 14 years as a peer-counselor for the Oregon Attorney Assistance Program (OAAP), I've helped lawyers work through all sorts of job and career crises: solo and small firm practitioners, lawyers in mid- and large-firms, government lawyers, judges. I remember one lawyer in particular: a distinguished man in his early 70's. One day, he dropped by our weekly career support group. When it was his turn to speak, he said he had been a sole practitioner for more than 40 years, and once had a wide network of lawyers who referred him cases. But over time, his contacts had either retired or died. And without their referrals, it was getting increasingly difficult to make ends meet. He hoped our group could introduce him to attorneys new to practice who would be interested in having him help them with cases. Why this remains such a vivid memory is because it was so sad to watch this distinguished lawyer try to sell himself to new admittees 40 years his junior. Sadder still, his situation need not have been so dire.

In recent years, I've witnessed other pre-retirement scenarios just as preventable. For example:

- Lawyers in their 50's and 60's with nearly nothing saved for retirement or emergencies who faced mental and physical health impairments.
- Lawyers who chose to retire, but soon after leaving the law felt purposeless or devalued without their lawyer role and lawyer identity.
- Lawyers who could no longer meet the performance expectations of their firms but couldn't envision or find employment alternatives.
- Aging lawyers who could afford to retire, but didn't know what they would do if they couldn't practice law.
- Lawyers who experience anxiety and depression when they put their retirement plans in motion.

When I recommended that the OAAP offer retirement workshops for lawyers and judges, I found a number of decent books on retirement; even a *Dummies* guide. But when it came to helping one particular group—lawyers—navigate the personal, financial, and professional challenges of what the ABA calls the "second season of service", I didn't find much of anything. Lacking such a resource, I decided to join with my co-authors John and Pat to write one.

Lawyers at Midlife is not a light read, and it's not a feel-good retirement book. At its core, it's a workbook; a planning tool intended to help mid- and late-career lawyers look down the road and lay the groundwork for the next chapter of their lives. Our goals for the book are modest: we want to prompt you with important questions…to share the insights of other lawyers…to help you take inventory of your retirement needs…and to develop and implement a plan to meet your goals and objectives. We understand that your time is critical. And in the world of billable hours, you might be tempted to skim these pages. We urge you not to. The book's greatest value will come from completing the self-assessment exercises, financial inventories, and worksheets. If you commit to making the most of this book, you will be better prepared to lay the groundwork for a richer, more satisfying retirement transition.

Michael Long, Esq.
John Clyde, CFP
Pat Funk
August, 2008

CONTENTS

The Five Myths of Retirement

If retirement isn't here yet, you don't need to think about it.

Retirement is simple: you just need to stop working.

Retirement will be a permanent vacation.

If you have enough money to retire, you will be fine.

You are going to love spending all that extra time with your spouse.

—JOHN TRAUTH, *YOUR RETIREMENT, YOUR WAY*

CHAPTER 1

Should We Even Call it Retirement?

"The other day a colleague called me and said, 'I'm thinking about changing my practice. I don't know exactly what I want to do, but I definitely don't want to call it 'retirement.'"

—A FORMER STATE SUPREME COURT JUSTICE.

Once upon a time, retirement meant a final withdrawal or exit from the world of work. Retirees lived off pensions, savings and/or investments, and pursued a life free of schedules, external expectations, and the stress of employment. It was a time to finally do what they wanted when they wanted. This once-traditional view of retirement was based on several assumptions: a) retirees did not like their work, b) their ability to perform inevitably deteriorated, and c) they considered leisure more satisfying than work.[1]

The American model of retirement never really applied to lawyers, though, and it will probably be even less true for Boomer lawyers (born between 1946 and 1964) and the generations of lawyers behind them. Here are just three examples of how differently some Boomers are approaching their so-called "retirement" years:

- *Bill*, a former Navy aviator, spent more than 20 years in small, medium and large firms, and the last 11 in solo practice. In his spare time, he kept adding to his flight log. By his late 50's, what Bill called the "novelty of law" had worn thin, and he was mourning the death of several friends and clients. "You keep practicing law for much longer," said his wife one day, "and you'll be just like them." Bill agreed, and at 62 decided to close his law practice and return to flying full-time as a flight instructor and aviation tour guide.

- *Stan* spent most of his 31-year career as an in-house counsel to a major corporation and retired from full-time practice in his mid-50s to establish a part-time practice. Now 64, he's got more referral work than he wants, and his schedule is still his own. "At my age, I don't mind turning down work. I've gotten used to being able to go where I want and when I want."

- *John*, a career lawyer, saw himself headed for the same traditional retirement as his father. So, in his 50's, he closed his practice, bought a boat, and sailed to Central America. After a year, John joined the Peace Corps, and helped establish a library in a Guatemalan village. "No one ever hugged me as a lawyer," he told me, "But as a teacher I got hugged all the time". John is now back in the US, helping develop low-income housing. His law practice is still closed, but he doesn't consider himself retired. "I think of myself as having been on sabbatical since 1996."

Hundreds of thousands of Boomer lawyers are expected to start retiring over the next 10 to 15 years (as many as a quarter-million by 2011, according to the ABA), but what sort of *retirement* will it be…or should we even call it *retirement*? In fact, most of the lawyers interviewed for this book—men and women in their 50's, 60's, 70's (even 80's)—have no desire to turn their back on work for a life of leisure. Why? Because as lawyers, most of us derive a high degree of purpose, meaning, and satisfaction from our work and our service to clients. This was amply confirmed in the Lawyer Satisfaction Survey conducted in 2007 by the Oregon Attorney Assistance Program (see Appendix 2).

Here in the Pacific Northwest, the OAAP has offered retirement-planning workshops since 2001. As one of its developers, I made a point of evaluating several retirement surveys in hopes of finding one specific to the legal profession. Unable to find one, we developed our own, and set out to contact active and inactive members of our State Bar age 50 and older, and a second, younger, group of Boomers born between 1957 and 1964. In all, 1,100 Oregon lawyers (a third of them women) shared their insights, observations, and concerns about retirement

A discussion of the Oregon Lawyer Retirement Survey has been included as Appendix 1. A few results worth noting here:

• Most Boomer lawyers in our survey plan to continue working well into the so-called "retirement years", with 40 percent planning to continue practicing after age 70, and 11 percent planning to practice full or part-time until they die or are no longer capable of practicing.

• The motivation to continue to practice is economic for some, however, for most it is mainly for the stimulation, sense of purpose and satisfaction that it provides.

• Boomer lawyers are generally optimistic about the next chapter of life. Almost half of the 50-and-older lawyers reported feeling *very optimistic* about their retirement years, 39 percent reported feeling *somewhat optimistic* about their retirement years, and only 15 percent reported not feeling *optimistic* about their retirement years.

- In looking ahead toward retirement, their primary concerns were: projecting their long-term financial and health care needs; and anticipating that retirement will result in the loss of intellectual stimulation and professional affiliations and camaraderie.
- A noteworthy 71 percent see retirement as a time to begin a new chapter in life, being active and involved, starting new activities and setting new goals.

In short, the healthiest, longest-lived, best educated, most affluent generation of lawyers this country has ever produced is eager to stay in the game, and is busy creating a new model of retirement. One phenomenon powering this new model is that today's lawyers at midlife are maintaining a much higher level of mental and physical functioning through midlife and into late adulthood. The average healthy 65-year-old American today is functioning mentally and physically at the level that our parent's generation functioned when they were 50, and the majority of the extra 20 or 30 years of longevity added in the last century have really been added to the middle of life when we are still at our prime, rather than at the end of aging. Consequently, this "down-aging" phenomenon is adding many extra innings of active engagement.

> ▶ The healthiest, longest-lived, best-educated, most affluent generation of lawyers this country ever produced is eager to stay in the game, and is busy creating a new model of retirement.

We hope that our book will help you envision, explore and plan for your personal transition from midlife to the retirement you choose to create. As you begin, give careful consideration to the following 10 questions:

- Do you really want to retire, and if so, when?
- What is your vision of retirement, and do you and your spouse/partner share the same the vision?
- Where do you want to retire to?
- What's your strategy for building and preserving a nest egg?
- What assets do you have for retirement, and are they invested in the most beneficial ways to achieve your goals?
- How much money will you need to support your lifestyle in retirement?
- What kind of relationships—personal and financial—do you want to have with your children and parents in later life?
- How will you and your spouse/partner approach, and manage, getting older?
- Do you have an estate plan?
- What will your legacy be?

CHAPTER 2

The Elements of Transition

"Leaving my firm felt like diving off a cliff without
knowing if the tide was in or out. To some extent,
I still feel that way two years later."

—Frank, retired after 31 years in large-firm practice

As lawyers, we like to imagine retirement as being within our control (rather than having it imposed on us), and we look forward to it as a time when we finally have the freedom and resources to do what we want when we want.

And yet, even when the stars align, and our planning and preparation produce the freedom of choice we imagined, retirement is a time of psychological and emotional adjustment, a roller coaster capable of unanticipated endings, losses, beginnings, and new perspectives. In short, in an age-defying culture, retirement has become a phase of life that no one—least of all the retiree—can accurately predict how it will play out.

Consider Dennis' situation: After 30 years as a successful plaintiff's lawyer, he had earned enough from his practice and his investments that he no longer needed to work. Over a period of years, he reduced his caseload, and handed off the cases he wasn't able to settle to junior partners for trial. Increasingly, he began taking more time off from work, he established a foundation for abused and neglected children, and he even flirted with the idea of working there after leaving his practice.

> . . . I've always been very busy in my practice. Always had a lot of clients, a lot of trial work. Always enjoyed the challenge of a law practice. But as I get close to retirement age, the question I have the most trouble with is, 'Why have I not totally given up my practice'? My kids and my wife are all pushing me to do it, so I really can't say why I still come to the office. It is just very, very difficult to make this transition from being a lawyer to doing philanthropic work. I used to think retirement was all about money: would we have enough, would our kids be secure? But now, as I think about retiring from my practice, it reminds me that this is not just the end of a career, but a step toward eventual death. That kind of hits you like a ton of bricks.

Dennis did finally set a date to retire, and soon after began to experience a shortness of breath. On one occasion he thought he was suffering a heart attack and was rushed to an emergency room. He had suffered a panic attack instead.

We experience change every day. Most of it is mundane; but some of it significant enough to disturb the status quo and transform how we see ourselves and life itself. For example:

Attending law school and becoming licensed to practice
Falling in love and choosing a life partner
The end of an intimate relationship
Our first law job
Marriage
The birth of a child
The death of a parent or significant other
Divorce
Making (or not making) partner
Losing a job
Serious injury or personal illness

Some of these events are developmental and predictable, others are like bolts of summer lightning. Either way, they usually set in motion a period of psychological and emotional adjustment, demanding that we let go of the way things used to be before we can establish a new homeostasis and emotional equilibrium. Our culture doesn't adequately prepare us for these "periods of transition". Instead, what we accept as the norm (or what we hope for anyway) is a smooth progression through life's developmental stages. Ultimately, though, reality trumps expectation, and all of us will experience varying periods of relative stability interrupted by change, loss and instability. In my experience, too many lawyers approaching the retirement years focus on financial and health-related issues, and fail to anticipate feelings of loss, discomfort and disorientation.

▶ Too many lawyers approaching retirement focus on financial and health-related issues, and fail to anticipate feelings of loss, discomfort and disorientation.

A few years ago, two University of Washington psychiatrists developed a scale that weighed the stress associated with major life events. They found that retirement was the 11th most stressful of 43 major life events, and that it was as stressful as attempting a marriage reconciliation, and nearly as stressful as being fired from a job. As a peer-counselor who works with lawyers, I completely agree. In my work, I have observed that at the point a lawyer decides to retire and begins to take concrete steps toward leaving the practice of law it triggers significant stress and anxiety.

Lawyers at midlife. Each of us moves through transitional periods in our own way. There are, however, predictable feelings, emotions and stages. And for the retiring lawyer, the experience is different for individuals fortunate enough to have chosen the timing of their retirement…than those who are not so fortunate.

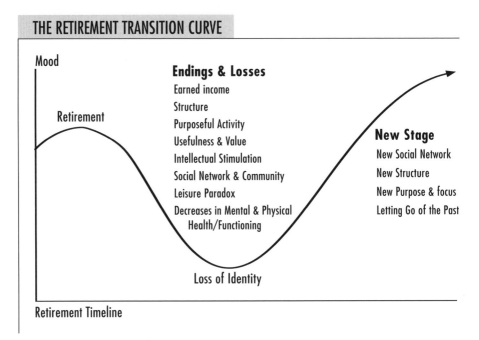

THE RETIREMENT TRANSITION CURVE

Mood

Retirement

Endings & Losses
Earned income
Structure
Purposeful Activity
Usefulness & Value
Intellectual Stimulation
Social Network & Community
Leisure Paradox
Decreases in Mental & Physical
      Health/Functioning

New Stage
New Social Network
New Structure
New Purpose & focus
Letting Go of the Past

Loss of Identity

Retirement Timeline

If you're fortunate to have chosen the timing of your retirement from law—and you have accumulated sufficient financial resources to maintain your lifestyle—you're likely to enjoy a positive swing in mood and outlook. For this reason, many of the retired lawyers I've met, counseled, or interviewed, report a tremendous sense of new-found freedom: for the first time in a long, long time they can travel, spend time with family, and engage in creative, long-deferred activities and exploration without having to measure life in two-tenths-of-an-hour increments.

What they don't yet realize is that their new-found freedom is just another phase. Sometime later—and it's different for everyone—the new retiree begins experiencing unanticipated emotions and discomfort. It is the time when many lawyers struggle to find activities that provide a sense of purpose and meaning…when they feel less valuable and valued…when they wrestle with questions of personal and professional identity. This, too, is a stage. And as the newly retired lawyer moves through the retirement transition, he or she typically experiences a rise and fall in mood and level of satisfaction.

If, however, a lawyer's retirement is imposed because of declining health, a decline in their practice, or because of their firm's mandatory age restrictions, such individuals may immediately encounter feelings of anxiety and loss upon retiring. According to research, *"Involuntary retirees have the most negative retirement experience, whereas voluntary retirees (e.g., who retired to pursue their own interests) report high satisfaction with retirement."*

Elements of Transition: Endings & Losses

…As a solo practitioner, just thinking about retiring made me feel powerless. I couldn't sleep because my head was filled with what-ifs: what if retirement was the wrong choice, what if I retired and went broke, what if I couldn't handle retirement and had to face the humiliation of going back to work?' It wasn't as if we didn't have a healthy portfolio; we did. But I worried that we might not be able to generate the kind of income that would let us live well. Believe me, the anxiety kept me awake more than a few nights.

—DICK, **63**, RECALLING THE PERIOD PRECEDING HIS RETIREMENT.

One of the first endings many retiring lawyers experience is the loss of earned income—the end of a regular draw or paycheck. This comes with some anxiety, and with good reason. Too many lawyers live at the edge of their financial means, their lifestyle expanding in direct relationship to increases in their income. As long as they continue working, they don't mind incurring debt to pay for additional needs and wants. But when they finally decide to close down their practice or leave their firm or agency, the parameters of their lifestyle are suddenly determined by whatever pension they might receive, and whatever savings, investments and home equity they might have acquired. For most of us, this loss of income highlights whatever uncertainty we have about the ability of our nest egg to support us and our spouse or partner.

The loss of a revenue stream is a major turning point in anyone's career, but for lawyers there are at least six other endings and losses that merit close attention:

Loss of identity. Once a lawyer steps onto the practice treadmill, it's difficult to step off. And after years, more often decades, of living and working reactively and postponing non-law pursuits and pleasures, it can be difficult to get in touch with your non-law interests and potential passions. You forget how to explore these parts of yourself in the way you did so naturally when you were a child, an adolescent, and a young pre-lawyer adult. Fearing the loss of one's professional identity is frequently voiced by lawyer's contemplating retirement, and, in fact, lawyers do experience a loss of part of their identity in the early stages of their retirement.

Until the last few years, I really did see myself only as a lawyer, and that's why I thought I would continue practicing law as long as I'm healthy. But I got involved in remodeling residential properties, and now it's grabbed my attention enough that I could probably be persuaded to leave my practice. —JOANNE, A FAMILY LAW ATTORNEY IN HER 60'S.

Loss of intellectual stimulation. Lawyers place a high value on intellectual stimulation, and are drawn to analyzing and solving complex problems. Practicing law fulfills that need for intellectual stimulation. But as we choose to transition from the practice of law, it is imperative to find other activities and endeavors that can quench this intellectual thirst. The lawyer in retirement needs something more than the New York Times crossword puzzle to keep their mind active. "It was true for me," said one lawyer. "After leaving work and volunteering for two years, I was going nuts. I really yearned for something I could sink my teeth into."

Loss of feeling useful and valued. Despite the demands of a full-time practice, most lawyers have a strong desire to help others even when it seems everyone wants a piece of them. In the early stages of retirement, though, lawyers often miss being in demand, and they feel less useful as a consequence. It was true for Tom, who left large firm practice after 20 years. "As stressful as the project deadlines or the crisis calls were," he said, "I always had a sense of really helping people and helping their business run smoothly. That's what I miss most about the practice of law." Several lawyers I interviewed noticed a related phenomenon: in the "phase-down"

> ▶ Lawyers in retirement need something more than the New York Times crossword puzzle to keep their minds active. "It was true for me," said one lawyer. "After leaving work and volunteering for two years, I was going nuts. I really yearned for something I could sink my teeth into."

of their practices, they experienced a sense of failure upon realizing that they no longer had the energy or motivation to take on the type of complex matters they once did without a second thought. And, as phase-down partners, they felt less valued by their firms because, unlike full-time partners, they didn't take on ownership of a case and see it through to resolution.

Loss of social and professional network. A loss regularly reported by lawyers who have retired is the loss of regular contact with coworkers and colleagues. Most lawyers work long hours. Many spend far more time with their coworkers and colleagues than with anyone else in their social network, and coworkers and colleagues serve to satisfy a significant part of their social needs. If a lawyer hasn't taken the opportunity to broaden their social network prior to retiring, retirement will result in a significant social loss and in feeling far less connected to others. "No matter how much fun you plan to have in retirement, you've got to expect losses," said John, who closed his practice at 52. "After I retired, some of the people who I thought were friends stopped returning my calls. You've got to be ready for things like this. You've got to accept that you're moving on, and just move. That's part of retirement planning, too."

Loss of leisure. By its nature, retirement provides more time for leisure…or does it? According to psychologist Richard Johnson, there is a catch. In his book, *The New Retirement*, he writes, "One of the paradoxes of leisure is that for an activity to be leisure it must be a diversion: a vacation, a breather, a break, a new space. Making leisure the central, and perhaps the only focus of our retired lives, we risk not having any leisure at all. When leisure becomes the primary focal point of living, it ceases to provide the essential pleasure and rejuvenation that it is intended to provide. Leisure loses its luster when it takes central stage in our lives. The paradox of leisure is that it must remain secondary to what is the primary focus of our life if it is to retain its ability to refresh us."[1]

▶ When you practice, your schedule is influenced by court calendars and clients. Without that external structure, retired lawyers often experience an uncomfortable loss of focus and direction.

Loss of structure and purpose. When you practice law, you don't have to decide how you are going to spend each day. Your schedule is influenced by court calendars or client needs and expectations. But without the external structure that work provides, retired lawyers often experience an uncomfortable loss of focus and direction. And those who haven't developed regularly scheduled activities—contract work, volunteering, hobbies, educational outlets—learn how stressful retirement can be. One lawyer, now semi-retired after almost 40 years as a business and real estate lawyer, says some of his colleagues refuse to retire because they can't cope with unstructured time. "Some," he says, "Are even afraid to take a sabbatical. They can't conceive how they might spend even a few months away from the practice of law."

Elements of Transition: What Do I Do Now?

In my consulting work with lawyers, they often recall with pleasure the activities for which they were so passionate before law school—music, athletics, politics, science, outdoor activities, and intellectual exploration, to name just a few. Many describe how these activities were sacrificed when they enrolled in law school and made the pursuit of academic and employment opportunities their top priority. Musical instruments were packed away, fiction and nonfiction were replaced by casebooks, and leisure time with family, friends and life partners was cut short. Sitting for the bar exam followed, after which there was the search for one's first job, and the subsequent discovery that the law is indeed a jealous mistress.

In the tug-of-war between the personal and the professional, all too often our clients and our practice require—or are willingly given—priority. And somewhere along the way we lose touch with aspects of our interests, our passions, our own identity. For so many of us, it reads like a grim re-enactment of Herman Hesse's *Beneath the Wheel*.

When it comes to a satisfying retirement, there is no one-size-fits-all formula. Because, like the life stages that precede it, each person approaches the retirement years with individual preferences, interests, values, experiences, strengths, challenges, hopes, dreams and concerns. And together with a life partner, you shape a life in retirement that works for you. What are you meant to do at this stage of your life?

What follows are the profiles of two lawyers who thought it important enough to ask the question before they retired.

PROFILES IN RETIREMENT: FRANK'S STORY

At age 55, Frank—a senior partner at a large Philadelphia law firm—preceded retirement with a year-long sabbatical. He chose to be a Jesuit volunteer, working in a residential treatment program for indigent men in Portland, Oregon. Taking his leave of absence in Portland was no coincidence; three of his four children lived there. At the end of his leave, Frank and his wife returned to Philadelphia, and he resumed his practice. However, when their first grandchild was born, Frank's wife returned to Portland to help out, and after several months they purchased a home there. For about a year, Frank commuted between Philadelphia and the Pacific Northwest, having reduced his caseload and taken a voluntary pay-cut. One day, he was visiting a childhood friend who was terminally ill when the treatment center where he had volunteered called to offer him a full-time position as a counselor. It was an agonizing decision; it meant retiring after 32 years in law. In the end, Frank accepted the offer.

"…Back in law school, my short-term goal was to be a Vista Lawyer for a couple of years. But by the time I finished law school, my wife and I had two children. So, I put my dream of service on a back burner for about 30 years. In that time, I felt that making a change…other than to go to another law firm…was not really an option for me because by then we had four children, and there never seemed to be enough money. In those early years, the practice of law felt oppressive to me. At times, it was challenging and exciting, but mostly oppressive. So at a pretty early age I decided to retire before I was 60. My sabbatical year was good, and I was very happy doing the work. But I don't think I fully realized how much anxiety I would have about leaving Philadelphia. I don't do real well with change, and leaving the practice of law—let alone my firm, my friends and the city where I grew up—would be a pretty drastic thing to do. But after consulting a financial planner I realized that if we adopted a slightly more frugal lifestyle we would have enough money to retire and relocate. And that's what we did. To this day, I don't believe all that's happened to me. In my head I do, but not in my gut. I mean, the combination of getting that call to be a counselor just at the time in my life when I was faced with the idea that I would not live forever…and that if I wanted to do other things I had better start doing them…persuaded me to accept the job and leave my practice. I don't regret my decision for a moment. But as much as I like Portland and playing with my grandsons, I miss Philadelphia, I miss the Phillies, I miss the Eagles, and I miss the intellectual challenge of practicing law." ●

At a time when most of his peers were protesting the Vietnam War, Bill enlisted and was accepted into the Naval Aviation Program. Upon graduating from college, and successfully completing flight training, Bill was assigned to a carrier–based jet squadron…and the next three years were the fulfillment of a dream. In 1969, Bill, now married, chose not to re-enlist, and decided instead to return to his hometown of Madison, WI, to start law school at the University of Wisconsin. In time, Bill would work in small, medium, and large firms in Madison, Phoenix, Arizona, and Portland, OR. As a sole practitioner the last 11 years, he successfully practiced across a broad spectrum of litigation and transactional practice areas. Throughout most of his legal career, Bill continued to fly, serving stints in both the Air National Guard and the Army National Guard, flying both fixed-wing aircraft and helicopters. At age 62, Bill decided to close his law practice and return to aviation full-time as a flight instructor with his own training company.

▶ "What really got me thinking about retiring was the death of friends and clients, even a young colleague who died at the gym. I remember my wife saying to me, 'With your schedule, if you continue working much longer, you're going to end up just like them."

—A PARTNER AT A MIDSIZED FIRM

"I gave it a lot of thought, but I just felt that after 33 years the novelty of practicing law was wearing thin. The pressures of practicing law have increased dramatically. Collegiality is elusive, everyone is concerned with how many hours you bill, and, because of the type of clients I represent, I don't always get paid. But what really got me thinking about retiring was the death of a few friends, including one relatively young male lawyer who died while exercising at the gym. And there were several clients and dear friends who lost their battle with cancer and heart disease. I remember one night my wife saying to me, 'You keep up this crap (a grueling schedule) for many more years, and you are going to be just like them.' Before I actually made the decision to retire, I started telling other lawyers I wanted to close my practice to start a new flight instruction business, I thought they would say I was crazy to give up my practice at my age. They didn't. They said things like, 'Gee, I wish I had something like that.' I think they were a little envious that they didn't have something to transition to. I love teaching flying. It's a hoot, and it doesn't seem fair because it's too much fun and I get paid to do it. Do I have any regrets? Well, I am leaving the profession with a sadness because of how many of my peers and friends appear to be more unhappy practicing law than being fulfilled by it." ●

Elements of Transition: Women Lawyers & Retirement

"For me, full retirement would mean a series of losses—a loss of contact with friends, a loss of stimulating work, a loss of structure. But of all of them, the loss of my identity as a lawyer would be the hardest because it was so difficult for women of my generation to get where we are now." —KATHERINE, SEMI-RETIRED CIVIL LITIGATION ATTORNEY

Historically, retirement was considered a male life stage or life event. Men were perceived as much more identified than women with their occupations and professions. As a consequence, men were supposed to experience a greater identity loss than women at the time of retirement. Recent research, though, indicates just the opposite; the challenges and losses professional women experience at retirement are more *similar* than different to those of their male counterparts. The research shows:

- Women see retirement as an ending to a significant chapter in their lives;
- They believe they will feel a loss of social status after retirement; and,
- They will miss the social interaction their work provides, even if they maintain contact with work related friends after retirement.[2]

But in other ways, retirement as a life event is often different for women lawyers (and non-lawyer women in general) than for men:

- Women assume responsibility for a disproportionate amount of the caregiving of children, aging or infirm spouses, and aging parents or relatives; and, they are more likely to move in and out of work and active practice to administer these responsibilities. In Year 2000, for example, the median age for retired/inactive male lawyers was 74; for women it was 50.
- For women, the opportunity costs of moving in and out of practice/employment include a reduced likelihood of earning promotions/making partner...reduced opportunity for developing a private practice and for professional growth and development...and lost opportunities for matching contributions and compound returns on 401(k) accounts.
- Women lawyers earn less than male lawyers (the Bureau of Labor Statistics reported that in 2005 the median weekly salary of women lawyers was about three-quarters of male lawyers). And women lawyers have been more likely than men to work in the public and nonprofit sectors where compensation is typically lower than in private practice. Consequently, they have fewer opportunities to save and accumulate wealth over their careers.

▶ Women lawyers report higher levels of retirement-related financial concerns, particularly concerning health insurance, Medicare and long-term care insurance.

- Women live longer and are more likely to live alone in old age as a result of being widowed, divorced, separated, or never married. Consequently, they are more likely to require long-term care at the end of their lives.

My mother was a registered nurse who worked until she was 80. After her death, I was struck by how little financial planning she had done, and I wondered how she managed to reach the end of her life with so little savings. Now, as a solo practitioner—and a single mom—the question of saving for the future haunts me, too. Sometimes I feel like I'm walking a tightrope without a net. After law school graduation, I found myself working as a staff lawyer for a county government. I never meant to turn it into a career, but somehow I managed to stick around for nine years. Ultimately, the insanity of local politics took a health toll—physically and mentally. I decided to start a private practice. But to do that I would have to cash in my retirement. I did, and wiped out what little savings I had accumulated, and the relative security of promised future savings as well. The choice I made was as an investment in myself. It gave me the freedom to break free of a toxic situation and create something meaningful for myself. But right now, security feels a long way off.

As I raise my daughter as a single mother, I find myself wondering what sort of lessons I'm leaving her with. Is she going to come out of this experience thinking that a job—any job—is better than self-employment, even if it costs you your health? Is she going to remember my stress at work or my stress over paying bills and providing for our futures? Or is she going to remember the fact that I was there for her where once I was not? I want her to grow up, as I did not—and have struggled to obtain my whole life—with a sense of the value of money and an understanding of the importance of saving. My parents "protected" me from such issues, and I've always wished they hadn't. I've had to acquire such knowledge the hard way, and I think it would have been much easier to grow up with this new-found frugality than to achieve it afterwards as an adult. That extends to retirement. I have no net, and that scares me.

Will I be working when I'm 80 like my mother did? And if so, will I be doing it because I love it, or because I need to?

Right now, I focus on day-to-day survival. But that won't last forever. By the end of my first full year in practice, I intend to set aside money for retirement. Once I have a certain amount saved in a low-risk vehicle, I'll look for a higher-risk, higher-yield potential fund in which to expand my savings. My daughter will be expected to get scholarships and grants, and to contribute to her own college fund. And I'm teaching her how to budget, how to save, how to think about money as something other than merely a means to an immediate gratification.

I wouldn't recommend my path to others; given the circumstances, it was the right thing for me at the time. But perhaps I won't really know that until much later in my life. I would suggest that others in my situation think not only about financial wealth but other forms of wealth as well—your health, your sense of accomplishment and fulfillment, and—most important—the legacy you want to impart to your children.

—SHERYL SISK SCHELIN (THEINSPIREDSOLO.COM) IS A SOLO LAWYER AND BUSINESS COACH PRACTICING IN SOUTH CAROLINA.

All things considered, our lawyer retirement survey (see Appendix I) found that women lawyers reported higher levels of retirement-related financial concerns, particularly concerning health insurance, Medicare and long-term care insurance. These results are consistent with the 2005 survey done by the

Society of Actuaries, which found that women reported higher levels of concern than men that:

> ▶ "Will I be working when I'm 80 like my mother did? And if so, will I be doing it because I love it…or because I need to?"
>
> —SHERYL, A SOLE PRACTITIONER

- They might not be able to maintain a reasonable standard of living for the rest of their (and their spouses) life;
- They might not have enough money to pay for adequate health care; and
- They might deplete all of their savings and be left only with Social Security.

"Women tend to be much more focused on fear and being alone," says Susan Hirshman, a managing director at JPMorgan Funds. *"For men, it's more of a competition: 'Did I get a five percent return?'"*

Elements of Transition: Relationships in Retirement

"I didn't think I'd retire from practice until 60 or later, and then the bomb hit: at age 52, my husband accepted an early-retirement offer from his employer of 30 years."

—MARILYN, SEMI-RETIRED FORMER SOLE PRACTITIONER.

Retirement isn't usually a singular experience; it involves a network of relationships, including a spouse or partner, children, extended family, friends, colleagues, acquaintances. And if you imagine your personal network as a kind of suspended mobile, you know that any movement on your part will affect the rest of the structure. Clearly the one person your retirement will most directly impact is your spouse/partner. Experience has shown that retirement removes a key organizing structure of one's relationship and shakes up old patterns and routines. Or, as that old joke goes, retirement too often means *"twice the husband and half the income."* If you have been fortunate enough to have enjoyed a long-term marriage or relationship, think back at the various issues and decisions you have worked through during your relationship. For example:

How you discovered common interests and activities.
How you both pursued your jobs/careers.
Where you decided to live.
Whether you had, or did not have, children.
How you shared parenting responsibilities and the daily tasks of life.
How you decided where to vacation.
How you dealt with money and financial issues.
What type of relationships you established with your extended families.

How you handled relationships with friends?

And how each of you became involved in your larger community and in what capacity.

Some issues are resolved more successfully than others, while others have a way of remaining emotional loose ends. And when one or both of you retire, many of these same issues often have a way of finding their way "back on the table" for *de novo* review. How stressful this becomes—and I'll introduce that aspect later in the chapter—depends on the communication and conflict resolution skills you developed over the course of your relationship. Hopefully, most lawyers nearing retirement age have discovered that the skills and behaviors that go with a successful legal practice (especially if your practice has been litigation-oriented), are not the same skills and behaviors that make for a close, intimate relationship with your partner and children. Of course, if you have not discovered this, you will certainly have another opportunity to discover it post-retirement.

> ▶ You probably already know that the skills and behaviors that go with a successful legal practice aren't the same ones that make for a close relationship. If you haven't learned it yet, you'll get another opportunity in retirement.

Deciding To Retire

A generation ago, most lawyers approaching retirement were male, and their wives were unlikely to be working outside the home or to have a career of their own. Retirement decisions were typically dictated by the accumulated wealth and health of the lawyer spouse. These days, lawyers approaching retirement are more likely to be one half of a dual-earner couple, which means that retirement decisions require more coordination. And coordinating retirement decisions as a couple is even more difficult when either/both spouses have strong ties to their jobs/careers.

The research of retirement planning and decision-making of couples tells us that:

- Men tend to give more thought to retirement, and to make financial and other plans earlier than women.
- Men are more likely to make unilateral decisions about when they retire, and are more likely to retire as a result of financial incentives and financial factors than women.
- Men are more apt to discuss retirement with friends and co-workers than women.

- Women plan for their future health care needs more than men.
- Women are more likely to report that they retired because their spouse/partner retired.
- About half of couples choose to retire within two years of each other. The likelihood of choosing to retire within two years of each other increases when couples differ in age by not more than two years.
- Individuals with younger spouses are more likely to retire later than those with older spouses, and individuals are more likely to retire if their spouses/partners have already retired.[3]

How Retirement Affects Couples

Researchers at Cornell University looked at 534 married men and women between the ages of 50 and 74 in upstate New York.[4]

Among their findings: both men and women in dual-earner households report greater marital conflict and decreased marital quality during the actual transition to retirement from their primary career jobs.

According to the Cornell study, "(The) evidence shows, for both men and women, that the retirement transition itself is related to decreased marital satisfaction and increased marital conflict. Newly retired men and women report the lowest marital satisfaction and the highest marital conflict, compared with those who are either retired continuously (two or more years) or not yet retired from their primary career jobs. Becoming retired is related to heightened marital conflict when one's spouse remains employed regardless of gender. Yet couples who have been retired for two or more years enjoy higher marital quality than those who have not yet retired."

Men. For men in late mid-life, retiring from one's primary career job is the strongest negative predictor of marital quality: it is related to both lower marital satisfaction and higher marital conflict. Newly retired men tend to report higher marital conflict than those who remain employed in their primary career jobs, or those retired from those jobs for two or more years. And recently retired men whose spouses are employed report the highest marital conflict. Recently retired men whose spouses are not employed report lower levels of conflict in their marriages than those whose spouses are employed.

Women. Women with employed husbands who retire from their primary career and become re-employed report the highest marital satisfaction, followed by retired and re-employed women whose husbands are no longer employed, and women in couples in which both are retired and not working. Retired and re-employed women with employed husbands tend to work fewer hours (22.5) than not yet retired women (42.4 hours). Not-yet retired women with employed husbands report the lowest marital satisfaction. And newly retired women were more depressed than long-retired women, or not-yet-retired women, especially if their husbands remained employed.

For couples, the transition to retirement—like the transition for the individual lawyer—is a gradual one. And couples who do not make the time to discuss their individual hopes and plans for retirement and later life often hit rough patches early in their retirement. "Developing realistic expectations about what retirement will be like, when it will begin, and what it should and should not include is important for couples to address early and revisit often."[5]

How can you and your spouse/partner improve your chances of achieving a smooth transition? By being sensitive to, and making the effort, to improving your conflict management skills. According to Atlanta psychologist David Woodsfellow, "Retirement is one of those times in life when conflict management skills are strongly predictive of how well the couple does or how poorly the couple does. Because all the issues you put off dealing with because you were too busy (before retirement)…well, that's what you're going to deal with when you retire."[6]

Losing a Spouse or Partner

If you are married or have a life partner, you envision sharing your retirement with that person. That assumption is part of the foundation of your retirement plan. Losing that person through death or divorce as you approach retirement, or after you've already retired, only compounds the sense of loss and grief.

One lawyer I know did all the right things to position himself for retirement. He built a successful transactional solo practice…saved and invested well…kept fit…and, when he got within range of retirement, he recruited a younger lawyer to join him and purchase his practice. He structured the purchase over a period of several years so that he could make a slow transition and allow the younger attorney time to cement his relationship with clients. Finally, in his late 60's, with all the pieces in place, my friend retired. A few months later, his wife of 30 years filed for divorce. He made it through, but the experience had a negative impact on his first few years of retirement.

Another attorney of my acquaintance, a Federal criminal defense lawyer, was also making plans for retirement when his wife was diagnosed with lung cancer. "Our dream of retirement died when she passed away," he told me.

"There were her four kids, my stepchildren, and all the grandchildren, and we were going to stay close after I retired. A family kind of life in Philadelphia, close to all the things we enjoyed—the opera, the orchestra, the restaurants. That would have been the kind of life we would have led."

While some older lawyers might have quit or cut back on their practice to reassess their life, John did the opposite. "After my wife's death, my grief reaction was to plunge back into my work for the last five years," he said. "It was stupid, but that's what I did, and it hasn't been successful. I did take in a partner, and that has been helpful. But I find myself accepting cases every month so that she will have a stable flow of cases until she gets established…and it's just a trap that keeps me practicing when I should have retired."

But what if it is the lawyer who passes on? What then for the surviving spouse? In Chapter 8, read, *"Closing a Spouse's Practice: What I Wish My Husband Had Told Me."* It's the personal account of a Connecticut woman whose attorney husband died after a long battle with cancer.

A Circle of Friends

As we all know, the unrelenting pressures of practicing law make it difficult to keep up with the daily demands of life and to be available for our families. Friendships are even more difficult to maintain, and we pay a high price for that isolation.

A large and growing number of studies report that as we transition away from full-time practice into retirement, our circle of friends plays an increased role in determining our satisfaction with life and even how long we live. Furthermore, individuals who enjoy close relationships with others live longer and healthier lives than those who don't. One University of Michigan study of 100 recent retirees concluded that *the most powerful predictor of life satisfaction after retirement was the size of a person's social network.* Those who expressed satisfaction with life averaged social networks made up of 16 people while those less satisfied had social networks of fewer than 10 people. The reverse is also true: people who are isolated and lonely are more likely to become ill and die prematurely.[7]

In New Haven, CT, a study involving more than 2,800 men and women 65 years of age and older investigated the relationship between longevity, social activity, purposeful activity (working, volunteering, etc.), and physical fitness. It found that socially active men and women lived an average of two-and-a-half years longer than those who were not socially active.[8]

A few years ago, Ralph Warner, attorney and founder of Nolo Press, the do-it-yourself legal publisher, wrote, *Get A Life: You Don't Need a Million to Retire Well* (*nolo.com*). It's a unique retirement guide that focuses on non-financial issues as well as the traditional retirement concerns. The financial planning chapters are not as complete as readers might want, but the book does a profound service by focusing on the importance of broadening one's circle of friends, relying on one's extended family, and developing hobbies and non-work activities. In the excerpt that follows, Warner shares this very personal observation about his father, a retired lawyer:

▶ Lifelong learning—the notion of use-it-or-lose-it—is a key factor in maintaining cognitive functioning and aging well.

"…Having observed, with sadness, how lonely and increasingly isolated my father was in the years before he died at age 80, I understand first-hand how impoverished a retirement can be without friends. My father's loneliness was palpable. For days at a time he had no one except my mother to do things with or to even talk to. Undoubtedly he would have been happier—and probably would have lived longer—if he had even a few confidants. Dad hadn't always been lonely. For many years, as a partner in a small firm, he worked with lots of interesting people and made a few real friends. On the weekends, he relished the time he spent with a half-dozen or more golf and tennis buddies. Add to this the busy-ness of raising two sons, staying on friendly terms with the neighbors, belonging to several clubs, chairing the town recreation commission and playing semi-serious bridge, and it is fair to say that my dad was actively engaged with all sorts of people. So why was he so alone in the years before his death? I think he would have explained it something like this:

- *'My law partners and most of my old law business friends retired.*
- *'Many of my friends moved to Florida while I stayed in New York.*
- *'My physical strength declined, and I couldn't play golf or tennis with anyone except a dwindling number of old friends.*
- *'In my mid-60s, my older friends began to die or become senile… in my 70's the same thing began to happen to friends my own age… and before long, my address book consisted of little more than columns of crossed-out names.*
- *'My two sons—my only close family—chose to live thousands of miles away, and I saw them only a few times a year. As a result, I never really became close to my grandchildren.'*

The heart of his problem is that my dad lost his ability to make new friends."[9]

To expand and maintain your circle of friends throughout adulthood, consider these commonly cited suggestions:

- Commit yourself to continue making friends in midlife.

- Continue to make at least some younger friends.

- If you are married or living with someone, it is a good idea for each of you to have some friends of your own in addition to the ones you share.

- So that you improve your chances of forming new friendships, involve yourself in group activities.

Whether you are married, in a long-term committed relationship or single, you will need a strong network of relationships in retirement. Take a moment to complete the following Relationship and Personal Support System Worksheets.

Retirement Relationship Worksheet

Married or single, we all need strong relationships. This worksheet will help you examine your current relationships and expectations into retirement.

Existing Relationships (Name)	Basis For Relationship (Related, work, church, etc.)	Expect Relationship to Continue Into Retirement	Expect Relationship to End At Retirement

What does your worksheet tell you about your current relationships and those in the future? Will there be significant gaps? If so, some planning now will prevent one of the losses that can occur at retirement.

Personal Support System Worksheet

From the worksheet on the previous page, transfer you relationships to this circle of support. Those persons who you are closest to belong in your inner circle and so on.

Our Personal Support System

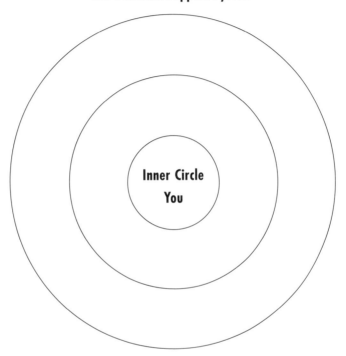

**Inner Circle
You**

It is Time to Build and Strengthen Your Relationships

…If you find someone in the outer edge of your circle that you wish to move closer.

…If your inner circle is more empty than you would like it.

…If you feel a personal void anywhere in your support network.

Elements of Transition: Work, Service & Education

"My dad worked for one company his entire career, and when he left he bought a retirement home and played golf. That was his model of retirement… and mine… until I realized what I was headed for. At that point, I decided to do something completely outside my experience and learned more about myself in the process."—JOHN, WHO CLOSED HIS PRACTICE AT 52.

Retirement *is* personal… very personal. And at the point one is ready to retire, the subject of what you want to retire *to* becomes much more relevant than what you are retiring *from*. Consider:

- In his book, *Breaking the Watch: The Meanings of Retirement in America*, longevity researcher Joel Savishinsky writes, "…One of the most frequent pieces of advice (from the retirees in our study) was that one should plan finances and pensions far in advance, but also enter retirement passionate about something that gives you a sense of purpose."
- Earlier, I cited a Connecticut study involving more than 2,800 men and women 65 years of age and older that investigated the relationship between longevity, social activity, purposeful activity, and physical fitness. It found that purposeful activity increased longevity the most! Men and women who engaged in purposeful activity lived an average of four years longer than those who did not.[10]
- Retirement frees up 25 hours a week for men and 18 hours a week for women, according to time-diary studies conducted by the University of Maryland's Survey Research Center."[11]

So, the question becomes, 'What are you going to do with all that time'?

Consider John Ryan, a plaintiff's lawyer whose career spanned more than 50 years. John developed a life-long love for literature in college, but never even attempted to write poetry until the age of 68, following the death of his wife. Now, for the past 20 years, writing poetry has been his passion and source of engagement and rejuvenation. He wrote three books of poems between 1988-1999, and published them as a single volume (*Expressions*). John's other passion is cooking, for which he has also published a cookbook.

Author Richard Bolles, in his book, *The Three Boxes of Life, And How To Get Out Of Them*, suggests that as products of our culture we think of education, work, and retirement as a series of "boxes" to inhabit and then move on. Bolles argues that this lock-step life sequence is obsolete, and that we owe it to ourselves to blend the three together whatever our stage of development. Thus, one's education years should also include a time to work and a time to play…one's working years should include continued education and a time to play, and—more to the point here—our retirement should include educational opportunities, a chance to work if we choose, and a time to enjoy the leisure activities we once set aside.

How you go about blending work, education and leisure into your retirement will depend on your values and priorities. But the process is made easier by asking yourself these five simple questions:

- What are your interests?
- How would you like to spend your time?

- What activities would give you purpose and a sense of being useful?
- What would provide the intellectual stimulation to which you've become accustomed?
- What leisure activities would rejuvenate and re-energize you?

Profile in Retirement: John's Story

A career lawyer, John looked over the horizon and saw himself headed for the same sedentary retirement as his father. So, in his 50's, he decided—in his words—*"to get out of my comfort zone before I got too old"*. He purchased an ocean-going sailboat, rented his home, arranged for someone to handle his clients, and set sail from Oregon to Central America. Upon concluding his year-long voyage, John enrolled in a Guatemalan language school, joined the Peace Corps there as an instructor, and helped establish his village's first library. "No one ever hugged me as a lawyer," he told me, "But as a teacher I got hugged all the time".

"A lot of people don't have any other models of retirement, so they do what their parents and everyone else does. I was lucky. I did something completely outside my experience, and the world opened up to me. It wasn't easy. Out there on the water, you don't have a phone, a secretary, a newspaper, a computer, and you don't have your status as a lawyer. But the trip helped me understand there are so many other ways to live, and that you don't need a lot of money to do it. Now that I'm back, I make a point of talking with lawyers who are thinking about retiring, and I tell them, 'Get out of your comfort zone. Find out what you enjoy and what opportunities are out there for you.' The sooner you get outside your routine and start exploring new things, the better off you are. Sure, there's always uncertainty, but if you don't get too scared… and you keep putting one foot in front of another… things will develop. Life has a way of redoing your plans if you're open to it."

Author's note: John eventually returned to Oregon a different man. These days, he's in a partnership developing low-income housing. And even though his law practice is still closed, he doesn't consider himself retired. As he puts it, "I think of myself as having been on sabbatical since 1996."

Working in Retirement

The most recent studies suggest that a significant percentage of current retirees are choosing to continue to work full-time or part-time after retiring from their primary job or profession. A report by the Pew Research Center found that 71 percent of current workers thought they would continue to work after retirement—more out of desire than necessity. A study by Merrill Lynch found that 76 percent of Boomers expected to retire from their current jobs around age 64, and then start an entirely new job or career. And a MetLife/Civic Ventures survey of 1,000 Americans ages 50 to 70,[12] the participants were quite specific about their post-retirement plans and motivations. Among the findings:

- More than half believed retirement is a time to begin a new chapter by getting active and involved, rather than a time to take it easy and to take a much-deserved rest from work and daily responsibilities.
- Nearly two-thirds of the boomers plan to continue working in retirement.
- Only a minority of the participants believe that retirement is the end of one's productive years.

The MetLife study also reported that for most adults ages 50-70, the concept of working in retirement had four important elements:

- 59 percent says it offered the opportunity to stay involved with others.
- 57 percent says it would give them a sense of purpose.
- 52 percent says it would provide additional income.
- 48 percent say it would help them improve the quality of life in their community.

And when it came to the kind of work they wanted to do in retirement, two-thirds of the leading-edge boomers were quite specific; they said it should benefit their community in at least one of three ways:

- Help improve the quality of life;
- Provide an opportunity to help the poor, the elderly, and other people in need;
- Provide the opportunity to work with children and young people.

Considering the results of these studies, it was no coincidence when we heard about the retirement plans of one Northwest attorney named Jeff:

Background: After a year in medical school, and another year serving on a medical ship in Vietnam, Jeff decided to go into law. His legal career included stints as a public defender, assistant US Attorney, City Attorney, and three years in private practice. In his mid-50s, Jeff started work on a Master's in counseling. When he finally retired as City Attorney, he completed his degree and opened a part-time counseling practice. As a veteran, he has also been volunteering with other veterans returning from Afghanistan and Iraq.

"When I started out, I did public defender work. I defended a number of clients involving the insanity defense, and I got very involved in working up at the medical school. Later, I became chair of the Oregon Psychiatric Review Board. What always grabbed me in law was working with individual clients, especially on the psychological or emotional issues affecting what was going on in their life. These are the things that I look back on with the most satisfaction, when I really made a difference in somebody's life. So throughout my career, there's been a mental health component to my practice. I don't see my move to counseling as something entirely different (from the practice of law). It's a very logical extension of what I've always done."

Jeff's experience with an "encore career" happens to correlate with what the ABA has learned about lawyers at midlife. In February, 2007, the ABA's Commission on Second Season survey found that boomer lawyers were eager for more information in two areas: having a second career within the law, and having a second career outside the law. In Chapter 7, we discuss how you can reassess your work and career aspirations, and we provide some self-assessment exercises and resources for exploring options and opportunities for work in your own "second season".

Volunteering in Retirement

An AARP-sponsored retirement survey reports that more than half of boomers expect to dedicate time to community service and volunteering during their retirement years. Traditional volunteering is not what they have in mind, though. According to the survey, what drives Boomers is the need to use their skills, develop meaningful or purposeful relationships, and to make a significant impact. This was brought home in my interview with a now-retired state supreme court justice, who told me, "A lot of us older lawyers, myself included, still want to make a difference. We don't want to feel like has-been's, or that we're no longer needed. We believe there is something that we can still do that is going to contribute to society."

I discovered that many lawyers feel this way, and that they seek out opportunities for community service that will provide intellectual stimulation and utilize their skills and experience. Ralph, who retired after more than 40 years in private practice, did just that.

Before he closed his practice, Ralph went in search of volunteer work that would, in his words, "keep my mind active, and that I could really dig into." In time, he found himself on the advising council of a local behavioral health council that reviews and grades his county's mental health services contracts. In his case, connecting with a nonprofit before he retired was the key to making a meaningful connection. "There are so many opportunities for a lawyer to make a difference in the nonprofit world," he said. "But developing that interest should not be put off until retirement. If you wait too long, it's probably too late to have a genuine affection for the possibilities that are available."

In fact, some lawyers may experience frustration and disappointment if they postpone their volunteering or pro bono work until after they retire. One now-retired college administrator said of his experience, "I thought that if a person with my experience came to an organization and told them that I wanted to give them a chunk of my time, they would be enthusiastic. I was wrong. The nonprofit world is not as permeable as I expected. Maybe it was me. But it also seems that it's as much the mind-set of organizations; a certain reluctance, hesitation, and lack of experience involving older people."[13]

One who agrees is Marc Freedman, author of *Prime Time: How Baby Boomers Will Revolutionize Retirement and Transform America* (2002). Freedman argues that our culture lacks the institutional infrastructure to provide current retirees and approaching Boomers with the sort of opportunities that would allow them to channel their considerable knowledge, skills and experiences into community service. Says Freedman, "The roles and opportunities of our society simply haven't caught up to the capacities and interests of today's 50- 60- or 70-year olds, much less the aging boomers of the coming decades. We face a burgeoning mismatch between demographics and opportunities—and the demographics are way ahead."[14]

Boomers have had to compete for opportunities with one another throughout their lives. If the infrastructure inducing and supporting volunteer opportunities does not change dramatically in the coming decades, they will once again be competing with one another for the types of volunteer opportunities that they desire and would find meaningful. The moral of this story is that if you are envisioning finding purpose and meaning through volunteer opportunities in retirement, you better start establishing those relationships well before you retire.

Education in Retirement

Most lawyers share a thirst for intellectual stimulation.

The Oregon Lawyer Satisfaction Survey cited in Chapter One found that the desire for intellectual stimulation is the primary motivator to go to law school, and the one continuous aspect of law that lawyers enjoy most. Not surprisingly, the loss of that intellectual stimulation was the personal concern most frequently cited in the Oregon Lawyer Retirement Survey. Later in the book, we examine the relationship between continued learning and cognitive function.

For now, we want to make the point that lifelong learning—the notion of *use-it-or-lose-it*—is a key factor in maintaining cognitive functioning and aging well.

In this country, there are some 400 colleges and universities with an on-campus Institute for Learning in Retirement (ILR) that offer continued learning in a flexible, informal and noncompetitive environment. To find an ILR campus in your area, type in the terms *Institute for Learning in Retirement* in the search box for any of the big search engines to find the name of a campus in your state. For information about other courses and educational programs, visit the following Web sites: *distancelearn.about.com, classesUSA.com, quickknowledge.com,* and *thirdage.com.*

There are also many opportunities to combine study with travel. Among them:

- *Elderhostel* (*elderhostel.org*)—A wonderful program that combines travel and education for those over the age of 60 (note: a spouse can be under 60 if traveling together). International in scope, Elderhostel provides a sample of college life (dorms, cafeterias) all while taking college-level courses at a very reduced rate in non-busy seasons. There are over a thousand Elderhostel sites around the world.
- *Smithsonian's Journeys Travel Adventures* (*smithsonianjourneys.org*)—A well-respected international travel/study program.
- *Earthwatch Institute* (*earthwatch.org*)—Earthwatch engages people worldwide in scientific field research and education.

See Appendix 3 (Resources) for many more travel-related Web sites.

Where Are You Retiring To?

Retirement may still be several years away. But that doesn't mean you can't think about where you might spend those years.

A US News & World Report cover story (Oct. 1, 2007) reported on what the magazine described as "the best places to retire", and assembled a first-cut of 2,000 American communities with a population above 15,000. Then they narrowed that list to just over a thousand communities, using criteria that included cost of living, climate, crime rate, access to healthcare, educational opportunities, and cultural and recreational amenities. Among the favorite US communities were Hillsboro, OR, Bozeman MT, Prescott AZ, Lawrence KS, Fayetteville AR, Smyrna TN, Peachtree City GA, Concord NH, and Venice FL.

For many boomers, retiring abroad has even greater appeal; this despite a sharply weakened dollar, and the obstacles of language, culture, and disconnection from family and friends. According to the Social Security Administration, nearly a half-million beneficiaries (about one percent of those in the system) had their Social Security checks sent abroad in 2005. And of all the international locations, the top 10 were Canada, Mexico, Italy, Germany, Britain (the entire U.K), Greece, the Philippines, Portugal, France and Spain.

Where do you plan to call home in retirement?

A study by AARP reported that only two out of ten boomers will move to a new geographic area when they retire. Most retirees age in place in their own homes and hometowns, a pattern that has remained stable over the past 40 years. According to the study, the most significant factor in the decision is whether to live near adult children and grandchildren. Other important factors include:

> Low crime rate
> Active, clean, safe downtown
> Good hospitals nearby
> Low overall tax rate
> Mild climate
> Scenic beauty nearby
> Low cost of living
> Good recreational facilities
> Low housing costs
> Active social/cultural environment
> Nearby airport with commercial service
> Major city nearby
> No state income tax
> Continuing-care retirement communities available
> Full or part-time employment opportunities available
> College town with adult education available

Profile in Retirement: Marilyn's Story

At the age of 50, Marilyn had a thriving solo practice in Cincinnati. She assumed she wouldn't retire for at least another 10 years. But out of the blue, her husband received an early-retirement offer from his long-time employer... and he accepted it.

"It all happened so quickly. We didn't know what to do. Fortunately, my husband got some tuition as part of his retirement package, so we were able to postpone our next move while he went back to school. But then we really had to make some hard choices. So, we read books on relocation, read about all the Best Places in Money *magazine, and took some exploratory trips. Our criteria was only that we didn't want to live anywhere as*

hot as Cincinnati...or as cold. We finally settled on the Pacific Northwest, close to our two kids and our granddaughter. My husband spent a week house-hunting in Portland, and then we made an offer on a house we both liked. Once we were settled, we joined a church and I met two members who were attorneys. When I said I was interested in doing some work utilizing my legal skills and experience, one of them suggested I look for opportunities to work as a JD paralegal. So, I did. For the past eight years, I've worked as a freelance probate paralegal. In between assignments, I can spend time with our granddaughter."

If you think you might move, I recommend the relocation questionnaire on the next page. I also recommend reading, *The New Retirement: The Ultimate Guide to the Rest of Your Life*, by Jan Cullinane and Cathy Fitzgerald. In their book, they make the following suggestions:

- Visit for extended periods at different times of the year.
- Look at financial concerns such as taxes, cost of living, and business activity.
- Look at the employment opportunities should you want or need to work.
- Look at the availability and cost of medical care including health insurance.
- Look at the opportunities to pursue leisure and volunteer activities, continuing education...and just plain fun.
- Look at the effect of a move on your support system. Moving closer to or further from family and friends may have positive or negative effects.

Taking Inventory

As I mentioned earlier, for nearly 15 years I have facilitated workshops for lawyers actively involved in job or career transition, and for six of those years I have facilitated—and continue to facilitate—retirement-planning workshops for lawyers. In both, I observed that attendees benefitted enormously from engaging in self-assessment exercises and the opportunity to exchange with others their thoughts, experiences and concerns. For that reason, I recommend that you seek out one of the many community college and university campuses that have begun to offer retirement-planning workshops and classes.

One nationally respected resource is the North Carolina Center for Creative Retirement at the University of North Carolina, Asheville (*unca.edu/ncccr*). While researching this book, I had the privilege of attending one of their weekend workshops. Happily, it minimized lectures and presentations in favor of facilitated group discussions, exercises, and panel discussions, and concluded with each participant doing a five-minute presentation of the first steps they intended to take toward planning or implementing their plans for retirement.

TO RELOCATE OR NOT TO RELOCATE

Complete the following questionnaire to learn whether you're a candidate for relocating. If you have a Significant Other, he or she should also complete this short quiz.

1. Do you have a significant other?
   a. Yes
   b. No

2. How is your physical health?
   a. Never felt better
   b. More good days than bad
   c. Physician on speed-dial

3. How is your financial health?
   a. Rolling in dough
   b. Enough (even though I would like more)
   c. Thank heaven for Social Security

4. Is the climate in your current location...
   a. Something you want to flee
   b. Tolerable
   c. Ideal

5. To what extent does your children's location influence where you live?
   a. Not an issue
   b. Could play a role
   c. Would be a priority in choosing a location

6. What is the level of social support in your current location?
   a. Low/none
   b. Medium
   c. High

7. What is your level of involvement in your current community?
   a. Low/none
   b. Medium
   c. High

8. When making a decision, you usually...
   a. Carefully weigh alternatives
   b. Do your homework, but also trust your instincts
   c. Rely on your "gut" or intuition

9. What is your history of moving to new areas?
   a. Story of my life
   b. A few times
   c. Born and raised in current area

10. Which of these most closely describes your attitude?
    a. New relationships are the spice of life
    b. "Make new friends, but keep the old"
    c. Old friends are the best friends

11. Which of the following phrases most closely describes you?
    a. Extroverted
    b. Combination extroverted/introverted
    c. Introverted

12. I am:

    a. Not responsible for aging parents

    b. Not fully responsible for aging parents

    c. Responsible for aging parents

13. I am:

    a. Not into babysitting, or have no grandkids

    b. Someone who loves every minutes with my grandkids, but…

    c. Crazy about my grandkids; a high priority

14. I tend to:

    a. Enjoy travel to new locations

    b. Return to favorite spots

    c. Be a homebody

15. How do you feel about change?

    a. Ready and willing

    b. Generally accepting

    c. Dread it

16. Outside interests:

    a. Many and varied

    b. Some

    c. Hardly any

Scoring—

Give yourself one point for each (a), two points for each (b), and three points for each c.

16-29 points: Start packing. You have the characteristics that make you a good candidate for relocation.

30-38 points: Think carefully about moving. You're on the fence.

39-47 points: Probably best to stay put! Your characteristics and feelings about relationships and community could make relocating difficult.

—Excerpted from *The New Retirement*, by Jan Cullinane (Rodale Books). Reprinted with permission.

What was so encouraging is that in just three days workshop participants learned how to begin to articulate with clarity the life they wanted in retirement, and the initial steps they could take toward creating that life. I encourage you to investigate this resource and other such group experiences in your own community.

In addition there are several online retirement-planning tools. A few are free; most require a modest fee, and the results must be interpreted by an executive coach at an hourly rate. Here are a few online tools of which I am aware: *retirementwellbeing.com*, *mynextphase.com*, *retirementoptions.com*, and Turning Points Navigator (*tpnavigator.com*).

But now, to jumpstart your retirement self-assessment, please complete Retirement Inventory I and II that concludes this chapter.

RETIREMENT INVENTORY I

To begin a personal examination of your expectations about retirement, place an "X" at the point that best describes your level of concern.

	No Concern	Some Concern	Concerned
Not wanting to let partners/clients down			
Second career opportunities			
Economic security			
Reduction in lifestyle			
Productive & purposeful use of time			
Leisure activities			
Usefulness & value			
Maintaining self-esteem			
Professional status			
Professional relationships			
Staying healthy			
Being involved in community			
Involvement with family			
Care-giving responsibilities			
Making new friends			
Possible relocation			
Availability of medical care			
Getting older			
Remaining independent			

Others:

_____

_____

_____

Those issues which are causing the most concern are the ones that you need to address and invest additional time exploring. It will help you in your planning if you identify personal concerns on the lines below and begin the process of problem solving.

Areas of concern	Actions I (we) plan to take

RETIREMENT INVENTORY II

In the chart below, mark each value according to how you feel about it. Add others not on the list.

VI= Very important   SS= So-so   DNI= Definitely not important

I= Important   NI= Not too important

Value	VI	I	SS	NI	DNI
Being with other people					
Being with family					
Making decisions					
Helping others					
Doing exciting things					
Being alone at times					
Accepting responsibility					
Influencing others					
Developing new ideas					
Sense of well being					
Time out of doors					
Standard of living					
Being challenged					
Adventure					
Compatibility					
Winning					
Independence					
Having fun					
Prestige					
Public contact					
Social contribution					
Variety					
Appearance, self					
Appearance, surroundings					
Effective use of time					
Physical well being					
Mental stimulation					
Keeping busy					
Sense of belonging					
Power of authority					
Achievement					
Other:					

CHAPTER 3

The Financial Planner

"My most successful clients are those who start planning their transition three to five years in advance." —David Corbett, a Boston retirement consultant

For generations, retirement planning always had a single focus: *Will I have enough retirement income to replace my salary?* It's still a valid question, especially in this economy. But experience shows that each of us has a different vision of this thing called "retirement", so our financial plan for it needs to be tailored to fit our personal frame of reference. Couples, especially, should consider the hopes and aspirations of *both* parties so they can develop a joint retirement plan. To that end, this chapter will explore three important questions:

What is the current state of your finances?

How do you picture your retirement, and how much will that vision of retirement cost?

How will you get from where you are today to where you want to be?

The journey metaphor is appropriate here because the process of retirement-planning is not that much different from planning a trip. You identify the starting point and destination, and then proceed to work out the best route and methods of travel…with the understanding that the "journey" that works for your neighbor or colleague will probably not be the best in your own circumstances. In the sections that follow, we will look at each of the above three questions in detail. The answers you generate will take you a long way toward answering the most-often asked retirement-planning question: *"Do I have enough money to retire?"*

Step 1: The Current State of Your Finances

Determining your current financial status is essentially an exercise in organization. To complete this exercise, you need to inventory your assets, calculate your net worth, and examine your current expenses.

Inventory your assets. For some of you, this will be as easy as clicking into your personal financial software (e.g., *Quicken, Managing Your Money*) and printing a report. For others, it means slogging through the files (shoeboxes?) holding all your investment account reports, your insurance policies, your Social Security statements, etc. Whatever the case, this really is an important first step. If you already have a system for organizing and managing your financial records, you can proceed to the next section. If not, we invite you to use the *Financial Assets Record* we include at the end of this chapter to organize your financial records for easy retrieval.

To prepare your own Financial Assets Record, and to complete the worksheets and exercises in this chapter, you will need to assemble several important financial records/statements, including:

Income tax records
Pension plan records and documents (Retirement Account (401(k), Keogh, SEP, IRA's, etc.)
Social Security annual or customized statement
Bank accounts
Savings accounts
Stocks, bonds, and other securities accounts
Business interests
Deeds to property
Insurance policies
Wills & other estate planning documents

Measuring your net worth. To plan for financial independence, we urge you to also establish your net worth. This personal balance sheet is a compilation of what you own (assets) less what you owe (debts or liabilities). When striving for financial independence, your current net worth represents an essential baseline for an effective future plan. Those of you with personal financial software should be able to print a Net Worth Statement if all your assets and liabilities have been entered into your database. To post periodic updates (and ascertain your financial progress), use the net worth program with your personal software package or use the *Net Worth Worksheet* at the end of this chapter.

▶ You must have a clear idea of your current monthly expenses in order to make accurate projections. That's one of the foundations of financial planning, especially as it relates to retirement.

Calculating net worth isn't easy the first time. But you've already done much of the work if you have completed your *Financial Assets Record.* Or, if you recently applied for a loan, use the application as a starting point. Note: a Net Worth Statement only reflects a particular point in time and is quickly out of date. At a minimum, you should determine your net worth on an annual basis. Why make the effort? Because your Net Worth Statement is a baseline against which you can chart your progress toward achieving financial independence. Speaking of progress, financial advisors regard a 10 to 15 percent growth in net worth per year a feasible goal, particularly in the middle years when one's income is likely to be at its peak and family obligations have begun to wane. So, if you ever wondered how much you should save from year to year, or if your assets are properly deployed, or whether you have taken on too much debt, the changes in your net worth can help answer these questions. You can make your net worth statement as simple or as detailed as you wish. But, it should be complete enough to show you how you stand now in order to measure your financial progress in the future. Simple or detailed, though, keep your value estimates conservative. You will eventually be living off your net worth. So, keep this in mind:

- Your assets are worth only what you can sell them for...not what you originally paid.
- Your stocks and bonds should be valued at the market price as of the date of your calculation.
- Your net worth includes your 401(k), IRAs, and/or your share in the firm's profit-sharing plan.
- The cash and other conversion values of your insurance (your insurance company can supply these figures) are included.
- Your home or other real property is worth no more than it would bring on the market minus sales costs.
- Your household goods are worth only what they would bring on the second-hand market (unless you have antiques or art objects).

Quantifying your expenses. One of the foundations of financial planning—especially as it relates to retirement—is that you must have a clear idea of your current monthly expenses in order to make accurate projections. So, our next stop is an exploration of how and where you spend your money.

Let's be honest, many of us don't take the time to systematically record and calculate our recurring monthly expenses. We go month-to-month, draw-to-draw, and either have money left at the end of the month, or an increased balance on our credit cards or home equity line of credit. But at the risk of repetition: *you must have a clear idea of your current monthly expenses in order to make accurate projections.* To do so, use the monthly expense program in your personal financial software, or complete the *Personal Expense Log* at the end of this chapter. Quantifying your current expenses will enable you to project your retirement expenses more accurately, and may help you identify options for reducing high-interest debt or increasing your savings for retirement.

Projecting your expenses in retirement is a very personal process. For a long time, the so-called *Three-Fourths Rule* was the working formula: you estimated your current monthly expenses and multiplied them by three-fourths. Today, though, that traditional formula may be outmoded. In fact, it probably isn't prudent to assume or anticipate that your expenses are going to decrease in retirement...especially in *early* retirement. For example, if you choose to do the sort of travel you have had to put off while practicing law, or you wish to engage in new leisure or business activities, your early retirement expenses are likely to be more than your current expenses. Later, your medical and care-giving expenses will most certainly increase your budget. Remember, retirement is not a "finish line" you cross at the end of your career; it's a series of phases, and the expenses associated with your 60's and 70's will most likely look very different than those in your 80's and 90's.

So, how much money will you need to retire?

It will depend on three factors—your health, your health-related expenses, and the lifestyle you choose (including where you live and how you spend your time and energies). Which brings us to the second—and probably the most important—of our three retirement-planning questions.

Step 2: How Do You Picture Your Retirement... and How Much Will That Vision of it Cost?

As noted earlier, increased longevity and a phenomenon called *down-aging* (i.e., maintaining a high level of physical and cognitive functioning into later adulthood) has spawned a new vision of retirement that calls for a paradigm shift in retirement planning as well. Author John Nelson echoes this sentiment in his book, *What Color is Your Parachute? For Retirement.* In it he writes, "Our parents and grandparents were mostly focused on how to retire *from something.* But for those of us at midlife today, he says, "Retirement planning can (and must) focus on retiring *to something...*"

> ▶ What's your vision of retirement? You must define it before calculating the costs associated with that vision. It's truer for couples; a joint retirement plan needs to reflect the aspirations of both partners.

For this reason, the lawyer at midlife needs to define what he or she wants in the next phase of life *before* calculating the costs associated with those aspirations. This task is even more important for couples, whose joint retirement plan needs to reflect the aspirations of both partners. Not an easy task, according to a study published by Fidelity Investments. The 2007 study underscored what financial planners already know—that wives and husbands are not taking the time to discuss and plan for later life. In the survey of 502 married couples approaching retirement, the couples often had different understandings of their plans and preparations for life after the office.

- 61 percent disagreed on their primary source of funds in retirement.
- 41 percent disagreed whether at least one partner would work in retirement.
- 35 percent differed when asked about each other's expected retirement age.
- In all, only 38 percent said they worked together on financial planning for later life.

In response to the survey, the Wall Street Journal[1] polled financial advisers and couples to identify the most important questions spouses should ask each other in the five or so years before retirement. While the article addressed couples, singles should be answering most of these as well. The questions were:

- Do we really want to retire, and if so, when?
- What is our vision of retirement, and do we share the same vision?
- Where do we want to retire?
- What's our strategy for building and preserving a nest egg?
- What assets do we have for retirement, and are they invested in the most beneficial ways to achieve our goals?
- How much money will we need to support our lifestyle in retirement?
- Do we have an estate plan, and where is it?
- What kind of relationships—personal and financial—do we want to have with our children and parents in later life?
- How will each of us approach, and manage, getting older?
- What will our legacy be (both financial & non-financial)?

What will be *your* legacy? The answer is important as you begin turning your assets into retirement income.

For many of us, leaving a financial legacy to our heirs, or to our favorite charity or institution, is of primary importance. Others may choose to burn the candle at both ends and die broke. For the first group, the desire to leave an estate calls for structuring your retirement income streams such that you can live off the interest and earnings of your assets, preserving much of the principal for your estate. Which means you will need to save more or spend less of your assets. The "die broke" group may be able to spend more enjoying their retirement, but they must still plan their income and expenses so their money doesn't run out before their life does.

Again, how you feel about your financial legacy is critical to the design of your retirement financial plan. And while you may not have all your answers now, do begin to fill in the "In Retirement" column of *The Expense Log*. Assume that prices will not be different from what they are now; we will adjust for inflation later. Projecting retirement expenses is always a challenge, and never completely accurate because plans change…especially over the course of a retirement lasting 20 or more years. So, think of this as a process; not an absolute! In any event, associating your retirement dreams with hard cold costs now will be an eye-opener, and will help you project your retirement income needs.

Step 3: How to Get From Where You Are to Where You Want to Be

If "journey" is the working metaphor for retirement planning, then financial planning needs a metaphor of its own—and what better image than a three-legged stool. Think of it this way: one leg (0-20 percent) represents Social Security, a second leg (0-50 percent) represents your pension and/or retirement accounts, and the third (0-50 percent) represents your non-retirement savings and investments. In this section, we will begin projecting your income and expenses in retirement one "leg" at a time. Your task will be to identify sources of income that will replace your current salary, and create a financially balanced retirement.

For now, here's what you can expect from the known sources of retirement income:

Social Security. Proposed and signed into law in 1935 by President Roosevelt, Social Security was the first social insurance of its kind for elderly Americans. A safety net, it was intended for workers who retired without adequate savings and wealth to maintain economic independence, and whose wives would be left unprotected after their husband's death. Back then, the life expectancy in the US was 62, but Social Security benefits didn't kick in until age 65. Today, Social Security benefits are not a significant factor in the retirement income for all lawyers, but for many these benefits will provide one of several important income streams for retirement. Note: As of July, 2008, the Social Security Administration rolled out the first stage of a new, faster retirement benefit estimator (*ssa.gov/estimator*). A later, even more streamlined version was expected in late Fall 2008.

Who is eligible?

Self. Minimum eligibility is established by accumulating 40 Social Security credits. You can accumulate a maximum of four credits per year, so you must have worked a minimum of 10 years to qualify for benefits. Your benefit is based upon your highest 35 years of paying into the Social Security system. For most, the first few years that we paid into the System will not be used in the calculation since they reflect both low earnings and are beyond the 35 years needed. Those taking an "early retirement" may find themselves without 35 years of earnings in which case any years less than 35 will have zeros used in their calculation, thus reducing their benefit. Working part time in retirement before drawing your first benefit check will not reduce your benefit as the highest 35 years are used.

Spouse. Social Security provides retirement benefits to the spouse of any retired worker collecting Social Security retirement benefits. These spousal benefits are based upon the retired worker's Social Security record. The spousal benefit can be as much as one-half of the retired worker's full benefit depending upon whether a spouse begins to collect these benefits at full retirement age or earlier.

Divorced spouse. A divorced spouse may be eligible for benefits on a former husband's or wife's Social Security record if the marriage lasted at least 10 years. The divorced spouse must be 62 or older and unmarried. For a divorced spouse to receive benefits, the worker also must be 62 or older. If they have been divorced at least two years, he or she can get benefits even if the worker is not retired. The amount of benefits a divorced spouse receives has no effect on the amount of benefits a current spouse may receive.

Widowed spouse. A widowed spouse's benefits jump to the deceased spouse's higher benefit amount. A widowed spouse can remarry at age 60 and still receive his/her spousal benefit. A disabled widowed spouse can remarry at age 50 or older and receive his/her spousal benefit. If you, your spouse, or a divorced former spouse who has not remarried, or a widow/widower, have accumulated the 40 credits to qualify for benefits independently, Social Security will pay whichever benefit is greater.

When can you start collecting benefits?

Full retirement benefits. Between 2002 and 2008 the age for receiving full benefits gradually increased from 65 to 66. From 2008 to 2019, full retirement age will be 66. From 2020-2025, full-retirement age will gradually increase from 66 to 67.

Early retirement benefits. You can begin collecting Social Security anytime between age 62 and your full retirement age. Almost three-quarters of current Social Security recipients elected to start collecting their benefits early. The opportunity cost for electing to collect Social Security before your full retirement age will be a permanent reduction in your monthly benefit. The amount of this reduction will depend on the year you were born and your corresponding full-retirement age. A spouse, divorced spouse or widow/widower, may also elect to receive reduced spousal benefits before full retirement age. Refer to the *Benefit Reduction Table for Early Retirement* for the early-retirement penalty you would incur if you choose to begin collecting early. For a couple who plans on utilizing the 50 percent spousal benefit, the decision to take "early" retirement can have a dramatic impact on the family finances.

For example:

If Ray is eligible to receive $2,000/month at his full retirement age of 66, and his wife June waits until her full-retirement age to receive the 50 percent benefit of $1,000, the couple would receive $3,000/month. However, if Ray decides to take his first check at age 62, it will be reduced to $1,500, and if June also collects her first check at age 62, she will receive about $525 (half of $1,500 less 30 percent). The monthly family total is now $2,025, or $975 less than if they had waited for full retirement age.

When you consider that future Cost of Living Adjustments (COLA) will also be applied to this lower benefit, the impact of taking the lesser early-retirement benefit is felt year after year.

BENEFIT REDUCTION FOR EARLY RETIREMENT*

Year of Birth[1]	Full (normal) Retirement Age	Months between age 62 and full retirement age	At Age 62[2]			
			A $1000 retirement benefit would be reduced to	The retirement benefit is reduced by[3]	A $500 spouse's benefit would be reduced to	The spouse's benefit is reduced by[4]
1943–54	66	48	$750	25.00%	$350	30.00%
1955	66 + 2 mo's	50	$741	25.83%	$345	30.83%
1956	66 + 4 mo's	52	$733	26.67%	$341	31.67%
1957	66 + 6 mo's	54	$725	27.50%	$337	32.50%
1958	66 + 8 mo's	56	$716	28.33%	$333	33.33%
1959	66 + 10 mo's	58	$708	29.17%	$329	34.17%
1960 +	67	60	$700	30.00%	$325	35.00%

[1] If you were born on January 1st, you should refer to the previous year. [2] If you were born on the 1st of the month, we figure the benefit as if your birthday was in the previous month. You must be at least 62 for the entire month to receive benefits. [3] Percentages are approximate due to rounding. [4] The maximum benefit for the spouse is 50 percent of the benefit the worker would receive at full retirement age. The % reduction for the spouse should be applied after the automatic 50 percent reductions. Percentages are approximate due to rounding. * SOURCE: US SOCIAL SECURITY ADMINISTRATION

When Should You Start Collecting Benefits?

There are several factors to consider about when to start receiving Social Security:

- Are you planning to continue to work between age 62 and your full retirement age?
- What are the tax consequences of your starting Social Security?
- What is your anticipated life expectancy, and, if married, that of your spouse?
- Are you eligible for benefits on your work record and as a spouse?
- What other moneys are available to you at retirement that would allow you to delay starting Social Security at full retirement age and realizing increased monthly benefits (benefits increase 7.5 to 8 percent for every year you delay up to age 70).

▶ If you start collecting Social Security before full retirement age—and you continue to work—your benefits may be reduced if your earned income exceeds the maximum amount allowed.

Earning limitations. If you do start collecting Social Security before full retirement age and continue to work, your benefits may be reduced if your earned income exceeds the maximum amount allowed. For the current earned-income limitation, go to the Social Security Web site (*ssa.gov/pubs*), and go to the section for Retirement Benefit publications (specifically, "*If you work and get benefits at the same time*"). In 2008, the earnings limit was just over $1,000/month. After you reach your full retirement age, you can work as much as you want, and earn as much as you like, without having your benefits reduced.

Taxation of Social Security. Part of your Social Security benefits may be subject to federal income tax if your "total income" (adjusted gross income plus any tax-exempt interest income and 50 percent of your Social Security benefits) exceeds a base amount. Up to 50 percent of benefits are taxable if you are single with total income over a base amount of $25,000 or married filing jointly with income over $32,000. Up to 85 percent of Social Security benefits are taxable for singles with total income over $34,000 and married taxpayers filing jointly with total income over $44,000. So there may be tax advantages in not starting to collect benefits until your full retirement age, and even until age 70, if you anticipate that your total income will be less in these later years.

Longevity. If you expect that your Social Security benefits will be a significant component of your retirement income and that of your spouse, then how long you and your spouse live is an important factor in deciding whether to start Social Security early, or at full retirement age, or at age 70. You can estimate your life expectancy using The Healthspan Calculator (*agingreaearch.org*) , or The Life Expectancy Calculator (*livingto100.com*), or The Real Age Calculator (*Realage.com*). Although an individual at 65 may expect to live 18.2 more years, the joint life expectancy of a 65-year-old couple is 26.2 years.

Break-even age. To determine the age when the total amount of benefits you would receive if you wait until full retirement age begins to exceed the total amount you would receive if you start Social Security early, check out the Break-Even Calculator at *ssa.gov/OACT/quickcald/when2retire.htm*. If you choose to start receiving benefits early and invest those benefits instead of spending them, your break-even age will be extended out to a later date.

It's OK to change you mind. What if you started collecting your benefits early and decided later that you should have waited until full retirement age or later? Social Security will let you change your mind. If you stop your benefits and repay all the benefits you received, you may then collect your full benefits at full retirement age, or even enhanced benefits if you choose to delay receiving your benefits until a date beyond your full retirement age.

Your annual Social Security statement. Social Security sends workers age 25 and older who are not already receiving Social Security benefits an annual statement that contains an estimate of the retirement benefits you are projected to receive at age 62 and at full retirement age. There is also a year-by-year record of past wages covered by the Social Security tax so that you can verify that your earnings for each taxable year were correctly reported. It is your responsibility to correct any errors by using W-2 forms or employer records. If you have not been receiving your annual statement, you can request it online at . If you prefer to mail your request, you can download your Request for Social Security Statement (Form SSA-7004) at *ssa.gov/online/ssa-7004.html*.

Customized statements. Using what you learned earlier in this chapter, you are able to obtain a benefit statement customized to your particular circumstances. You can ask Social Security to provide benefit amounts based on different retirement scenarios. You provide information as to when you plan to retire from your current employment, whether you will have any future income and if so how much and for how long. For example, Jennifer plans to leave her practice at age 59. She will then work for an additional seven years earning $24,000 per year. Jennifer can provide this data to Social Security in order to receive a customized statement specific to her circumstances. She will not receive her annual statement in any year she requests a customized statement.

Applying for Social Security. You can apply for Social Security by phone (800-772-1213), or online (*ssa.gov*), or schedule an appointment at your local

Social Security office. We recommend that you start this process several months before you hope to start receiving your benefits. We also recommend that you consult with a Social Security representative and review your options before choosing to apply for your benefits.

Pension and Retirement Accounts

If you are fortunate enough to have a defined-benefit retirement plan (in which your employer will provide you with a monthly pension), you need to review your annual statement or talk to your benefits manager to learn the options you have at retirement. If you're married, you should consider taking an option that will continue to pay a monthly benefit if you, the pension holder, should die. This generally reduces the monthly benefit available, but would provide much needed security for your family.

If you're like most lawyers in private practice, the second leg of your "three-legged stool" consists of a defined-contribution plan. You have been responsible for this yourself with such tax-deferred retirement accounts as a 401(k), a Keogh, 403(b), Deferred Compensation (457), SEP, SIMPLE, and/or Traditional IRA's. The big attraction of these plans is that the amount of your annual contributions is deducted from income and not subject to current federal income taxes. This tax-deferral benefit can add hundreds of dollars to your savings each year. When you retire, your contributions, and the income from such plans, is then subject to regular income taxes in the year it is withdrawn. Some firms offer automatically deducted investment programs, and some may partially match your contributions, thereby accelerating the growth of your account.

For some of you, this "leg" of the stool may be in two sections. The first, and in most cases the largest, section will include your pension and/or pre-tax accounts. The second consists of your Roth IRA and Roth 401(k) accounts. The difference between the two is when taxes are paid on the funds. With Roth-type accounts, your contributions are made with after-tax dollars, but these are the last tax dollars you will pay on these accounts. The contributions plus all the income and growth accumulated over the years in the account is withdrawn tax-free after age $59\,^1/_2$.

You'll find a more detailed description and a discussion of these retirement plans in the next chapter.

Personal Savings

The third leg of the stool—your non-retirement personal savings—may be invested in many different asset classes, among them CD's, money market accounts, stocks, bonds, mutual funds, annuities, and some life insurance accounts. Hard-asset savings include investments in real estate, gold and other commodities, art and antiques. For those planning retirement before eligibility for penalty-free withdrawals from retirement accounts, this third leg of the stool will be the source of funds. In the next chapter, we'll discuss how to best construct this leg of the stool while saving for retirement and during retirement.

▶ How much money can you withdraw from your retirement/investment accounts each year, and not deplete the accounts before you die? About four cent. By raising your distribution to five or six percent, you risk outliving your assets.

When contemplating retirement, one of the most-often asked questions attorneys have for their financial adviser is, *"How much money can I withdraw from my retirement/investment accounts each year and not deplete the accounts before I die?"* The next chapter has a detailed discussion of strategies for withdrawing from your retirement next egg. For now, the quick answer is about four percent. You could raise your distribution to five or six percent, but you would risk outliving the assets you have set aside for you and your spouse/partner. To help with your calculations, we've created a quick reference at the end of this chapter. It's called *The Dipping Table*, and it will help you estimate how much you can withdraw from your investment and retirement accounts over varying amounts of time before they're depleted, as well as the amounts you can withdraw while still preserving your principal. Keep in mind that deciding when to start dipping/withdrawing from your accounts requires consideration of multiple factors, including:

- How much you will need to withdraw.
- How long can you withdraw without depleting the account.
- The rate of return you are earning on your accounts.
- The tax implications of your withdrawal plan
- How capable you are in coping with inflation.
- Your timing on certain events, like the $59\frac{1}{2}$ withdrawal age and the age $70\frac{1}{2}$ minimum distribution rules:

Now, let's see how your known income sources and your expenses will match up with one another:

Spend some time now so that you have an idea of how much retirement income you might expect from the first two legs of your stool. If you have completed the *Financial Assets Record*, you will have listed the amounts you and your spouse/partner can reasonably expect from Social Security, your retirement accounts, insurance, or any other arrangements you may have made for retirement income. For the time being, we are concerned only with the resources listed on the Financial Assets Record that are available to provide you and your spouse/partner regular retirement income. These include your Social Security, pension and retirement accounts. Your personal savings in bank accounts, stocks, investment real estate, etc., generally represent other resources that can be converted to retirement income. How close does this estimate come to matching what you think your financial needs will be? The next exercise will help you answer this question as we put your income up against your expenses.

Personal Retirement Graph

Drawing your own income-and-expense graph is simple. Once done, it's a useful aid in your retirement planning. In fact, this projection will create a remarkably accurate financial picture of your retirement years. There are five steps:

Step 1. Refer to your Expense Log (Page 62) for your monthly retirement expense target. Draw a dotted line across your Income and Expense Graph at this monthly expense level. The example for a couple retiring at age 60 shows monthly retirement expenses as $8,000.

Step 2. Enter your age at the year you plan to retire, and do the same for your spouse. The couple illustrated below are both retiring in the year 2010.

Step 3. Now, plot the monthly withdrawal from retirement plans and Social Security benefits you expect to receive with the year the benefits will start. On top of this, plot the any benefits your spouse expects.

EXAMPLE ONE: A HUSBAND & WIFE RETIRING TOGETHER (BOTH AGE 66)

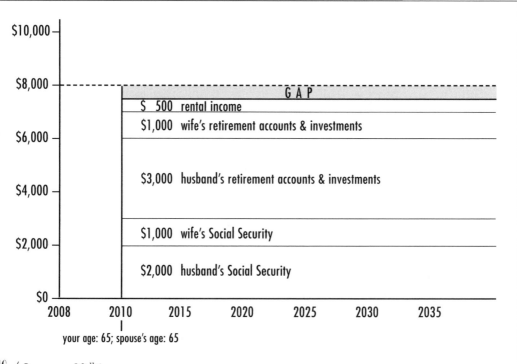

Step 4. On top of your spouse's Social Security income, plot any other regular monthly income you or your spouse will receive in retirement. In the first example, they have a rental paying $500 per month.

Step 5. Now compare your expected monthly retirement income with the dotted expense line and determine what additional supplemental monthly income, if any, is needed. In the first example, the couple will have a gap of only $500 per month; yours may be more.

Income & Expense #2: Single Person Retiring at 60

This second example is the projection for a single person who wants to retire at age 60 with a monthly income of $6,000. Notice that in this situation the person's retirement will be starting before he/she is eligible to receive their Social Security, creating a "stair-step" approach to this projection. In making the decision to retire early, this person creates a $2,000/month short-fall for six years, as well as some $400 for the rest of his/her life. Meeting these income gaps requires careful financial planning, possibly part-time work, and maybe reassessing their retirement lifestyle.

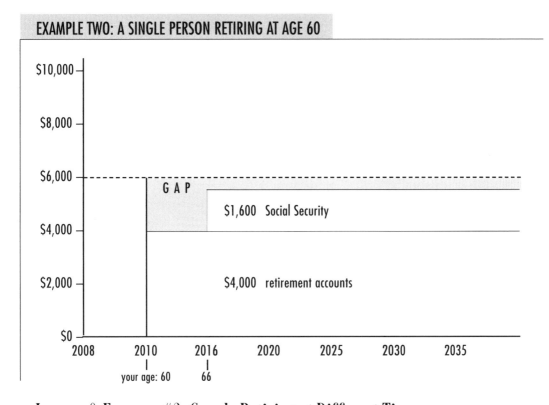

EXAMPLE TWO: A SINGLE PERSON RETIRING AT AGE 60

Income & Expense #3: Couple Retiring at Different Times

This third example shows a couple retiring at different times. They have estimated their monthly expenses at $10,000. In this case, too, there is a sizable

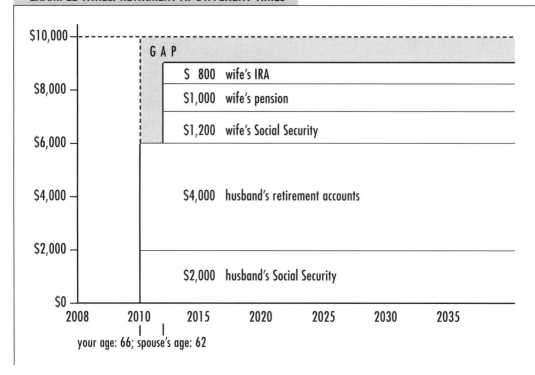

income gap in the years between the first and second retirements, as well as a $1,000/month gap afterwards.

Your Income & Expense Projection

Now it's your turn. From the steps and examples given above, chart your own projection on the next page.

What to do if you have a gap? If, after having completed your income and expense projections, the gap between the two is larger than your other savings and investments can address, we offer some options here. If you need to develop supplemental retirement income, even for just a few years, consider one of the following alternatives, or a combination thereof:

Delay retirement. Delaying your retirement by even one to three years can have a dramatic impact on your financial well-being. The combination of having several more years of what could be your highest income, the opportunity to save more of your income, and the delay in incurring retirement expenditures such as health insurance has a geometric benefit on your overall financial picture.

Employment of a spouse. If one spouse is presently working only part-time or not at all, consideration could be given to finding paid full-time employment. These additional earnings, even for just a few years, will provide income to bridge a gap. An essential aspect of this strategy is to make sure the additional income is saved for retirement, preferably through an automatic deposit plan, not used for current expenses. Remember, this is a retirement savings strategy not a strategy to upgrade your current lifestyle.

Reduce your expenses. If working longer is not an option, reducing your monthly expenses will reduce your gap dollar for dollar. Some have accomplished this by downsizing their residence, thus reducing the many expenses related to home ownership. Perhaps playing golf on public courses is a better financial decision than a club membership. Review all line items on your retirement budget for reduction possibilities.

Work in retirement. Supplementing retirement income with contract work or

YOUR INCOME AND EXPENSE PROJECTION

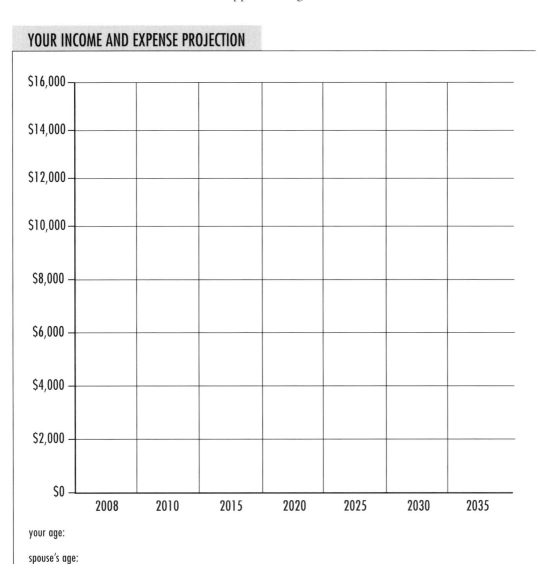

your age:

spouse's age:

a part-time practice has helped many attorneys. There are many creative arrangements retiring attorneys have worked out with their firms. For others, a hobby has been turned into a satisfying small business. You may have some thoughts about other things you want to do when you have finished your legal career, so thinking about these activities now as possible revenue-generators makes good sense. You should prepare for this new activity several years before retirement. Turn to Chapter 7 for more discussion on working after retirement, and go to *LawyerAvenue.com* to find a national roster of lawyer/career counselors and coaches, many of them with JD's themselves.

Increase savings. Another option is to increase the amount of savings for retirement now to provide for your shortfall. These funds may come from reducing current expenses or from any future increases in income. In addition to saving more, each of us can probably improve the way we manage our expenses and investments. Periodically, it is prudent to review how your investments are performing, and research whether there are financial institutions that may provide higher returns and/or lower costs. Be aware of the hidden costs in having someone else do your investing.

Invest more aggressively. We are not suggesting speculation as a way to fill the gap, but many people become far too conservative in their investments prior to, and during, their retirement years. As a consequence they lose several percentage points of return that could be used to make their nest egg more profitable and rewarding. Yes, many of your parents and grandparents did convert all their assets to bonds and CD's at retirement. But doing so today puts you at risk of running out of money well before you run out of life. With 20 to 30+ years to fund, you need your investments to grow above and beyond the rate of inflation.

Rethink your commitment to preserving an estate for heirs. Too often, we hear from both pre- and post-retirees that they only want to spend the earnings from their retirement accounts, and save the principle for their heirs. This concept often vanishes under closer inspection and may not be legally possible under the IRS' minimum-distribution rules on retirement accounts.

However you choose to fill an income/expense gap, remember that just identifying it is the most important thing you can do as you work through the financial aspects of your transition planning. Once you have the target in mind, you will find the best path to get there based on your particular life situation. As you consider strategies for filling in projected income gaps, keep the following basics in mind:

- Living beneath your means is one of the keys to a great retirement.
- Invest savings wisely (see Ch. 4).

- Eliminating debt can go a long way towards reducing your monthly income needs.
- Doing what is necessary to prevent any financial disruptions is also important.

The incidence of divorce is often elevated during the retirement transition as couples get to spend more time with each other than they have during their careers. Taking the time to nurture your relationship and deal with differences beforehand can have a dramatic impact on your financial viability. Other financial disruptions include children that are not prepared to be responsible for themselves financially, and the need to care for aging parents who perhaps did not do their own planning. For resources in this area, go to Appendix 3.

What Inflation Can Do to Retirement Income & Taxes

Inflation is one economic force that can chip away at our financial foundations.

The primary objective of financial planning is to save and invest your money at a rate of return that equals or exceeds the rate of inflation and taxation, thus maintaining the dollar value needed to purchase goods and services after retirement. No one can forecast future prices. But it is possible to take steps to avoid some of the financial difficulties inflation can cause. To deal effectively with expenses in retirement, one must maintain or improve the purchasing power of the funds set aside for that purpose. Over the past few years, inflation has been around three percent, very different from the double-digit levels we experienced two decades earlier. Being able to retire and have adequate purchasing power for the next 10, 20 or 30 years is an important objective. This is why you need a clear picture of how inflation is likely to affect the income we will need.

Consider:

Social Security. Social Security benefits are tied to the cost of living. Generally, if a couple determines that they will have benefits of $3,000/month, then that amount will be increased each year as the cost of living is increased. Your purchasing power will be maintained over future years as a matter of law unless Congress makes changes to the COLA. Many public pension plans (state systems, civil service, military, etc.) automatically adjust benefits as the cost of living rises too.

Private pension plans. The majority of private pension plans call for the payment of a fixed-dollar annuity that is the same amount of money each month for the life of the retiring person. Often this fixed-dollar annuity plan is extended to dependent survivors. Over time, the income stream can be greatly eroded by inflation. At four percent inflation, a dollar's purchasing power is reduced to 50 cents in about 15 years.

Investments. Monies invested in a balanced portfolio should provide a cushion against the ravages of inflation as one would expect the world's investment marketplace/economy to have returns greater than inflation. Your money is invested and you hope for the best returns, but experts agree that market "down years" may deplete your equity investments and raise problems with inflation-proofing. A partial remedy may include some investment in Treasury Inflation Protected Securities (TIPS), where a part of your income comes from these conservative but income-protected securities. Syndicated financial columnist Scott Burns (*scottburns.com*) has an online calculator for working with inflation assumptions and real returns on various investments.

> ▶ Experts agree that market "down years" may deplete your equity investments and raise problems with inflation-proofing. A partial remedy may include some investment in Treasury Inflation Protected Securities (TIPS).

Annuities. Basically there are two types of annuity payouts—fixed and variable. The fixed guarantees a fixed income for a specified period, such as 10 or 20 years, or for life. The amount of the annuity remains the same for the entire period with no adjustment for the cost of living reducing your purchasing power. Variable annuities will vary the amount of income paid out depending upon the equity investment and its rate of return. The claimed advantages of the variable annuity concept are a) protection against long-term erosion of purchasing power, and b) possible performance surpassing that of fixed-dollar annuities. The disadvantage of a variable annuity is the risk of loss of capital during the down times.

There are also two different time-frames associated with annuities: deferred and immediate. *Deferred Annuities* are sold by insurance agents and financial advisors as tax-deferred retirement savings vehicles. After-tax investments in Deferred Annuities grow on a tax-deferred basis inside the annuity. *Immediate Annuities* are purchased at or in retirement for the purpose of providing a guaranteed income stream. A lump sum of money is invested in an Immediate Annuity in return for payments back to the investor starting almost immediately.

Income taxes. For the purposes of example, let's say your salary increases in direct proportion to the cost of living. If the cost of living goes up seven percent, your salary would increase by seven percent as well. This would allow you to maintain your purchasing power … except for one factor: income tax rates take a bigger bite (e.g., *bracket creep*) as our income goes up. As a result, you would actually lose purchasing power because a larger percentage of your income would go to taxes. There are legal and appropriate ways to avoid certain taxes;

all of us need to look more closely at the tax consequences of any savings or investment decisions we make. We'll explore this topic more in the next chapter.

Cash, Risk Management & Home Equity

Thus far, this chapter has explored three basic questions:

What is the current state of your finances?
How do you picture your retirement, and how much will that vision of retirement cost?
How do you get from where you are to where you want to be?

But as you ease into retirement mode, it's important to think about three other major financial building blocks to determine what changes may make sense at this point in your life. They are:

• Emergency cash
• Risk management (insurance or self-insure).
• Home equity

Emergency cash. Emergency cash is money set aside in liquid investments (money market accounts, savings accounts, laddered Certificates of Deposit), so you can continue to pay essential monthly expenses (home, food, utilities, insurance, etc.) if your income stream is disrupted for any reason. During our working years, the suggested amount is between three-to-six months of expenses. Thus, if your essential monthly expenses are $6,000, your emergency cash fund should be between $18,000 and $36,000 depending on your circumstances.

▶ For peace of mind, expand your emergency fund from three-to-six months of available funds to one-to-three years. In this way, you're not likely to have to sell an asset at a loss in order to pay your bills.

As we move into the retirement environment where we are taking distributions from our investment accounts in order to supplement pensions (if available) and Social Security, the definition of emergency cash may change more to readily available liquid funds. Since you may be selling stocks, bonds, and real estate in order to generate needed cash for expenses you need to consider the reality of market volatility. In retirement you want to avoid having to sell assets in a "down" market to meet your monthly bills. Therefore we encourage you to expand the three-to-six month concept to one-to-three years of highly liquid available funds. By setting aside this amount, you give yourself the peace of mind of never having to sell an asset at a loss in order to pay your bills. We will discuss later how you might implement this concept in your retirement plan.

Risk management. Risk management has both a document component and an insurance component.

Risk management (documents). These are the documents that all of us should have throughout our adulthood, and midlife is an opportune time to review and revise them as necessary. We discuss these documents in greater detail in Chapter 6 (The Estate Planner). They include:

- *Will and/or Living Trust.* Provides for the disbursement of your assets.
- *Financial Durable Power of Attorney.* Gives someone you designate the power to make financial decisions for you if you're incapacitated.
- *Health Directive.* Creates an advanced medical directive that states your wishes about your medical care. With a Durable Power of Attorney for Health Care, you name a person called your health-care agent who is authorized to make medical decisions for you if you are unable to make them yourself.
- *Do Not Resuscitate Card/Document.* Many states require an additional form or card to be carried if you would choose not to have emergency personnel (911) perform life-sustaining activities. This document must be available to show emergency personnel or else they are obligated to perform life saving procedures.
- *Letter of Instruction.* A document that communicates to key individuals the specifics of your financial life. It lists your various bank and investment account locations, your insurance providers, your attorney, your accountant, your financial planner and other professional advisors. See Chapter 6 for additional details.
- *Beneficiaries.* It is advisable to verify that the beneficiaries on all your retirement and insurance accounts are as you want them. Many a second spouse has been stunned to learn that since a beneficiary was not changed on a document that the ex-spouse would be inheriting the asset. Remember, beneficiary designations take precedence over the Will and/or trust.

Risk management (insurance). The financial side of risk management deals with acquiring insurance to manage the risks associated with our lives and our assets. Evaluate whether you have managed your risks appropriately with insurance in these areas:

- *Health insurance & long-term care coverage:* Health care costs are one of the major expenses for retirees. Because of the importance to your successful retirement plan of decisions related to your health and long-term care insurance, we have devoted an entire chapter to assist you. Please refer to

Chapter 5 for a detailed discussion of several important topics.

- *Home and auto policies.* Are you gaining the benefit of discounts available when you insure both with the same company? Does your home insurance increase in value as building costs increase? Do you have the proper extra protection for environmental conditions in your area, i.e., flood insurance, earthquake coverage, etc? Take this time to review your policies and assure that your risks are properly covered.

- *Personal umbrella policy.* When you determined your net worth, you determined the total amount of money you would have if you hypothetically sold everything you owned and paid off all your debts. This amount is exposed in litigation in the event of a future lawsuit not covered by insurance. For peace of mind—and at a very reasonable cost—it is highly recommended that you acquire a Personal Umbrella Policy to cover whatever your net worth is at any point in time. This policy pays after your home and auto policies limits are reached and is far less expensive than purchasing $1 million + liability on the home and auto policy.

- *Business policies.* Chapter 8 (Closing a Practice) includes a discussion of tail-end malpractice coverage. Also, consider a Key Person Policy that allows for the financial transition between partners in a practice.

- *Disability insurance.* If you will depend upon income from work during your retirement, you need to protect this income with a disability policy that will replace generally around 60 percent of this income.

- *Life insurance:* If you died today, would your spouse/partner be able to continue to live comfortably, and have sufficient financial resources to support and educate your dependent children? Life insurance is an important risk-management tool to ensure that your spouse and dependents are financially protected in the event of your death if "self-insurance" isn't realistic.

▶ If you died today, would your spouse/partner be able to continue to live comfortably? Life insurance is a risk-management tool that ensures your spouse and dependents are financially protected.

How much insurance is enough?

The answer is different for each of us, depending on marital status, the age and number of dependents, the earning potential of each spouse/partner, and the lifestyle or standard of living you want to insure. Historically, the life insurance industry's rule of thumb is that your life insurance policy should be at least 10 times your annual salary. Online life insurance calculators allow you to manipulate variables to develop an estimate based on your specific needs. One such calculator is provided by the Life and Health Insurance Foundation for

Education calculator (*lifeline.org*). Some financial experts suggest that life insurance be used only for the protection of dependents, and they recommend less-costly term insurance to provide that protection. Although life insurance is normally not considered an investment product, there are life insurance products with investment components. In the section below, we offer a brief description of some of the most common types of life insurance policies:

Term insurance. A type of life insurance purchased for a limited number of years that has to be renewed periodically at a higher premium rate based on age. Some companies offer term policies which run to age 60 or 65. Further, a term policy may be convertible; that is, you may be able to exchange for permanent insurance with level premiums while accumulating cash values. A term policy normally accumulates no cash value. Group term insurance often is paid for in whole or in part by a firm. This is a valuable fringe benefit of some kinds of employment. Group insurance also may be purchased through other groups and organizations. Group insurance is normally convertible; you can keep the policy when you leave the firm by converting it to an individual policy and paying for it yourself, normally at a little higher rate. Some firms continue group term insurance for a former employee after retirement. The face value may drop drastically at 65, and continue dropping as the retiree ages. Another important thing to know about any policy is whether it contains a disability provision (a waiver of premium), and/or the payment of monthly income, if the policyholder becomes totally and permanently disabled.

Whole life policies. Whole life policies are normally written for the life of the policyholder, and at death pay the face value to the beneficiary. The face value is the amount stated on the face of the policy that will be paid at death or at the maturity of the contract. It does not include amounts payable under accidental death or other special provisions. Whole life policies are offered on the level premium plan, which means the premium stays the same even though the policy holder grows older. Such policies usually accumulate a cash and loan value after a specified number of years. A type of whole life, sometimes called pension maximization, is sold as income protection for the surviving spouse. While this product may in some cases prove a better protection tool than the survivorship options offered in many employer pension plans and annuity payouts, it is important to evaluate all aspects, especially the impact of inflation.

Universal life insurance. This type of policy falls somewhere between term and whole life. It provides term insurance with a tax-deferred savings account. The account earns interest at market rates. Often, the option exists to change the amount of protection periodically, use the savings account to make premium payments, or make larger payments to the account. Since insurance agents make a lower initial commission on selling universal than whole life, it is not unusual to pay annual administration fees of three to 10 percent of each year's premiums. Note: investing in life insurance for purposes of producing income for one's own retirement has both advantages and disadvantages. A major advantage is the certainty that the benefit will be paid under the stated conditions, either as an annuity, or as a lump sum death payment, to the beneficiary. Insurance is also used as a way of passing wealth to survivors escaping certain tax liabilities. A major disadvantage is the low rate of return that is earned on the savings accumulated under the whole life policies. Under such policies, a part of your premium payment pays for the protection in the event of death, and the remainder is accumulated as your savings, which is called cash value. The return on these excess premiums is often about four percent a year and set by state insurance commissions. Life insurance policies, therefore, are often strong on protection of dependents and weak on the return.

Single premium deferred annuities. Due to tax advantages, single-premium deferred annuities have become popular as retirement savings tools in addition to employer pension plans. They are purchased more as an investment product than protection since a considerable portion of the single premium amount goes to work immediately earning a respectable return tax deferred until the policy is redeemed. The policyholder will often have the option of selecting either a fixed or variable (varies with the investment and market conditions) rate of return.

Two important tax advantages of life insurance to consider: at death, the proceeds from a policy are delivered to the beneficiary tax free, and in some policies part of the premium is tax-deferred.

Regardless of the type of insurance you have chosen, the transition period provides a good time for review of how much insurance you really need. Typically, you bought life insurance in order to provide income for your spouse, to pay the monthly mortgage and other debt obligations, and to provide children's college funds. To the degree that you have grown your investment accounts, paid down your mortgage and debt expenses, and your children have completed college or have funds in place to do so, the amount of insurance that you may need on your life might be less than before. Choosing to reduce the amount of insurance may provide additional funds for retirement savings investment.

On the other hand, if you chose pension or annuity options that will not provide income for your spouse upon your death, you may find yourself with the need to maintain or acquire life insurance as an income protection plan.

Again, like many other decisions at this stage of life, your own particular circumstances will dictate the best course of action. Consulting with your financial advisor and insurance representative will provide you with specific recommendations for action.

Home Equity

Notwithstanding the current state of the housing market, home ownership is still a valuable investment for most of us. Home values have appreciated during our lifetimes, and in many cases this appreciation is one of the largest assets we own. Home equity is defined as the difference between what our home would sell for today (less selling expenses) and the mortgage we owe.

Home ownership in and of itself offers financial advantages beyond the equity "savings account" built through the combined forces of appreciating home prices and the gradual monthly reduction of our mortgage. With a fixed-rate mortgage, we experience the "freezing" of the monthly mortgage expense associated with keeping a roof over our heads. There are also the current benefits of yearly tax deductions for property taxes and mortgage interest. Home equity is a building block that offers many alternatives during our retirement years. How this home equity may be used to your advantage is dependent on what your plans are for your retirement lifestyle. Are you planning on staying in this home until you die, or are you planning on selling this home in order to downsize in the same geographic area or to move to a new state or even another country? Let's explore the possibilities under either circumstance.

Want to stay in your home forever? First, for those of you who decide to stay in your home. How can you gain access to some of this home equity if you do not actually sell your home? There are several options depending on the type of need that you have. Staying in your home will require continued maintenance. On fixed incomes the need for a new roof or other major expenses is probably not in your monthly budget. These periodic needs for additional funds can be satisfied by using a home equity loan or a home equity line of credit (HELOC), loans that are paid back in monthly installments.

With a home equity loan you get a lump sum of money, at a fixed interest rate for a specific period of time (usually no more than 15 years). A fixed amount (principle and interest) is paid back monthly until the loan is repaid. A home equity line of credit is another alternative. With a HELOC, you arrange to borrow up to a specific amount, say the same $25,000 as above, but you do not take the full $25,000 at one time. You can spend only $10,000 on a new roof today, and not use any of the balance until a later date...or never. This is a line of credit that you can access as needed by writing a check provided by your lender. You will pay interest only on the amount you have actually borrowed to spend. Most of these loans are at variable interest rate, which means that when interest rates change, you will be paying more or less for your monies borrowed. Since these loans often require that you just pay the interest on a monthly basis, borrowers need to have the discipline to pay some of the principle down each month along with the required interest or these can become very expensive loans over time.

While a home equity loan provides ways to tap the equity in your home for specific needs, some of us may need to convert our home equity into a monthly stream of income of a more permanent nature. In other words, our home may be used as a supporting leg of the income stool along with Social Security, pensions, and other savings and investments. The equity in your home can be used as a nest egg through the use of a reverse mortgage. As the name implies, a reverse mortgage is basically a loan that works backwards. You can borrow money based on the equity of your home and nothing has to be repaid until you move or die. The loan, with the accrued interest is repaid either from the proceeds of the sale or by your heirs obtaining a regular mortgage if they want to keep the property. These loans are available to anyone over age 62. Please note that these loans require that there be little or no current mortgage on the property. These loans generally have higher "closing costs", the expenses associated with getting the loan, and the interest rates are higher than standard mortgage rates. But, for those who face a decision of needing to sell their home in order to pay their monthly expenses, a reverse mortgage may offer a reasonable solution allowing you to stay in your home and yet providing you with needed funds. Due to their complexity, please consult a specialist if you choose to explore this financial alternative.

AARP has a good publication that describes the basics of reverse mortgages. Currently, federally insured reverse mortgages (Home Equity Conversion Mortgages) account for about 85 percent of reverse mortgages. The National Reverse Mortgage Lenders Association has a helpful online calculator to develop some estimates of loan amounts you may qualify for, and the costs you would incur. Go to *reversemortgages.org*.

Ready to move? Next, for those considering a move from your current place of residence to another, your home equity provides the funds for your next purchase whether it is in the same city, state, country or not. Under current tax law, a single person is exempt from paying capital gain taxes on $250,000 of appreciation and a married couple does not pay taxes on $500,000 of profit from selling a home, provided you have lived in the home as your principal residence for an aggregated two years out of the last five. At current rates, this saves a single person $37,500 and a married couple $75,000!

While this tax exemption applies to only your principal residence, the two out of five years residency requirement allows for some flexibility in your transition planning. Work with your tax advisor to determine the feasibility of making a vacation home a principal residence, or the ability to keep your current residence (as a rental or not) while you transition to a new home.

Whatever your plans are relating to your home, your real estate assets provide an important anchor point for your overall financial plan. Combined with planning for adequate cash reserve at all times and managing risks to your financial independence, these three key building blocks are essential to a strong financial foundation.

Heading Into the Home Stretch: 10 Mistakes You Don't Want to Make

- Continuing to accumulate debt rather than paying down debt at midlife.
- Inadequately projecting your monthly/annual expenses and overspending in early retirement.
- Withdrawing from your retirement accounts at an excessive or unsustainable rate.
- Inaccurately anticipating how long you will be able to continue to practice law (or remain employed full or part-time).
- Underestimating your life-expectancy or that of our spouse/partner, increasing the risk of running out of money before you run out of time.
- Failing to diversify your investments; getting overly concentrated in a few stocks, funds, or asset classes.
- Undertaking a leveraged investment position by buying stocks on the margin, or becoming over-leveraged in an inflationary real estate market.
- Locking into poor returns on your investments through long-term CDs or annuities.
- Failing to adequately project or defend against the erosive effect of inflation.
- Underestimating health-care costs in retirement.[22]

Date prepared _____

Pensions

Record all pensions you and your spouse expect to be paid, including Social Security income, employer pensions, and other pensions (e.g., military, government). For most pensions, it is difficult to obtain exact monthly income figures. However, estimates based on information from your pension fund representative of from your local Social Security office, should suffice for this exercise. To request an Earnings and Benefit Estimate from Social Security, call 800-772-1213.

- Source(s) of income
- Monthly income for you & spouse
- Monthly income for you as a survivor
- Monthly income for your surviving spouse

Retirement accounts

Record all tax-deferred retirement accounts (IRA, 401(k), 457 Deferred Compensation, etc.) owned by both you and your spouse:

- Source(s) of income
- Monthly income for you & spouse
- Monthly income for you as a survivor
- Monthly income for your surviving spouse

Bank, credit union & other accounts

Record all financial accounts owned by both you and your spouse:

- Company or institution/type of account
- Account number
- Listed owner
- Current balance

Stocks & bonds

List all stocks, bonds, and/or other securities, owned by both you and your spouse

- Company/type of security
- Number of shares
- Date purchased
- Certificate number
- Owner
- Current market value
- Cost

Insurance

Record all policies for you and your spouse that provide any death or living benefits. Don't forget that you may be included in a group insurance program through your company or organizations (e.g., your mortgage company, AAA or American Express).

- Insurance company
- Policy number
- Insured
- Beneficiary
- Policy owner
- Death benefit (natural/accidental)
- Cash value

Real estate

Record all of the real property owned by you and your spouse.

- Location/purchase date
- Purchase price
- Current market value
- Balance of mortgage
- Monthly payment
- Date mortgage paid off
- Owner title
- Net Rental Income

Other assets

List all items (e.g., jewelry, automobiles, collectibles) that could be converted to cash if necessary.

- Item description
- Date purchased/estimated cost
- Current market value

Regular Expenses: Current Budget Estimated Budget/Retired

Mortgage or Rent $ _____ $ _____
Utilities, Telephone _____ _____
Food (home and eating out) _____ _____
Work Expenses _____ _____
Entertainment, Recreation _____ _____
Clothing _____ _____
Laundry, Cleaning _____ _____
Personal _____ _____
Auto Operation _____ _____
Education _____ _____
Education of Children _____ _____
Contributions _____ _____
Support of Others _____ _____
Loans _____ _____
Regular Services _____ _____
Retirement Account _____ _____
Insurance (medical) _____ _____
Other _____ _____

Total Regular Expenses: $ _____ $ _____

Periodic Expenses: Current Monthly At Retirement

Property Taxes $ _____ $ _____
House Maintenance _____ _____
New Household Purchases _____ _____
Insurance (auto, home) _____ _____
Life Insurance _____ _____
Disability, Insurance _____ _____
Vacations _____ _____
Gifts _____ _____
Income Taxes (local, state, US) _____ _____
Legal Services _____ _____
Medical, Dental, Veterinarian _____ _____
Other _____ _____

Total Periodic: $ _____ $ _____
Total Monthly Expenses: $ _____ $ _____

YOUR NET WORTH

Date _____

Assets (what we own)		Liabilities (what we owe)	
Cash		**Home and auto**	
Cash on hand	$_____	Mortgage balance	$_____
Checking accounts	_____	Home equity loans	_____
Savings accounts	_____	Car loans	_____
Money market funds	_____		
Money owed to you	_____	**Loans**	
	_____	Credit card balances	$_____
Investments	_____	Education loans	_____
Stocks	$_____	Other loans	_____
Bonds	_____		
Mutual Funds	_____	**Other debts**	
Other investments	_____	Insurance premiums	$_____
	_____	Alimony/child support	_____
	_____	Taxes	_____
Personal property	_____	Debts to others	_____
Autos	$_____		
Home furnishings	_____		
Clothing	_____		
Jewelry	_____		
Art, antiques	_____		
Other collector items	_____		
Other assets			
Home (true cash value)	$_____		
Other real estate equity	_____		
Vested pension benefits	_____		
401k	_____		
IRA's	_____		
Life Insurance (cash value)	_____		
Annuities & Def. Comp.	_____		
Other assets	_____		
Total assets	$_____	**Total liabilities**	$_____

YOUR NET WORTH (Assets – Liabilities): $_____

THE DIPPING TABLE*

Starting with this lump sum	Amt. you can withdraw each month for a specific number of years, reducing your principal to zero					Amt. you can withdraw per month & keep your principal
	5 yrs.	10 yrs.	15 yrs.	20 yrs.	25 yrs.	
$ 50,000	$ 940	$ 529	$ 395	$ 330	$ 292	$ 208
75,000	1,411	794	592	495	438	313
100,000	1,881	1,058	790	659	585	417
200,000	3,762	2,116	1,579	1,319	1,169	833
300,000	5,643	3,175	2,369	1,978	1,753	1,250
500,000	9,405	5,291	3,948	3,297	2,922	2,083
750,000	14,108	7,936	5,922	4,945	4,384	3,125
1,000,000	18,811	10,582	7,896	6,594	5,845	4,167
1,500,000	28,216	15,873	11,843	9,891	8,767	6,250

*Rate of return for the above table is 5%.

CHAPTER 4

The Assets & Investments Planner

"Americans Delay Retirement as Housing,

Stocks Swoon" —*Wall Street Journal* HEADLINE

All of us are investors of one sort or another.

Some are more conservative, investing in the safest investments or just paying down the mortgage on our home; others are more aggressive, putting money into stocks, bonds, real estate, and commodities. Regardless of where you fall on the investment risk-taking spectrum, to maximize your investment return you must have a sound understanding of investment concepts and alternatives.

We have designed this chapter to provide you with the basic investment principles and financial strategies you will need to employ in building and spending your nest egg for and in retirement.

Depending on your investment experience, this chapter represents either an introduction to investment concepts or a review of known principles. We urge everyone to spend the time to either learn or revisit these investment basics. Like baseball spring training, even investment professionals review and practice the basics of investing in order to insure a strong consistent performance. Keep in mind that each of you have different objectives so the frame of reference you bring to the world of savings and investments will vary. Differences of opinion are the norm and are OK. You don't want to blindly follow your partner's or neighbor's investment strategies; their goals and tolerance for risk may be totally different than yours. Drawing from our discussion in Chapter 3, if you know where you are today and where you want to go—and have a basic knowledge of investment principles—you will be able to find the best path to reach your individual financial objectives.

For most of you, this basic knowledge will be used to communicate with your professional advisors. Knowing the language and concepts of investing is a primary way to assure that your advisors are working in your best interest to achieve your goals.

One lawyer we interviewed wondered, "It would be nice if I could find a financial professional who made moderate gains on my investments, kept the losses small, and gradually increased my money without charging a huge fee."

Many lawyers we know have found someone meeting that description; others weren't so lucky. Which brings to mind a story close to home: John Clyde, one of this book's co-authors, says he had been saving for years for his daughter's college educations when he was approached by an acquaintance. The acquaintance, an investment broker, recommended that John and his wife invest $11,000 of their college fund in two investment-grade diamonds. Everything worked out well…for a while. Within a year his investment doubled in value. But within three years, the bottom dropped out of investment diamonds, and the value of the stones was eventually worth a quarter of what John originally paid!

On Financial Advisors

It shouldn't come as a surprise that the financial advisor specializing in stocks is likely to recommend investments in stocks; the insurance specialist will probably suggest strengthening your insurance program; and the specialist in real estate will probably encourage you toward real estate strategies. Financial advisors tend to specialize, and human nature being what it is, they are likely to be more interested in, biased toward, and advocates of, what they themselves are selling. Accepting that financial experts are as prone to human shortcomings as the rest of us, we are better prepared to employ the analytical skills we use as lawyers to make effective use of the valuable information and services they can provide.

Sometimes, the concerns we have about the integrity of financial consultants may cause us to avoid or delay developing and employing an investment game plan. *But in the long-run, that could prove fatal to achieving financial independence.*

▶ Concerns about the integrity of financial consultants can sometimes cause us to avoid or delay developing an investment game plan. In the long-run, that could prove fatal to achieving financial independence.

Knowledgeable, hard-working, financial experts (i.e., bankers, accountants, financial planners, insurance agents, stock brokers) stand ready to help you invest. And while they can be an excellent source of information, their recommendations should never automatically become your decisions. The people who represent themselves as "experts" have the obligation to communicate the facts, both pros and cons, in a way that is clear, accurate, and understandable. So, keep asking questions and requesting the information you need to understand all of your options and your own needs well enough to make decisions. If necessary, shop until you find experts who have the communication skills to clearly understand your needs, your goals, your risk tolerance, your objectives.

How to find a financial adviser. In the US today, there are nearly 400,000 professionals providing financial advice, many of whom are professional brokers and planners. Wall Street Journal columnist Jonathan Clements put into words the skepticism/cynicism most of us entertain at times about the financial services industry, "the investment advice business doesn't inspire confidence, (and) given a choice between signing on with the typical financial adviser or simply dumping everything into Treasury bonds, I would take the Treasuries every time." Clements recommends using fee-only advisers (those who charge an hourly fee, a percentage of your portfolio's value, or a fixed annual retainer). In addition, he recommends working with brokers, planners, and insurance agents who have taken the time to become certified (a CFP, or Certified Financial planner, a Chartered Financial Consultant, a Chartered Financial Analyst, or CPA/personal financial specialist). Any of these, should have the requisite credentials and expertise to assist you in developing investment strategies and managing your portfolio.

We would include the following questions when interviewing financial advisor candidates:

- What are your qualifications/credentials?
- Are you a CFP? If so, how long have you been practicing as a financial planner?
- Are you a Registered Investment Advisor?
- What other licenses or certificates do you have, and when did you obtain them?
- How are you compensated for your services? Do you charge by the hour, by a flat fee, or by commission on the sale of products?
- What is your approach and/or philosophy of financial planning and investing?
- Do you sell/recommend specific investment products?
- What experience do you have working with lawyers or other professionals?
- Is there a minimum account balance that you require?
- What size accounts do you typically handle?
- How frequently do you review your accounts?
- Who will be the person(s) working on my account?
- May I have the names and contact information for 10 current clients for reference? You will then randomly select several to call.

To help sort the wheat from the chaff, here are some of the better-known and well-established designations you might see behind the names of financial advisors looking to win your business:

CFA (*Chartered Financial Analyst*). Awarded by the CFA Institute, this designation goes to investment professionals who successfully complete a rigorous three-year, three-exam program of study in the fields of portfolio management and investment analysis. While held by some personal financial advisors, the designation is especially popular among Wall Street security analysts and money managers who cater to institutional investors.

CFP (*Certified Financial Planner*). Awarded by the Certified Financial Planner Board of Standards to candidates who complete a personal financial planning curriculum, pass a 10-hour, two-day exam, and provide evidence of financial planning-related work experience. It is increasingly becoming the most well-known designation for financial planners.

ChFC (*Charter Financial Consultant*). To become a Chartered Financial Consultant, financial advisers must complete an educational program offered by The American College, which cover financial planning, investments and insurance, meet experience and ethical standards, and complete 30 hours of continuing education biannually.

CPA/PFS (*Certified Public Accountant/Personal Financial Specialist*). CPAs who wish to specialize in financial planning can go on to earn the Personal Financial Specialist credential from the American Institute of Certified Public Accountants by accruing at least 1,400 hours of financial planning business experience, committing to continuing education in the field, and passing any one of six qualifying exams, including those required to a CFP, ChFC or CFA designation.

RIA (*Registered Investment Adviser*). A financial adviser who has registered with the Securities & Exchange Commission or his or her state securities regulator to manage the investments of others. To become an RIA, advisers typically must pass the Series 65 Uniform Investment Advisor Law Examination administered by the North American Securities Administrators Association, or have earned one of the following certifications: CFP, ChFC, or CPA/PFS.

* PREPARED BY THE *WALL STREET JOURNAL* AND THE FINANCIAL PLANNING ASSOCIATION ●

To make sure you're getting someone knowledgeable, search for a CFP at *cfp.com*. If you use a broker, check for disciplinary problems at *pdpi.nasdr.com/pdpi*. And if you want to find a fee-only adviser in your area, go to *feeonly.org* or to *garrettplanningnetwork.com*.

Keep in mind, if you are single you will want a planner who works with the issues of singles in retirement, and couples with children will want to associate with a family-oriented financial planner. And if you have any special circumstances, such as a special-needs family member, finding an advisor with experience in that area is all-important.

For many people, the best approach to financial planning is assembling a team of professionals. You serve as the general manager, making sure that your "team" communicates with each other. Members of your team might include your financial planner, your attorney (one knowledgeable with estate and elder law), your accountant, your real estate agent, and your insurance agent. By forming a team, you get the best of all worlds. In fact, you may find some of these professionals already aligned and sharing office space. Making the decision to hire an expert or team of experts doesn't relieve you of the responsibility of understanding investment concepts. You must ultimately take responsibility for your financial independence.

So, let's get down to some of the basics.

Keys to investment growth: the fundamentals

Progressing toward financial independence depends on making consistent savings contributions, harnessing the "power of return" (i.e., appreciation plus dividends or interest), and giving yourself the "power of time" to allow the "power of compounding" to multiply your accumulated wealth. Managing taxes is also important to the success of this equation.

> ▶ The one factor that distinguishes lawyers who attain financial independence from those who don't is NOT how much they earned practicing law. It's that they managed to save a percentage of their annual income.

Three fundamentals:

Spend less than you earn. You need to spend less than you earn if you want to accumulate wealth for retirement. That may be obvious to you, but in the course of our lawyer retirement workshops we're constantly amazed at how many lawyers ignore this financial reality. *In fact, the single most important factor that most often distinguishes lawyers who have attained financial independence from those who have not, is not the amount of money they earned practicing law. It's that, over a period of many years, lawyers who have succeeded in attaining financial independence had saved a percentage of their annual income.* Each year…good income or not…these lawyers had saved 10 to 15 percent of their net income, even if they had to borrow the money to make their maximum annual IRA or 401(k) contribution. Many lawyers seem not to have the discipline to accomplish this. However, living beneath your means is one of the keys to a great retirement.

Appreciate the power of compounding. Regardless of what we decide to invest in, our partner in investing is the "power of compounding", which no less than Albert Einstein once described as *the most powerful force in the universe.* The ultimate result of our savings and investments depends partly on the amount of our savings contributions, but mostly it is produced from the compounding of our gains over time. The earlier we begin an investment the more powerful the effect of compounding will be. As an example, a 20-year-old, who puts $2,500 a year in a Roth IRA for only 10 years (a savings total of $25,000) at a conservative five percent rate of return will have accumulated $200,790 at age 67. Someone who waits until age 40 and saves $2,500 a year until age 60, will have contributed $50,000, and yet will have only accumulated $122,134 at age 67.

A simple methodology for determining the growth of an investment is the "Rule of 72". If you want to know how long it will take for your investment to double at a given interest rate, or what interest rate you will need to get over a specific time period for your investment to double, you divide the known interest or years into 72. For example, if Pat can get six percent on a given investment, she can determine that it will take 12 years for her $5,000 investment to grow to $10,000 (72 @ 6 percent = 12 years). If she has only 10 years until the monies are needed she would need to get a 7.2% return (72 divided by 10 years = 7.2%).

Know your tolerance for risk. It's a cliche but true; higher return usually goes hand in hand with higher risk. So, if you can't afford to lose your investment, *minimize* your risk; if you want to *eliminate* risk almost entirely, expect to receive the lowest return on your investment. Evaluating investment alternatives is a matter of analyzing the risk/reward expectations of a given investment. Knowing your risk profile will allow you to select the appropriate investments to meet your goals while allowing you to sleep at night. Your financial planner can help you determine your risk profile; also, most investment Web sites will provide a risk-analysis tool as part of their asset-allocation section.

What risks are we talking about? Professionals agree that they generally fall into five categories:

- *Loss of purchasing power.* As discussed in Chapter 3, inflation is the enemy of purchasing power. Over time the same dollar buys less. So, even if we think we are choosing a very conservative investment approach, we risk losing the ability to cover our expenses as inflation silently, but consistently increases their cost.
- *Interest rate changes.* Interest rate changes have an inverse relationship to bond returns. When interest rates rise, the value of bonds paying a lower interest decline. An interest rate decline has the opposite effect. Because your existing bonds pay a higher interest rate, they are more valuable than newer bonds paying a lower interest rate. If you hold your bonds until their maturity date, you are not really impacted by these changes. Barring a default, you will get your expected interest rate and the bond's face value. It is when you trade bonds or invest in a bond mutual fund that you face the interest rate risk.

- *Financial risk* (business failure). When investing in any business, you run the risk that the business may not be successful and will therefore be unable to meet their financial commitments. If a company is unable to sell their goods or services for a profit, the value of their stock goes down and if cash flow is not sufficient, bond holders may experience missed interest payments or at worst default.

- *Business risk* (poor management). Sometimes the business premise is viable, but management is not able to achieve the expected results. Or, sometimes, fraud is involved (think Enron, World Com, Tyco). As an investor, you and your advisors must stay ever vigilant through research in order to minimize this risk.

- *Stock market risk* (fluctuation). This risk is a fairly general one. You know the market goes up and down. During these swings, even the best stocks are impacted to one degree or another. Down market experience has shown, however, that if the underlying fundamentals of a company are strong, it will rebound faster once the market turns up.

The risk-return pyramid below is helpful in portraying the levels of risk and return associated with the different categories and classes of investments. The base of the pyramid (risk management or forms of insurance to protect against the loss of assets) represents the safest (e.g., lowest-risk) investments offering the lowest anticipated rates of return. These conservative investments also carry the *greatest* potential for loss of purchasing power due to inflation. As you move up the pyramid, you increase your potential for higher returns by assuming increased exposure to higher market volatility. If you are not familiar with all of the investment categories/classes represented, we have included an investment glossary at the end of the chapter.

Along the left side of the pyramid are three categories of asset classes:

Conservative. These investments provide the greatest safety. Several are protected directly or indirectly by government safeguards and provide excellent savings vehicles though with lower returns.

Moderate. These investments generally consist of those that can provide a better return than the conservative investments but at greater risk.

Aggressive. This level represents those with a much higher degree of risk. The risk includes loss of principal, so they should be selected only as part of an overall diversified portfolio and with investment capital you can afford to

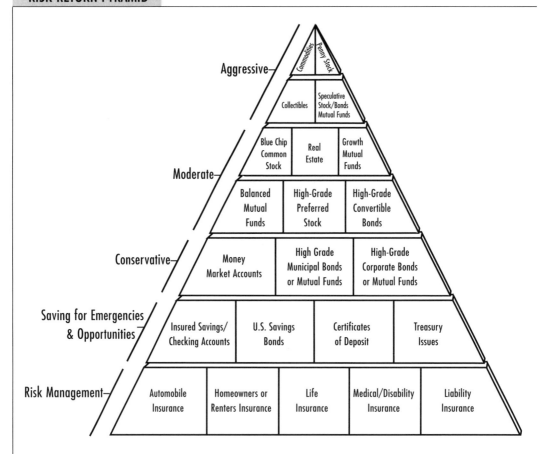

lose should you need it at a time when values have dropped. During 2000 and 2001, some portfolios heavily invested in high tech stocks lost 80–90%; in 2007 and 2008, portfolios heavily weighted toward real estate have suffered.

As you review the pyramid, perhaps locating the positions of your current investments along the risk/reward path, keep in mind that the increase in risk we are discussing relates to an increase in what is called volatility more so than a loss of capital. Volatility speaks to the fluctuation of value/prices over a period of time. As you move up the pyramid, you have a higher risk of prices fluctuating up and down more dramatically over the short term. But this same volatility can be managed over the long term in order to gain the advantage of higher overall returns.

Does it really make much difference where you put your money? Yes! Return is the all-important fuel behind the power of compounding and is essential to reaching your goals. On the next page, you'll find different rates of return with the same amount and time-frame.

Amount Invested	Time	Rate of Return	Total
$100/month	30 years	5%	83,712
Same	Same	9%	183,074
Same	Same	12%	349,496

Most successful investment portfolios will include an appropriate mix from all parts of the pyramid consistent with an investor's ability to assume risk (often determined by the investor's risk profile) and the time when the monies will be needed.

With all these choices, how do you determine what to invest in? Different asset classes perform better than others one year to the next. There have been years when bonds, investments we generally think of as conservative and therefore providing lower returns, have outperformed all classes of stock. Because you never know what the next year will bring, it is important to implement the investment concept of diversification.

Keys to Investment Growth: Diversification

We know a plaintiff's lawyer who invested two of the largest judgments of his career in the stock market in the late 1990s, and he rode the dot.com boom. Just about the time his portfolio was peaking, the lawyer—feeling financially independent—notified clients and others he might close his practice. Soon after, the dot.com boom turned into a dot.com-bust, and the lawyer was financially unable to retire after all. Worse, his long-time referral sources had gone away by this time, and he was forced to rebuild his practice from the ground up.

Lesson learned? Don't put all your eggs in one basket. Diversify.

Diversification, also known as *asset-allocation*, is extremely important to your ultimate success. Simply put, it is the breaking apart of your total capital into several investments that can meet your financial objectives. By investing in several complementary asset classes (stocks, bonds, inflation-protected securities, real estate investment trusts, etc.), you stand a better chance of reducing your risk by spreading the chance of loss over several unrelated investments. A setback in any one is likely to be counteracted by gains in the others. In fact, diversification can often produce better overall performance since it may allow you to select some investments with potentially higher returns. For example:

If you put $10,000 in one investment for 20 years with a 7.5 percent return, you would earn more than $42,000. Now assume that same $10,000 is divided into five equal parts and put into separate investments generating different rates of return for the same period— $2,000 @ 0 percent; $2,000 @ 5 percent; $2,000 @ 7.5 percent;

The Assets & Investments Planner / 73

$2,000 @ 10 percent; $2,000 @ 15 percent. Those investments would grow in excess of $62,000! Even with a single non-performer, the overall effect of diversification would not only have earned you more money but reduced your risk at the same time.

Studies show that asset-allocation accounts for up to 92 percent of your total return; investment selection (i.e., what you chose to invest in within an asset class) accounts for four percent; investment timing (i.e., when you buy and sell) two percent, and the differences in the cost of investing another two percent. *So, if you do nothing more than assure your monies are properly and truly diversified across the different asset classes, you will have taken a major step towards your financial success.*

> ▶ Want to have a diversified portfolio with little or no effort? Put your bond funds into a Total Bond Fund that has bonds with a mix of maturity dates and quality. Put 70-80 percent of your stock funds in a Total (US) Stock Market Fund, and 20-30 percent in a Total International Stock Fund.

Time-based asset-allocation. A second component of diversification calls for matching your risk profile with the time-horizon of when you will need to start pulling money from your portfolio. For example, suppose you don't intend to retire for another 10 years or more. Your stock investments may have wide fluctuations in that time, but historically they will probably out-perform either bonds or money-market accounts. On the other hand, if you think you'll need to draw on your portfolio in two or three years, lower-risk investments would avoid fluctuations and provide the money when needed. Your overall portfolio diversification may be comprised of several smaller diversification buckets that are aligned with the year you will need the funds within them. This time-horizon concept will be discussed in greater detail later as we explore how to best diversify our assets in order to fund our retirement needs.

Financial experts agree that asset-allocation is the single most important factor in producing stable, long-term investment results. Historically, financial planners suggest that the percentage of your assets you keep in interest-earning or conservative investments should match your age. So, if you are 35, put 35 percent of your assets in these investments; if you're 50, divide your assets between interest earning assets and equities. This rule of thumb may be challenged as you plan for increased life expectancy and therefore elongated years of needed retirement income. Later, we will explore the mix from another time-oriented perspective which may allow you to adjust the percentages based on your own financial picture. Whatever you determine your appropriate asset allocation mix to be, remember to consult with your financial advisor to review your portfolio at least annually to determine if it needs to be "rebalanced".

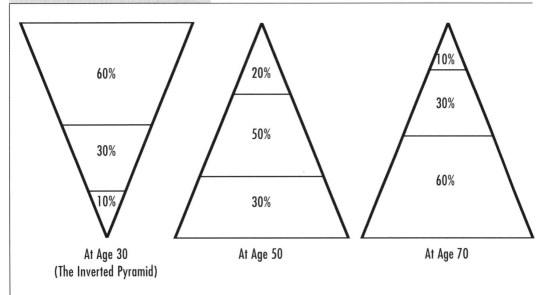

At Age 30
(The Inverted Pyramid)

At Age 50

At Age 70

A rule of thumb some financial planners endorse suggests the percentage of you assets that you keep in interest-earning investments (i.e. bonds, GIC's, CD's and Money Market funds) should match your age. In other words, if you are age 35, put 35% of your assets in these investments. If you are age 50, split your assets between interest earning assets and equities. ●

Rebalancing. Let's say that you have established an asset allocation of 60 percent stocks, 35 percent bonds, and five percent money market cash. Over the past year, stocks have done well but bonds have lagged a little, leaving you with an allocation of 70 percent stocks, 25 percent bonds and five percent conservative. You *rebalance* by selling 10 percent of the stocks and buying into the bonds, returning to your original 60-35-5 allocation. Why? Because asset classes are cyclical and tend to revert back to the mean. By rebalancing, you lock in the stock gains; plus, a 70 percent weighting in stocks is outside your risk tolerance as determined when you set up your asset allocation. If you are still actively contributing new funds to your accounts, you could choose to rebalance by allocating all new funds to bonds until you reach your desired allocation, but you may lose the advantage of capturing your stock gains.

▶ Trying to pick your own stocks is like trying to do your own appendectomy. If you're not prepared to rebalance your investments yourself, get an investment firm to handle your assets.

Targeted funds. If you don't want the responsibility of monitoring and managing your investment portfolio, you should know about *target-date* (or *life-cycle*) mutual funds. Here's how they work: if you planned to retire in 2020, you would put all of your retirement funds in a 2020 "targeted" fund. As you age, the investment mix would be reallocated toward less risk by increasing the percentage of such conservative vehicles as bonds and Treasury Inflation-Protected Securities (TIPS). There are many target-date mutual funds with different allocation strategies. Some reduce risk and allocate the investment mix to more conservative investments more quickly than others. You would need to research the design and investment objectives of each, and see which is consistent with your own objectives. Don't be concerned with the specific target date name, but rather the right mix for your risk profile. In some cases, the best fund for your 2020 retirement may be a fund titled "2025" or "2030".

Dollar-cost averaging. All investments have volatility. But timing only accounts for about two percent of your overall portfolio return. Most studies show that trying to time the market (attempting to profit by deciding when to jump into and out of a given stock, bond, or real estate market) is not an effective strategy and can in fact reduce your overall return. Advisors strongly recommend ignoring the ups and down of a market and using the concept of dollar-cost averaging to increase the effectiveness of your investment pyramid purchases, particularly those in the upper sections of the pyramid.

Dollar-cost averaging is a technique that goes to work for you when you purchase securities on a regular, systematic basis. It's a technique used by many investors who have the same amount of money deducted from their checks to purchase securities regardless of the ups or downs in the market. As a result, the investor buys more shares or units of the investment when the price is low and fewer shares when prices are high. To work successfully, share prices must rise following declines in value, with regular dividends going to purchase additional shares.

When it is time to begin spending your savings in retirement, a systemic withdrawal plan implements the dollar-cost averaging concept in reverse. If you need $500 a month, you will need to sell 10 shares if the price is $50, but only eight shares if the price increases to $62.50. You sell more shares when prices are down, and fewer shares when the price increases.

Keys to Investment Growth: Liquidity

As you make the transition towards the next phase of your life, the significance of planning for liquidity within your investment profile will become more important. During your working career your orientation has been to accumulate funds for retirement. When you ultimately make the transition from working to retirement, you need to make a critical mind shift away from saving towards spending these assets. In Chapter 3, you read about the need to change your planning mind-set from having three-to-six months of expenses in your cash reserve/emergency fund to perhaps one-to-three years.

Liquidity is the ability to readily convert an investment into cash at any time without loss of principle. For example, a US Savings Bond is liquid because one can redeem it for cash by simply redeeming it at a bank. On the other hand, while you can sell a stock or mutual fund at any time as well, you can not assure yourself that the sale will not be at a loss if the market or that particular investment is down at the time you need to sell. Real estate is not liquid because it could take months to sell even though you might be able to sell at a profit. Some investors desire liquidity since it does allow them to convert an investment to cash whenever they want to do so. With this desire in mind, many people approaching retirement believe they should convert their stocks and mutual funds to bonds or CD's in order to provide liquidity to fund their lifestyles. But remember, the penalty for liquidity is a lower rate of return and therefore the potential loss of purchasing power through inflation. You must balance the desire for liquidity with the need for growth to maintain purchasing power or you run the risk of running out of money.

> ▶ The penalty for liquidity is a lower rate of return and a potential loss of purchasing power through inflation. To maintain purchasing power, you must balance the desire for liquidity with the need for growth or you risk running out of money.

In light of your liquidity needs, your upcoming financial transition also gives an opportunity to re-analyze your investment portfolio in terms of income vs. growth.

Income vs. growth. Suppose you invest $100,000 in a way that provides you with an annual income of, say, $5,000. Your capital (the $100,000) stays the same year after year, generating a consistent annual income for you. On the other hand, if you choose to invest the money in stock or real estate, your capital might grow to as much as $200,000 in seven or eight years but it may not provide annual income. Traditional financial advice suggests that you accumulate as much capital as you can in your peak earning years, then switch from capital-growth to income-producing investments several years before retirement. While this strategy is still valid, it is important to maintain growth investments during retirement in order to compensate for inflation and the potential longevity of our retirement years. A strategy to accomplish both growth and income is to invest your growth dollars in dividend paying stocks or real estate that provides a positive cash flow. In the ideal world, when your growth investments (stocks, real estate, etc.) were nearing their highs, you would move them to the best income-producing investments you could find. But how do you know your investment is nearing its highs? When there is a buzz about how well your investment is performing (and your doctor friends are buying into it).

Unfortunately, the better your investment returns, whether from appreciation or income, the more you may need to share your profits with Uncle Sam and perhaps your state & local governments. In all investment planning, it is important that we not forget our governmental partners that want their share of our gains.

Tax Planning

Tax planning is the process of looking at various tax options in order to determine when, whether, and how to conduct personal transactions so that taxes are eliminated or reduced. Two types of taxes will often play a role in your investment decisions—income through interest & dividends and capital gains. Capital gains taxes are based on the difference between the price we pay to buy an asset and the price we receive upon the sale of the asset. Buying an asset for $3,000 and selling it for $6,000 after sale expenses produces a capital gain of $3,000. While doubling your money is definitely a good thing, where that asset was held and how long will dictate what type of taxes you owe.

Our progressive federal income tax system is currently bracketed between 10 and 35 percent, depending upon annual taxable income...and many states and some localities also tax individual income. Based upon past income, you probably have an idea of your combined federal and local tax bracket, which could translate into the high 30's or low 40's, a pretty big number. However, making investment trades in retirement accounts normally generates no immediate or annual taxes. Rather, the increase in value or profit from a trade builds the value of the retirement asset, tax-deferred. At a later date, however, the annual proceeds withdrawn are taxed as regular income at your combined federal and state income tax rate. So, withdrawals from your pre-tax retirement accounts, whether they are the original dollars invested, interest or dividend income, or capital gains from growth, are all taxed the same at your then combined income tax rate. Roth 401(k) or Roth IRA accounts have no taxes at withdrawal since the taxes were paid on the money deposited; nor are taxes generated from the increase through interest and dividends or growth (capital gain) in the Roth accounts.

Investments in taxable accounts (e.g., non-retirement, after-tax accounts; the 3rd leg of your three-legged stool) have profits and dividends taxed as capital gains and interest income taxed as regular income. Taxes on interest and dividend income are paid on an annual basis. Capital gains taxes are only due upon the sale of an asset. Short-term capital gains (on assets held less than one year) are taxed at your combined income bracket and long term gains (on assets held more than a year) are currently taxed at a 15 percent or 10 percent rate. As you can see, the length of time an asset is held plays not only an important part in the investment's value, but in its taxation.

TAX IMPACT

Account Type	How Taxed	When
Non-Roth Retirement Accounts	Ordinary Income	Annual
Roth Retirement Accounts	Tax-Free	N/A
Non-Retirement Accounts:		
Long Term Capital Gains	Capital Gains 15 or 10%	Sold
Dividends	15 or 10%	Annual
Short Term Capital Gains	Ordinary Income	Sold
Interest	Ordinary Income	Annual

The higher your tax bracket, the more attractive tax-free investments become. While the interest rate paid on tax-free investments such as municipal bonds is generally lower than that paid on US Government or Corporate bonds, they oftentimes yield more on an after-tax basis. The following table may help you assess the advantage of tax-free investments in certain interest rate markets. If you are in the 35 percent tax bracket you would need to find a bond paying at least 4.6 percent to have an equivalent return to a muni paying only three percent. If you are in a higher income bracket and are investing in municipal bonds, work with your financial advisor and accountant to make sure the interest income earned will not trigger the Alternative Minimum Tax (AMT).

TAX-FREE VS TAXABLE—EQUIVALENT YIELDS

Tax Free	15%	25%	28%	33%	35%
3%	3.5	4.0	4.2	4.5	4.6
3.5%	4.1	4.7	4.9	5.2	5.4
4.0%	4.7	5.3	5.6	6.0	6.2
4.5%	5.3	6.0	6.3	6.7	6.9
5.0%	5.9	6.7	6.9	7.5	7.7

If you are in one of the higher federal tax brackets, you have experienced a substantial bite in your income taxes over the past several years. This is a result of IRS regulations in which more and more taxpayers are losing certain tax deductions based on their mid-to-high annual incomes. Consulting your CPA or tax advisor may help you better understand what tax-reducing strategies may be available to you, including minimizing the Alternative Minimum Tax (AMT).

Tax diversification. While understanding the tax ramifications of individual investments is important, the overall structure of your investment portfolio can also be viewed from a tax perspective. Earlier, we discussed above the importance of *asset diversification* (having your assets invested across the risk pyramid), and *time diversification* (having your assets invested in the appropriate level of the asset pyramid for the time the monies will be needed). The third important component for which to plan is *tax diversification.*

There are essentially three different tax categories for our investments. As we have discussed, assets invested in your non-Roth retirement accounts are tax-deferred. Your Roth assets and most life insurance-based investment accounts are tax-free. All your other investments are taxable.

Note: Tax diversification is different than *asset diversification.* Most of you will have multiple accounts falling into these three different tax categories. And while it is important to be broadly asset-diversified amongst your accounts, it is not necessary to be asset-diversified within any one account. For example, if you have $300,000 in six different accounts, the $300,000 should be asset-diversified, but each of the six accounts may be weighted differently in terms of the assets they hold. There may be funds offered in your 401(k) that you would not be able to purchase on your own or maybe you can gain an expense advantage by "buying in bulk". You may then choose to concentrate that investment in this account and balance your other stock and bond funds in your other accounts. For management and IRS regulation purposes, you may put your investment real estate assets with one custodian.

When are taxes paid? In the taxable account, you pay taxes on an annual basis (income taxes on any interest or dividends received and capital gains tax on any investments you or your mutual fund manager have sold during the year). You pay regular income tax on any withdrawals from your tax-deferred retirement accounts when you withdraw the monies after age $59\frac{1}{2}$. Note: if you withdraw funds prior to age $59\frac{1}{2}$, you will be subject to a 10 percent penalty on the withdrawal amount unless you establish a Systematic Withdrawal plan under Section 72(t) of the IRS code. As the name implies, there are no taxes on your tax-free investments.

To implement tax diversification, we begin by exploring which of our chosen diversified investment vehicles should be placed in which type of account. While there are always exceptions, the rules of thumb are:

- Place investments that generate annual income tax in such tax-deferred accounts as Treasury Inflation Protected Assets and Real Estate Investment Trusts (REITS).
- Place assets that produce the lower dividend and capital gain tax of 15 percent in taxable accounts.
- In Roth or tax-free accounts, you can place anything since taxes are not an issue. But, you should concentrate the assets from which you expect the most significant growth over time as that appreciation will not be shared with Uncle Sam like it would be if it were in a tax-deferred or taxable account.

Another aspect of tax diversification is that it is advisable to spread your investment assets across the three tax categories. Because there's no predicting what Congress will do insofar as future tax legislation, by having funds in all three pools you are better prepared to manage the impact of future changes. The objective is to put you in control of what taxes you pay and when you pay them. As you approach retirement, you will be transitioning from many years of savings to many years of spending your investments. By being aware and managing your tax diversification you can gain the most from each saved dollar. Part of your control will also come from effectively using insurance as a risk management tool (See Chapter 3 page 57) against unplanned circumstances. Without insurance, you might need to quickly liquidate accounts to meet what could be a very large unplanned need, losing control of the tax implications.

> ▶ Many lawyers retire with too much money in their pre-tax retirement accounts. Welcome to the concept of tax diversification.

While you might consider it an enviable problem, many lawyers retire with too much money in their pre-tax retirement accounts. The problem lies in the fact that at age 70$\frac{1}{2}$, you must begin withdrawing, and therefore paying taxes, on a portion of your account(s) regardless of your need. Failure to take the IRS-mandated minimum distributions incurs a 50 percent penalty on top of the income taxes due. So, don't get caught in this tax trap. It may be advisable for you to spend and pay taxes on some of these funds prior to age 70$\frac{1}{2}$. Or you may decide to pay the taxes and convert them to tax-free Roth accounts if you really do not have a use for the funds.

For many of you, the tax-free category may be smaller than you would like. Income limits may have prevented you from contributing to a Roth IRA. For those of you that will not need some of your tax-deferred funds for 10 years or more, you might consider paying income taxes now by converting some of your current tax deferred accounts to a Roth IRA account. By paying the income tax now, you will allow your accounts to grow tax free from the conversion date forward. The decision factors on whether to convert or not include:

• Do you have funds outside your retirement account to pay the conversion tax bill. It rarely makes sense to pay the bill from within the retirement account with your tax advantaged dollars.
• Do you expect your retirement tax bracket to be the same or higher in retirement? If so, paying taxes at today's lower interest rates may be a wise move.
• Do you have time before you plan to withdraw the funds so that they are able to gain the benefit of compounding in a tax-free environment. Financial advisors and many financial Web sites can assist you with determining the break-even point for paying taxes now with fund conversion vs. later with fund withdrawal.

Until 2010, only those with an adjusted gross income of $100,000 or less can/could do a conversion. In 2010, however, the income limitation will be removed and anyone can convert from tax-deferred to tax-free accounts as long as they are prepared to pay the taxes on the converted amount. To encourage these conversions, thereby generating much needed tax dollars for the government, the IRS regulations will allow you to delay your tax payments until 2011 and will allow you to spread the tax bill over two years (2011 & 2012).

Retirement Accounts

Retirement accounts are an important part of a successful financial plan. They represent the second leg of the three-legged stool.

Up until now, we've discussed retirement accounts and their beneficial tax status without exploring the different accounts available to you. These accounts are permitted by the IRS, and for the purposes of illustration it may be helpful to think of them as *filing cabinets*. The IRS has designed these so-called *cabinets* so that the government's taxing arm cannot penetrate as long as your investments remain inside. It is only when they are removed/withdrawn that the government may collect their share through taxation. Within these retirement accounts you are able to place most of the investments found in the investment pyramid. In other words, your individual investment decisions become like individual *files* within the protection of the *cabinet*. These include savings accounts, stocks, bonds, commodities, mutual funds and real estate. For the most part, the only investments **not** permitted are collectibles and life insurance. If you want to better understand the investment options described here, go to the investment glossary on pages 95–101.

Let's review several tax-deferral options that are currently used to channel funds into retirement savings. No attempt is made to give complete explanations of each since IRS regulations and investment sales representatives will produce volumes on demand, but rather to provide some information of how they might work for you. Use this section to identify your current retirement *file cabinet(s)* and determine if another *cabinet* is possible or is more beneficial.

Defined-benefit plans. Your retirement plan may be the defined-benefit type (pension) in which the dollar amount you receive each year in retirement is predetermined by the number of years you have participated in the plan, the amount of your wages, and—under some plans—your age. Defined-benefit plans are being replaced by other plans. If you have such a plan, consider yourself one of the lucky few. Many think all they can receive under an employer's pension plan is a retirement payout when they reach age 65. While this is its primary purpose, several types of retirement benefits may be available including:

- Retirement income benefits for the attorney and his or her spouse before age 65
- Benefits in the event his or her employment is terminated before reaching the minimum retirement age (vested benefits)
- Death benefits
- Widow's pension
- Disability and medical benefits

Defined-contribution plans. These days, defined-contribution plans are more common, and the retirement payout is based on what has been contributed to the account (usually by your firm and yourself), and its earnings over the years.

There are several kinds of defined-contribution plans. They vary in terms of their structure and administrative requirements, their contribution limits (either in terms of a maximum percentage of your income and/or an annual maximum contribution), their tax treatment, and their policies (such as allowing for loans or whether they are plans that allow employees or not). Not all plans are available to everyone. The decision of what plan to use may be yours if you are a sole practitioner or managing partner of a firm. If you are a member of a firm or an employee of a corporation or governmental entity, the decision has been made by others and you must utilize their retirement plan structure and internal policies. Keep in mind that the IRS regulations provide the guidelines for each of these plans, but a firm or company can chose to implement a plan in their own fashion as long as they stay within the IRS guidelines. For instance, while the IRS permits loans from some of these plans, many organizations choose not to offer them due to added administrative requirements.

Recognizing that many baby boomers are behind the savings curve for retirement, the IRS now allows "catch-up" provisions in many plans allowing those over 50 or those within a certain number of years of retirement to contribute more than the standard amount. Taking advantage of these catch-up provisions will allow you to accelerate the growth of your retirement funds. The more you can save in these tax advantaged accounts, the more planning freedom you will have in retirement.

> ▶ Many Boomers are behind the savings curve for retirement, so the IRS now allows "catch-up" provisions, allowing those over 50—or within reach of retirement—to contribute more than the standard amount. Taking advantage of these provisions allows you to accelerate the growth of your retirement funds.

The following defined-contribution plans are accurate within today's regulations (although Congress and the IRS have made changes to contributions amounts, age-related options, etc., so there is every reason to believe they will do so in the future):

401(k) Plans. Many large and medium-size law firms and corporations offer a 401(k) plan. Lawyers working there authorize their firm or corporation to subtract a pre-tax maximum of $15,500/year ($20,500 if they're 50 or older), and put it into a fund to accumulate tax-deferred earnings until retirement. Please note that these amounts may change each year. Some firms also make matching contributions. 401(k) funds may be withdrawn or rolled over to another plan without penalty when a worker leaves the job. If permitted by your plan, the maximum amount that can be borrowed for hardships may be as much as $50,000 so long as the loan is repaid, with interest, within five years. Specific regulations govern such transactions and must be carefully followed.

The Roth 401(k). Allows for after-tax contributions to a separate account that grows tax-free. Contributions must accumulate for at least five years in this account with no distributions until after age 59 ½. This is an interesting opportunity for those who have a number of years until retirement and believe taxes may be higher during their retirement years.

Individual 401(k). For the solo practitioner, an Individual 401(k) offers the greatest opportunity for growing retirement accounts. This 401(k) is comprised of a 401(k) type component with the same maximum contribution amounts as other 401(k)'s, but also a profit sharing part that allows an individual to save up to $42,000 per year. This type of 401(k) allows you to put close to 100% of income into the 401(k) portion if your finances allow. Many attorneys who continue to work after retirement as independent contractors use this vehicle to increase their retirement savings.

Deferred compensation (457). This is a plan that may be available for lawyers who work in the public sector (city, county, state, or federal government). The maximum contribution is limited to $15,500/year, with an additional $5,000 for those age 50 or over. It works this way: your employer withholds part of your paycheck each pay period and deposits it in a special account at a financial institution. By deferring a portion of your salary, you reduce the amount of taxes withheld and your total yearly taxes. You will not pay taxes on the deducted income or the interest/growth it earns until it is withdrawn, normally when you leave employment or at retirement. There are additional catch-up provisions that allow accelerated contribution levels a few years before retirement.

Tax-deferred annuity (403b). These accounts are available only to employees of non-profit organizations (educational, social or religious). Some non-profit employers have both tax-deferred plans and a pension plan. Under 403b, an employee can elect to defer a maximum of $15,500 per year, and up to $20,500 if age 50 or over. As a person who has not previously used a TDA approaches retirement and chooses to do so, there is a formula for accelerating contributions. The amount deducted from the paycheck is not subject to current income taxes. Income received from the plan after retirement is subject to tax like any other income.

IRAs. As an attorney, you can contribute up to $5,000 per year of income into a traditional IRA ($6,000 if you're 50 or older), and not pay income taxes on it until the funds are withdrawn after age 59½. A non-working spouse may also contribute to a separate IRA account up to $4,000 each year. Regulations may limit tax-deductibility of the contribution, so getting specific information from your financial institution is advisable. Just don't let anyone tell you that because you earn too much you are ineligible for a non-deductible traditional IRA.

Other IRA's include:

- *Roth IRAs* (while not deductible at funding) allow taxpayers to withdraw funds completely tax-free, after a five-year period and age 59½. The contribution limits are the same as a traditional IRA and you are allowed to use both a Roth and a traditional IRA as long as the combined contributions do no exceed the annual maximum allowed. Your financial advisor can assist you on the merits of these IRAs for your particular purposes.

- *Rollover IRAs* are limited to the amount you are rolling over from another retirement plan and do not have contribution maximums. Attorneys with 25 to 35 years of work experience in several settings may find themselves with several accounts rolled into one Rollover IRA account.

- **SIMPLE IRA** plans allow solo practitioners and small firms (fewer than 100 employees) to contribute up to $10,000 of compensation a year (an additional $5,000 each year if age 50 or older). These plans have less administration and lower costs compared to a 401(k), and could be an attractive alternative. For details, talk to your financial institution or accountant. If you are able to save more, and qualify, look to an individual 401(k) for its greater flexibility.

- *SEP IRAs* may work for small firms that want to make the contributions for their employees. They work much like a profit-sharing arrangement with a maximum contribution of 25 percent of earned income up to $42,000. The contribution percentage can be changed from year to year. Many firms are choosing this plan over the old KEOGH plans that had cumbersome IRS regulations and paperwork.

Putting Your Objectives Together

As we look towards putting all these concepts and retirement savings plans together, you must make several decisions. Only you can make the decision of how much you can and are willing to save, and only you can determine how long those savings will grow until you need some of them. We have identified the major categories of financial objectives that you need to think about. You again are the only one who can make the determination of where you stand on each of these. They include:

- Your degree of risk comfort level/profile; conservative, moderate or aggressive;
- Your diversification across investment vehicles;
- Dollar-cost averaging implementation;
- Your time-horizon;
- How much liquidity you need;
- Your mix of growth and income; and
- Your tax considerations.

We suggest that you take the time to determine your risk profile and investment objectives, and evaluate how well your current investments match your self-determined profile and objectives. Here are several examples to get you started.

Example #1. The Cartwrights are in their 50's, and are both practicing attorneys with grown children. Their combined income is $262,000/year. Both take retirement planning seriously, and invest around 15 percent of their income each month. Insofar as growth, risk, liquidity, and taxes, their investment objectives are...

Growth. The Cartwrights have adopted a capital-growth strategy because they don't need income from their investments until they retire.

Higher degree of risk. Since the couple has 10 to 15 years before they expect to retire, they feel they can accept a higher degree of risk. Investments in certain types of stocks should provide a higher rate of growth. An index stock mutual fund and possibly an international fund would also provide a degree of diversification.

Liquidity. The Cartwrights feel there is little chance they would need their nest egg prior to retirement, and that only a small part of their investment needs to be liquid in case of some emergency. They would use a retirement time-horizon of 10 to 15 years.

Taxes. The Cartwrights have taken specific steps to minimize current income taxes by maximizing contributions to their firms' tax-deferred options. They are making plans to begin to convert some of their tax-deferred assets into a Roth IRA on an annual basis starting in 2010. Today, they are setting aside funds to meet the conversion tax bill. They have also made after-tax investments in government securities that are nontaxable. Their greatest concern is being subject to the Alternative Minimum Tax (AMT) for the last few years of their careers, and consequently losing the benefit of some of their deductions.

Example #2. Nan is single, in her late 40's, and is in private practice with an income of approximately $95,000/year. Because she's been thinking about retiring before age 60, she contributes each month into investments that will enhance her retirement income. Her investment objectives are...

Growth. Nan is investing for growth since she has an adequate income now.

Moderate degree of risk. Although not a big risk-taker, Nan sees retirement at least a dozen years away and can accept some risk in her investments. She has acquired several growth stocks and contributes regularly to a package of more aggressive growth mutual funds offered in a Roth 401(k).

Liquidity. Since her income is steady and likely to increase over the next few years, Nan has only a small nest egg set aside for an emergency (approximately three months income). Most of her funds, over and above living expenses, are tied up for several years.

Taxes. Nan has elected to pay more income taxes now using a Roth 401(k) for her retirement savings. Her thought is that tax brackets may creep higher in future years to pay for the current large federal budget deficits. As she withdraws money from this 401(k) account, there will be no taxation.

The point needs to be repeated here that each case is different, and an attorney's financial planning must be tailored to individual needs and objectives. To help clarify your own investment objectives, take a few minutes to consider the following questions:

Q: What degree of risk would you be comfortable with in order to earn an above-average return on investment?

Q: What are your short- and long-range financial goals, and what type of investments might you select for both?

Q: How would diversification play out in your investment portfolio, and what steps could you take to reduce risk and possibly increase return?

Q: When would it be advantageous to shift some of your investments from growth to income-producing, and how much income would you need/want?

Q: How liquid would you need to be to meet an unexpected emergency, and how much of your capital would you be willing to invest for a higher return?

Q: To what degree could you invest on a monthly basis for retirement?

Q: Do you know your approximate tax bracket...or the net (after taxes) return on any income your investments earn? Do you know what should be done to minimize your taxes and benefit your retirement nest egg?

Withdrawal Strategies

Without a withdrawal strategy, spending down your retirement nest egg can be dangerous. We don't know how long we'll live, what the inflation rate will be, or how the financial markets will fare. Consequently, how much one can...or should...withdraw from one's retirement accounts is a main topic in the financial planning industry today.

Early research gave rise to what financial planners call *The Four Percent Rule*, which states that four percent is the amount that can be annually withdrawn from your nest egg with a high probability that it would last 30 years. It's still pretty accurate. But here's where the dangers lay: if you raise the withdrawal rate to five or even six percent, the risk of your nest egg not holding up for 30 years increases dramatically. In fact, a six percent withdrawal rate has only a 50 percent chance of going the distance. (see chart on page 90.) These numbers are based upon an asset-allocation of 60 percent large company stocks and 40 percent intermediate-term U.S. bonds.

The effect of high withdrawal rates. Some financial planners suggest that you could increase or decrease the withdrawal percentage each year depending upon the account's return from the previous year, minus taxes. But this strategy is problematic. If you are dependent on the income stream for living expenses, what would you do in those years when the account has low returns or even loses money? Can you afford to constantly adjust your withdrawal from the account based upon its earnings? It is probably more prudent to save assets gained in any high return years for the leaner years that are sure to follow in the investment continuum.

Most of us don't have the flexibility or the discipline to make major adjustments in our spending habits, so we must depend upon a less volatile withdrawal strategy. One strategy most financial experts recommend is to set up an automatic withdrawal program from a low-risk fund (for example, a money market fund), and periodically replenish it from a more aggressive fund. Most financial experts advise drawing down your taxable accounts first, then turning to your tax-deferred accounts like your 401(k). If you have Roth accounts, save them to withdraw from last. Most brokerage houses and mutual funds will provide assistance with this process.

Let's explore some strategies and steps that you might consider as you approach retirement. One of the major challenges you might have is changing your financial mind-set from one of savings to one of spending. For savers, flipping that switch may not be so easy. Many savers have difficulty spending the monies they have saved for so long, and thereby place themselves on a less-fulfilling retirement path than their funds could actually allow. Those of you with more relaxed approaches to spending will need to curb your inclination to spend your retirement savings once you begin accessing them. An informed middle course may better serve both personalities.

Thus far, we have explored two of the three "D's" of retirement planning—asset-diversification and tax-diversification.

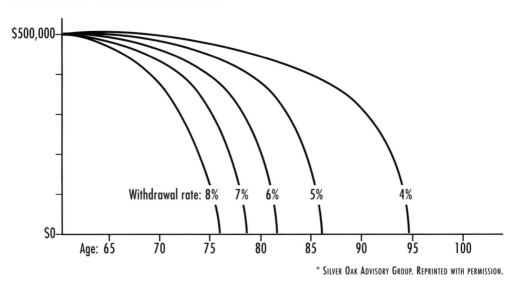

Simulated Portfolio Values (90% confidence level)

Withdrawal rate: 8% 7% 6% 5% 4%

* SILVER OAK ADVISORY GROUP. REPRINTED WITH PERMISSION.

The third "D" is time-diversification.

This concept was introduced earlier as we asked you to consider when you would need to spend certain amounts of your assets, and to make sure you had proper diversification for funds needed in two years for, say, a child's college education vs. funds needed 10+ years out for retirement. Funds needed in two years need to be invested fairly conservatively (i.e., low return for high liquidity) vs. funds that can be invested more aggressively in order to gain higher returns for a retirement 10 or more years off. We also discussed in Chapter 3 the concept of your three-to-six months of emergency cash expanding to a one-to-three year cash reserve in retirement. Another aspect of time diversification is the length of time specific funds may be required. For some financial needs, you may have a lifelong requirement such as the need to pay monthly health insurance. Other financial needs may only exist for a set number of years, such as a child's education expenses. How might these concepts unfold in retirement income planning?

As you approach retirement, you have so far learned here that it is essential to determine the lifestyle you want to have and then determine the expenses associated with that lifestyle. When you have accumulated the necessary funds to achieve your goals, you then need to develop a savings distribution plan that meets your specific income needs. Implementing the concept of time-diversification will allow you to have the current liquidity you need to sleep at night knowing your expenses are covered while allowing you to maintain the necessary growth of your other savings to wage the war against the ravages of inflation.

The case study below will further explain the integration of investment concepts as you prepare for the shift from a concentration on savings for retirement to an approach for managing savings and withdrawals in retirement. We have incorporated the "buckets" withdrawal strategy in this case study, which involves dividing your total nest egg into several investment accounts, or "buckets":

Bill, a teacher, and his wife, Peggy, a lawyer in a midsized firm, have saved $900,000 in the course of their careers.

According to their calculations, their monthly expenses in retirement will be $6,000. Bill's lifetime pension will provide $2,000/month (plus $1,000 more to his wife under a "survivor" option). Peggy has no pension benefits, but half of their savings ($450,000) is in her 401(k). Together, their Social Security benefit was conservatively estimated at $1,800/month. Combining the two known income streams leaves Bill and Peggy with a $2,200/month gap to make up from savings. Can they do it? They did a quick test of their ability to retire by using the Four Percent Rule. Since taxes will reduce the value of Peggy's 401(k) approximately 25 percent to $337,500, they use a total savings figure of $787,500 rather than the total $900,000. Four percent of $787,500 is $31,500, or $2,625/month. They are comfortable with coming up with this amount, and asked their financial planner to help them create a retirement investment plan.

Here is what Bill and Peggy developed:

In order to assure themselves of the capability to spend monies without worrying about selling assets each month, they decide to establish a three-year cash reserve to cover monthly expenses. This reserve will have $80,000 (36 months x $2,200/month needed to supplement Bill's pension and their Social Security checks). The $80,000 will be invested in the most liquid assets (e.g., money market, savings and checking accounts, CD's, short-term Treasury Bills and bonds). While these investments will pay the lowest return, the purpose of this bucket of money is not growth or income. Its purpose is to allow Bill and Peggy to sleep at night knowing that the money they spend on a daily basis is already there without the need to sell an asset at a loss. They understand that high liquidity comes at the price (the lowest returns), but that is OK with them for this needed pool of money.

Their financial advisor counsels them to put their income-oriented investments in another bucket to provide income needed four to 10 years out, and their growth-oriented investments in yet another bucket that would stay invested for 10+ years. Their advisor explains that in order to deal with inflation, and to protect their $6,000/month purchasing power, a major part of their assets need to remain invested for growth even though they are in retirement. The couple understand that with their three-year cash reserve bucket, these assets will not be needed in the short-term. They are comfortable with assuming more volatility risk in exchange for higher returns and therefore larger growth in this portion of their portfolio.

Among Bill and Peggy's investment options are medium-risk (e.g., medium-return) investments such as intermediate-term bonds, four- and five-year CD's, REITS (Real Estate Investment Trusts) that pay monthly or quarterly income, dividend-paying stocks...and annuities. Annuities were mentioned earlier, but let's digress a moment to discuss their potential role in your own retirement income planning:

Annuities are insurance products, and they are purchased from insurance companies in return for a guaranteed income stream. This is a way for individuals to convert their retirement savings into income streams similar to those enjoyed by people with defined-benefit plans. Buying an annuity amounts to handing over a portion of your savings to an insurer in return for a check every month for life. If the annuity is based on just your lifetime, you run the risk of dying before you get the full return of your monies. On the other hand, if you live beyond your calculated life expectancy, the insurance company will continue to pay.

Fixed annuities. This is where the interest rate—and therefore the monthly check—is set at the time of purchase. This may seem to be a little boring to some, but it will provide the security of insuring regular monthly payments for life or for an extended period of time. The downside is that inflation will reduce your monthly check's purchasing power over time. The size of the payments depends on the interest rate at the time you sign the contract, and on your life expectancy. For example, if a 65-year-old male puts $100,000 into an immediate annuity today, he would receive approximately $700/month as long as he lives. Go to *ImmediateAnnuities.com* to calculate annuity income streams.

Variable annuities. With this type, your funds are invested in mutual fund type vehicles instead of an interest rate vehicle. You gain the advantage of the potential for growth within your account which is translated to a higher check amount typically adjusted annually. While the insurance company may guarantee you a minimum check each month, the minimum will be less than a fixed annuity because your monies are at greater risk. So while investing $100,000 in a variable annuity allows your monthly check to grow beyond $700 over an improving stock market, your check may be reduced in a falling market to a guaranteed amount below $700. If you can live with the uncertainty, variable annuities are a way to combat inflation.

Today, there are many options you can add to annuities. If you are married, you may want to consider a joint and last survivor product which would pay as long as either you or your spouse is alive. Adding inflation protection to the payout would be prudent to consider. If you have children, you may want to add an option that provides some payout to them if you should die before a certain time.

> If you're retiring with a modest nest egg, you may want to consider buying an immediate annuity. Purchasing an annuity from a reliable company provides a secure stream of income as you age.

If you're retiring with a modest nest egg, you may want to consider buying an immediate annuity. Purchasing an annuity from a reliable company will indeed provide a secure stream of income as you age. Many annuity investors choose a combination of fixed and variable annuities. It can be advantageous not to purchase all your planned annuities at one time. Waiting until your later 60's or 70's will provide a higher monthly payout due to the life expectancy factor.

The downside on some annuities is that the fees can be steep, the products complex, and you lose control of your funds once you have handed over your money. However, if you see an annuity as prudent in your planning, compare quotes from large insurance companies or such mutual fund companies as Fidelity Investments or TIAA-CREF where the fees are lower. It is wise to have an investment advisor assist you in your annuity planning.

Now, let's return to Bill and Peggy:

Their advisor suggests they annuitize $200,000 of their savings, half to be allocated to a middle-term (four-to-eight-year) bucket to purchase a fixed annuity, and the remainder to the long-term bucket (eight-plus years) to be invested in a variable annuity. Along with the variable annuity, the couple's long-term bucket would include their stock and stock mutual fund investments and their investment real estate. These investments are characterized by their medium-to-low liquidity but proportionately higher returns than the middle bucket. By placing their riskier investments in the longer term bucket, Bill and Peggy can insulate themselves from daily market fluctuations. They would have time to recover from any potential paper losses because they would not be forced to sell a declining asset in order to pay this month's bills.

Once Bill and Peggy have distributed their savings into the appropriate time-diversified buckets, they will need to consider a plan to replenish the three-year bucket. This is a conceptual division of their assets, because in reality their retirement savings would stay in their respective funds whether they are Peggy's 401(k), their traditional and Roth IRA's, or their regular stock and savings accounts.

Time-diversification is more a mental philosophy rather than an actual structural organization process.

The replenishing of the three-year and four-to-eight-year buckets is done a number of ways. Key to this process is a change in approach from your career-savings years to your retirement distribution years.

While saving, you are advised to implement automatic reinvestment of interest and dividends. Your account growth is accelerated by never taking any monies out; every penny earned by your investments is plowed back into the investment. If having some of a particular stock is good, having more is better! So, you reinvest your investment earnings to buy more and gain through the power of compounding. Now, as you approach retirement, a switch is flipped. Instead of reinvesting dividends and interest into their producing asset, these payments will be channeled down to the next lower bucket. Interest and dividend income from the four-to-10 year funds will be placed in the three-year bucket. Interest and dividends from assets in the 10+ year bucket will be reinvested in assets in the four-to-eight-year category. Any monies harvested from assets during the rebalancing process or asset management decisions will again be channeled to the next lower time-frame. In this manner, the buckets are replenished on a continual basis.

The quantity and mix of assets in the second bucket needs to be sufficient to generate $26,400 plus the rate of inflation a year to meet Bill and Peggy's $2,200/month need for supplemental income. If they used a five percent composite rate of return as an underlying assumption of this bucket, they would allocate approximately $525,000 to this bucket. With $80,000 of their funds in the spending bucket, this leaves about $295,000 in their growth bucket. In percentage terms, Bill and Peggy's plan allocates nine percent to the spending-bucket, 58 percent to the income bucket and 33 percent to the growth bucket.

If for any reason Bill and Peggy were not comfortable with this planned allocation, they have several alternatives to consider like those discussed in Chapter 3, page 72. For instance, if either or both of them had plans to work some in retirement, their income could be deducted from the needed monthly $2,200, thereby allowing a reduction in the size of the spending and income bucket and a increase in the growth bucket.

If they live into their late 80's and 90's and own their residence, a reverse-mortgage might be used to create additional income. At that age, Bill or Peggy may need in-home or nursing home care. This added expense of several thousand dollars a month might justify considering a reverse-mortgage to increase their monthly cash flow. For more on reverse-mortgages, review the information on Page 59.

Investment Vehicles Glossary

The investment vehicles described below are intended to get you thinking about some additional options. Take a few minutes to look over this material, and identify each type of investment for which you want more information:

Savings accounts. A passbook, or savings account, earns a bank's lowest rate of return; on the other hand, a time-deposit or a Certificate of Deposit, earns its highest rate. With a passbook account, you can take your money out of your account any time; with a time deposit, you agree to leave it in your account for three months, six months, or perhaps several years. Since the bank can count on the money in your time-account, it gives the highest interest for such deposits, and you can also use it as loan collateral. Any withdrawals before the time is up, and you will be penalized—typically, three month's loss of interest and reversion to the regular interest rate for those funds withdrawn before the time period has expired. There are no special tax breaks on savings deposits, whether regular or time-deposit accounts. For the conservative investor, an attractive feature is the insured value of most accounts up to $100,000 by an agency of the federal government.

Money market funds. Money market funds, like other mutual funds, operate on a simple principle—pooling. They receive relatively small amounts of money, and lend it in the money market where large corporations, banks, and even the federal government borrow short-term cash. The interest earned is then passed along to a fund's investors or "shareholders" as dividends. Generally, the rate of return is a percentage point or two above regular savings. Your money is very liquid, with most funds offering check-writing privileges and no withdrawal charge (although some institutions limit the number of withdrawals each month). Unlike savings accounts and CDs, money market funds are not insured. It is not unusual for a fund to require $1,000 or more for the initial investment with a minimum account balance of $500. Withdrawals normally need to be in amounts of $500 or more.

Bonds. Bonds are basically IOUs from the issuer for a fixed return. The original principal plus interest must be paid to you at a given time in the future. Bonds, sometimes referred to as fixed income securities, are sold by all levels of government (federal, state, local) and by corporations. Some bonds are high quality while other more risky bonds are referred to as junk bonds. If the issuer of a bond goes bankrupt, bondholders are paid before stockholders.

U.S. Savings Bonds. With these bonds, you are assured of getting principal plus interest with safety. If you decide to hold a U.S. savings bond past its maturity date, the Series EE will continue to earn a similar percent of interest for a maximum of 30 years. Series HH bonds, which pay interest to the purchaser every six months, can be purchased in multiples of $500. There are some tax advantages with Series EE and HH bonds. The tax on EE bond interest does not have to be paid until the bonds are cashed in. Only the person who originally purchases a Series EE or HH government bond (or an heir) can cash it in—they are not "marketable" bonds. Most government bonds, though, are marketable, since one person can sell them to another before the bonds mature. This marketability means that such a bond can be converted to cash rather quickly. Marketability also means these bonds are subject to economic conditions that will cause the price of the bonds to rise and fall to some extent. Inflation-adjusted savings bonds, commonly called I-Bonds, consist of two parts: an inflation component that is adjusted for inflation every six months, and a fixed rate that stays the same for the life of the bond. Conservative investors like their high rates and purchase them through local banks or directly from the Treasury Department (www.savingsbanks.gov). They must be held for a minimum of 12 months and if you cash them before five years, you'll forfeit three months interest.

U.S. Government bonds. The two classes of U.S. Government bonds are issued by the U.S. Treasury, and by U.S. agencies such as the Federal Intermediate Credit Banks, Federal Home Loan Banks, Federal Land Banks and many others. Bonds issued by agencies generally have a return rate of from a fourth of a percent to one percent higher than those bonds issued by the U.S. Treasury. These bonds are also subject to price variations because of market conditions. In other words, the current price of a bond might be less or more than the price originally paid for the bond. Treasury bills, notes, and bonds have federal tax on interest earned but not state tax. Some agency bonds have similar tax advantages.

Municipal bonds. Municipal, or muni, bonds are issued by states, counties and cities. One of the major attractions of municipal bonds is that they are usually exempt from federal income taxes. Moreover, they are also often exempt from state income taxes in the state where they are issued. The quality of municipal bonds varies widely. One needs to be sure about the rating before purchasing a municipal bond as some bonds can be very risky. An attractive way for purchasing muni bonds is through mutual funds that trade exclusively in your state. A caution: high-income individuals may lose some of their tax advantages because they are subject to the Alternative Minimum Tax.

Corporate bonds. Corporate bonds vary greatly in quality; some are high quality while others offer little chance that you will get your investment back. They are "marketable", which allows you to sell them as you choose, and the price could be higher or lower than your original purchase price. Interest is paid directly to you semi-annually, so you do not have the advantage of compounding. A corporate bond is an IOU that is only as good as the corporation offering the bond. Because there are many different bond issues, many investors rely on the rating assigned to bonds by major financial service organizations such as Moody's and Standard and Poor's. Bonds with the smallest degree of risk are rated AAA, those with slightly more risk are rated AA, and so on down to a rating of C for the most risky. Most financial specialists advise the small or inexperienced investor to avoid buying bonds that have a rating of less than A to avoid too much risk. There are no special tax advantages to owning corporate bonds. Normally, high quality corporate bonds pay a higher return on your investment than federal or state agency bonds.

Zero coupon bonds. They could be almost any of the above-mentioned (muni, corporate, or Treasury) bonds. With these bonds, you pay a discounted amount at the beginning to receive a face value payout at a specified later date. Zero Coupon Bonds are excellent tools for planning for a college education or other future commitments like retirement. It is recommended that these bonds be held in tax deferred accounts so as to avoid paying taxes on the interest which is "earned" but not distributed on a yearly basis.

Inflation-adjusted securities. These fixed-income securities have built-in inflation protection mechanisms that keep their purchasing power close to par, based upon a national cost of living index. Some retirees find that this attribute is very important in planning for long-range retirement income. Brokerage firms and mutual fund companies are good sources for additional information.

Stocks. When you purchase stocks, you purchase part ownership in the companies issuing the stock. Stocks generate return in two basic ways: dividends and growth in market value. When you buy or sell stocks, you pay a commission to the broker who handles it for you. Many banks, credit unions and mutual fund companies have set up discount brokerages. They process only buy and sell orders, do not give advice, do not engage in underwriting new stock issues, or other securities dealings handled by regular brokers. Attorneys with sophistication and knowledge of particular stocks may save thousands of dollars in trading costs each year by using discount brokerage on-line services.

Preferred stock. These stocks get preferred treatment. Most pay a fixed dividend four times a year to the owner, and the amount of this dividend never changes. In other words, preferred stocks offer a fixed rate of return to their owners. Of course, the owner can sell the stock at any time and be paid the prevailing market price, which may be higher or lower than the original purchase price.

Common stock. Common stocks do not promise dividends, though many do pay them. When both dividend returns and the capital gains returns (the gain made between the purchase and selling price) are combined, U.S. common stocks have earned, on average, between 10 and 12 percent per year over a 10 to 20-year period. Of course, this is an average; you can gain a very high return with one stock and lose the entire investment with another. The best advisors have been wrong on many occasions. On the other hand, if one is prepared to accept the risk of market fluctuations and even the possible loss of the entire investment, then carefully selected stocks can be a means to above-average growth of the funds invested.

Mutual funds. Mutual funds pool the funds of many investors, creating large sums of money used to take advantage of investment opportunities. Mutual funds can afford to hire expert money managers to analyze and plan their investments. A person can invest directly in a mutual fund by sending money to it with an application, by going through a mutual fund sales person, or by contacting a broker. There are different types of mutual funds with different objectives. With almost 7,000 funds available, almost any type of investment that an individual can make directly can also be made through a mutual fund. Some mutual funds have a sales charge; some do not. The funds that do not charge a commission are called "no-load" funds. Mutual funds having a sales cost or a commission perform neither better nor worse than those that do not.

A mutual fund is only as good as the investments in which it invests. The idea is that while some investments in a fund may lose value, the average value of all the fund's investments may increase. Moreover, its professional managers can continually eliminate poor performers and add better investments. Until recent years, mutual funds concentrated on stocks and bonds. When the stock and bond markets dropped in early 2000, investors suffered. Mutual funds are more diversified and creative today, some using derivatives, hedging and other techniques. An investor needs solid information about a fund's objectives, investment strategy, past performance, and the fund's investment advisor. The Morningstar Reports and Value Line Mutual Investment Service publish a summary of mutual fund performance, and can be found online or in public libraries. Other resources include: the Mutual Fund Encyclopedia and Consumer's Guide Best Rated Mutual Funds.

Depending on your investment, some mutual funds offer a tax advantage. For example, if you put money into a mutual fund specializing in tax-free municipal bonds, you may not have federal or state income taxes on earnings from that investment. From a tax standpoint, owning these mutual funds is the same as personal ownership of the tax-free bonds. Over the last several years, Index Funds have become a popular choice due to their simplicity and their solid returns. They are a broadly diversified portfolio of stocks or bonds that buy and hold the securities in a particular index (S&P 500, Wilshire 5000, an international stock or bond index). Lower cost at purchase and lower yearly expenses are two of the primary benefits of these passively-managed mutual funds.

Exchanged-Traded Funds. ETF's are similar to index mutual funds, owning certain cluster or segments of stocks or bonds, but are traded like individual stocks on exchanges. They have gained in popularity due to this trading feature, their unique bundling of securities options and lower costs.

Mortgages. Ownership of first and second mortgages on property (homes or business sites) can produce handsome returns with second mortgages providing a possible return of 10–12 percent per year. You can make a good return…and you can also lose your shirt. You need to know the people taking the mortgage loan and the property being mortgaged. A first or second mortgage can be purchased from a financial institution or one can make a mortgage loan directly to another person with the assistance of an attorney familiar with mortgage loans. Most mortgages present no problems although some may require foreclosure and resale of the mortgaged property. If there is a foreclosure and you hold a second mortgage, the proceeds from a sale are first used to pay off the first mortgage. Any amount in excess is applied against the second mortgage. While the return on second mortgage investments is generally higher than on first mortgage investments, so are the risks. There are no special tax advantages for investing in mortgages.

Real estate. Investing in the residential or commercial property sectors can be attractive, especially in rising markets. Beside the benefit from appreciation in the value of property, there may be several tax advantages. Both the operating expenses and depreciation allowances can be deductions from gross income. Often the major portion of the funds used to buy the property is borrowed, producing both leverage and an additional tax deduction of the interest paid on the borrowed dollars. People who own rental property, however, are quick to talk about the downside of ownership. Before leaping into residential or commercial rentals, be aware of landlord-tenant responsibilities, the often-large amount of capital needed for the down payment, and the risks from market and economic changes. Buying bare land might solve the landlord problems but increases risk by not generating regular or adequate income to meet yearly property taxes and other expenses.

Two other options for owning real estate (while bypassing some of the headaches) are through real estate investment trusts (REITs) or limited partnerships. REITs are investment organizations regulated by the Securities and Exchange Commission that concentrate holdings in real estate. Limited Partnerships are a legal form of business organization in which the general partner assumes unlimited liability; the limited partners are liable only for their investment plus any additional money they have expressly agreed to risk. In exchange for this protection, they give up the right to participate in the management and some return from the property. Both options can be profitable when the properties they hold spin off rental income and increase in market value.

Options, commodities, metals, etc. These are grouped together because each requires special knowledge, experience (and some luck) to be successful. Options and commodities, for example, are investment vehicles that should be restricted to experienced investors with the time, interest, and money to spend on them:

• An option is a right or contract to buy or sell a security at a particular price. People buy and sell options to make a large profit by investing a relatively small amount of money. Options are used primarily by short-term speculators willing to lose the funds they use to purchase the option contract. However, more conservative investors may use a strategy of "covered calls", whereby they sell a call option against stocks in their investment portfolio in order to generate additional income.

• Commodities are goods like oil, wheat, corn, coffee and orange juice. When you invest in a commodity, you agree to buy a carload of wheat at a given price for delivery on a certain day. Of course, you do not want the wheat delivered, so you will sell your contract before the delivery date. If the price of wheat rises before then, you profit; if it doesn't, you lose. The commodity markets require a lot of money, time and luck. Only the sophisticated investor who knows a special area of commodities very well should consider investing in them.

• Precious metals (chiefly gold, silver, and platinum), are subject to international market forces and may be considered a hedge against inflation. There are commissions you must pay to buy, sell, assay and store precious metals. Chances are you would never lose all of your investment in precious metals; they might become more valuable than the money paid for them in the event of a serious depression, rampant inflation, or unsettling political events. Some investors find it much easier to invest in precious metals through mutual funds and ETF's.

CHAPTER 5

The Health & Insurance Planner

"Individuals who continue learning—especially in areas unfamiliar to them—not only live longer than individuals who don't, but they suffer significantly less from dementia and other diseases of the brain."—UCLA Brain Research Institute

My paternal grandfather was about 49 when he suffered a fatal heart attack.

In the years that followed, each of his three sons all suffered a catastrophic medical event: one died of a heart attack at age 49, another survived a cerebral aneurysm in his late 40's, and a third (my father) suffered his first stroke at the age of 66, and a second a few years later.

Aware of this family history, I have tried to take good physical care of myself. Growing up, competitive sports were my passion. But the long-term consequences of several youthful sports injuries required me to give up running, and engaging in most sports, in my late 30's and early 40's. By the time my daughters were old enough, I was spending more time driving them to their sports practices than exercising myself. And by age 49—the age at which both my grandfather and uncle died—I weighed 30 pounds more than when I was a teen.

One particularly stressful day at work, I felt a little light-headed, and my brain felt like it was pressing against my skull. So, I stopped by my doctor's office on the way home. The first thing they did was to take my blood pressure. It was 181/105, and not much better after waiting a few minutes. Next morning, I was still hypertensive. My doctor advised that we monitor my blood pressure for three or four weeks before deciding whether to start on medication. That same week, at an unrelated optometry appointment, my optometrist showed me a photograph he had taken of my eye during my annual examination that revealed signs of Stage One hypertension.

That week, I made four changes:

• I asked to be relieved of responsibility at work that was particularly stressful;

- I began exercising almost every day (walking after dinner and biking on weekends).
- I changed my diet (I started Weight Watchers).
- I purchased a blood-pressure cuff to monitor my blood pressure at work and home.

A month later, I was 10 pounds lighter and my blood pressure had dropped to the low 120's/low 80's range. My doctor said that medication for hypertension would be unnecessary. That was five years ago, and the changes I made—in diet and exercise—made all the difference.

Self Care: Your Life Depends On It

Several years ago I was facilitating a support group for lawyers suffering from depression. I asked the group what they were doing in the way of self-care that they found helpful in managing their depression. Lee, a solo, raised his hand: "What do you mean by self-care?" Lee had been a solo for almost 20 years, specializing in indigent criminal defense. He had never married or been in a significant relationship. He distanced himself from his immediate and extended family, had few friends, worked six to seven days a week, and had rarely taken a vacation or time off for almost his entire career. An extreme case, the concept of *self-care* was completely foreign to him.

Now, in each of the retirement workshops I do, I make sure to ask participants what they do to take care of themselves, and how satisfied they are with their self-care program. Typically, only a few of the participating lawyers have developed ongoing self-care practices.

Most have not, and the results are predictable.

- They continue to smoke.
- They don't engage in regular physical exercise.
- They continue to have a diet high in saturated fats and caffeinated beverages.
- They handle stress by drinking two (or four) alcoholic drinks at a sitting instead of taking a moment to engage in a deep breathing or progressive relaxation exercise.
- They escape from the demands, expectations and stress of work at the end of the day or week with TV, video games, or the Internet, instead of connecting with their spouse, partner, family or friends.

When these choices become habitual, and we fail to invest time and energy in self-care practices on a regular basis, the long-term, cumulative, negative consequences are significant, and for some fatal. Among lawyers, the most frequent (and predictable) excuses for not introducing self-care practices are: not enough time…one's obligations to clients and family…too stressed to change one's eating and exercise patterns…and (my favorite) *no one is paying me for doing self-care!* But the lawyers I meet who have become self-care converts usually have had a brush with their own mortality. And it was certainly a brush with my own that motivated me to make some long-overdue lifestyle changes.

▶ Stop smoking. As difficult as it is, kicking this one, single, self-destructive addiction may have the most positive influence on your retirement years than any other single lifestyle change you make.

So, in this chapter, I want to introduce the basic components of self-care that will be the most effective in preserving your mental and physical functioning.

First, if you smoke, stop smoking.

Granted, smoking involves physiological, behavioral, and psychological factors (all three of which need to be addressed, often repeatedly), but kicking this one, single, self-destructive addiction may have *the most positive influence on your retirement years than any other single lifestyle change you make.* Individuals who can stop smoking still face a risk of developing lung cancer. But the risk is substantially lower than if they continued to light up.[1]

Our circulatory system is amazingly resilient. And in recent years, doctors have learned that blood vessels and coronary tissue respond almost immediately to quitting smoking—even in smokers in their 60's and 70's. In fact, the risk of dying suddenly drops within the first weeks of quitting, and five years later one's circulatory system is nearly indistinguishable from that of someone who never smoked.[2]

Preserving Your Most Valuable Practice Asset

As lawyers, we value intellectual stimulation and utilizing our brains to address complex issues. After all, our entire legal education and professional experience is stored in our brain. So, even if we suffered other infirmities and disabilities, we could continue to practice law as long as our brains continued functioning well. Without a doubt, our brains are our most valuable practice asset.

It therefore certainly behooves us to take care of this most valued and valuable organ. And research has identified three factors that characterize individuals who maintain their mental abilities, particularly their memory, as they aged:

• They were more mentally active.
• They were more physically active.

- They maintained a sense of effectiveness and purpose in the world around them; that is, they continued to maintain a sense of control over their lives, felt they were contributing to their family or society, and generally felt good about themselves.[3]

The other components of self-care critical to caring for our brains and the rest of our bodies are:

- Eating a heart-healthy diet.
- Getting sufficient sleep and rest.
- Managing our stress level.
- Avoiding abuse or dependence on alcohol and/or prescription drugs.

The ROI on life-long learning. Years ago scientists thought the human brain was "hard-wired," meaning that during development, nerve cells would assume their proper positions and make myriad interconnections. Once in place and interconnected, they did not change. Now we know that concept is wrong.[4]

The brain is not a static organ. It continues to develop and reorganize itself throughout our lifetimes. Mental activities stimulate the brain to develop new connections between the cells of the brain, and to reorganize and reinforce the neural networks of the brain. This dynamic rewiring process is referred to as *neuroplasticity*. It is stimulated by exposing yourself to opportunities to learn new and different things. In other words, after practicing law for decades, handling your next complex case will not stimulate new connections in your brain as much as learning a foreign language or learning to play a musical instrument, tai chi, or chess.

▶ The brain is not a static organ. It continues to develop and reorganize, and is stimulated by opportunities to learn new and different things. The key is "new" and "different". Even a complex legal case will not stimulate new connections in your brain as much as learning a new language or learning to play a musical instrument, chess, or do tai chi.

Arnold Scheibel, head of UCLA's Brain Research Institute, believes that the brain's axons and the thread-like dendrites which send and receive messages, grow fastest when dealing with new material. So, when you think about laying the groundwork for the road ahead just remember, *"the most important thing is to stay actively involved in areas unfamiliar to you."*[5]

Individuals who remain active teaching and learning well into old age not only live longer than individuals who don't, but suffer significantly less from dementia and other diseases of the brain. Conversely, a brain that is not challenged to learn new things for an extended period will actually become smaller and less capable of learning in the future.[6]

Use it or lose it. Research also continues to confirm that those who remain physically active experience less mental decline and cognitive impairment than those who don't.

A five-year study of nearly 5,000 men and women over 65 found that those who exercised were less likely to lose their mental abilities or develop dementia including Alzheimer's. This study similarly found that the more a person exercises the greater the protective benefits for the brain, particularly in women. Inactive individuals were twice as likely to develop Alzheimer's, compared to those with the highest levels of activity (i.e., at least three times a week). But even light or moderate exercisers cut their risk significantly for Alzheimer's and mental decline.[7]

The benefits of exercise certainly extend beyond protecting the brain:

- A 1999 study of 25,000 men showed that, all others things being equal, men who were obese and physically fit had about the same risk of death over a 10-year period as men who were both physically fit and of normal weight. By contrast, men of normal weight who were unfit were twice as likely to die as the obese but fit men, while men who were both obese and inactive faced the worst odds: they were three times as likely to die of heart disease as physically fit men of normal weight.[8]
- Older adults who walk the equivalent of 30 minutes, six times per month had a 43 percent lower death rate than those who were sedentary.
- A study of more than 5,000 women with diabetes…found that those who walked the most (and at a brisk pace) lowered their risk of heart disease and stroke better than 40 percent.[9]

You (really) are what you eat. Our brains are dependent on our cardio-vascular system for the constant supply of oxygen and energy they need to continue functioning optimally.

Cardiovascular disease plays a major role in both strokes and certain kinds of dementia. After age 25, individuals experience approximately a one percent decrease per year in their metabolic rate."[10] If physical activity is not maintained, this metabolic slowdown would contribute to weight gain, and being over-weight increases your risk for diabetes, heart disease, stroke, and some sleep disorders."[11] It therefore makes sense to develop a habit of consuming a well-

Go to www.LawyerAvenue.com for more health resources. Click on Self & Family.

Between age 25 and 50, I had a pretty good understanding of how I should eat to maximize my health and wellness. And yet, I frequently deviated from following a healthy diet. In particular, I ate a lot of sweets and baked goods, gradually gaining about 30 pounds and adding six inches to my waist (from size 32 to 38). Periodically I vowed to lose weight, and made brief attempts to do so before surrendering to defeat and replacing my wardrobe with the next size of pants and shirts.

As I mentioned earlier, when my blood pressure spiked into the hypertensive zone, I committed myself to make positive changes. A good friend and my wife had both embraced Weight Watchers with success, so I decided to give it a try. I didn't go to meetings, I just started using their point system. The process of writing down everything I ate throughout the day, converting it to points, and staying within my allotted points over a period of several months proved successful. It made me much more conscious of what I chose to eat, and it helped over the long-term to decrease my fat intake, reduce the size of the portions I ate, and to increase my intake of fruits, vegetables, salads, fish and poultry.

If you have been idly threatening to change your diet or to lose weight, you may benefit from a system and support for doing so. There are a multitude of systems, pick one and get started. And when you fall off the wagon (and you will), get back on as soon as you can. In the June, 2007 Consumer Reports review of diets, obesity researcher Cathy Nonas, R.D., M.S., says: "The best diet is the one you can stay on." Weight Watchers had the best overall adherence rate of any that were studied and received the top ranking.

As we age, our bodies become less forgiving of dietary excesses. The margin of error for failing to eat wisely becomes more slight. Given the importance of positive nutrition for both our mental and physical functioning, embracing a heart-healthy diet in combination with maintaining our level of physical activity is well worth the effort.

---

balanced, heart-healthy diet. If you are overweight and/or your diet is not serving your brain and body well, please read on. It is not difficult to obtain all the information and guidelines you might need to develop a heart-healthy diet.

▶ One woman told her husband she wouldn't sign their joint tax return unless he made a doctor's appointment! He did. Tests revealed adult-onset diabetes and dangerously high blood sugar.

See your doctor…yesterday. A recent Wall Street Journal article posed this question:,"*Is Your Wife Pushing You to See a Doctor? Read This… and Go.*" In the article, Journal columnist Tara Parker-Pope profiled several men who learned of serious medical conditions only after prodding by their wives to visit a physician. In one case, prodding—even pleading—wasn't working. One woman finally told her husband she wouldn't sign their joint tax return unless he made a doctor's appointment! He did, and tests revealed adult-onset diabetes and dangerously high blood sugar. Today, with medication and lifestyle changes, his blood sugar is under control and he feels well. According to the Journal article, men who put off doctor visits are typically diagnosed with diseases at a later stage…when they are more serious and difficult to treat. All of which has major implications for a woman's long-term well-being: seven out of 10 female baby boomers will outlive their husbands and can expect to be widows for 15 or 20 years, and—according to the US Administration on Aging—more than half of the elderly widows living in poverty today weren't poor before the death of their husbands.

Stress can damage your brain. It's not difficult for lawyers to describe the stressors in their life.

But did you know that stress is more than an emotional/psychological phenomena? In fact, it has a broad generalized impact on most of the systems of our body.

There is increasing evidence now that stress actually damages the brain, particularly the regions associated with processing memories. The mechanism for this is thought to be the brain's response to hormones (called glucocorticoids) that increase during periods of stress. What can you do? Effectively managing stress requires developing strategies and tools for triggering the relaxation response of the body. Some of the strategies that have proven successful in triggering the relaxation response are: deep, diaphragmatic breathing; progressive muscle relaxation; meditation and prayer; visualization and guided imagery; and yoga and tai chi.[12] Which tool proves most helpful to you is just as individualized as what you find stressful. You just have to experiment until you develop a stress management plan that works best for you. For good measure, read *Stress Management for Lawyers* (3rd ed., 2007) by Amiram Elwork, JD/Ph.D., director of the Law-Psychology Graduate Training Program at Widener University.

Many of the lawyers participating in our retirement planning workshops envision retirement as the final liberation from the high levels of stress they experience practicing law. In fact, retirement does hold the promise of relief from the stressors of practice. However, retirement and aging present their own unique stressors. Some aspects of retirement and aging that lawyers have reported as stressful are:

- Boredom.
- Financial concerns and pressures.
- Loss of structure and focus that work provided, and the need to decide how to spend their time.

- Being with their spouse/partner 24/7 and renegotiating roles and responsibilities.
- Experiencing illness, mental and physical decline in functioning and chronic pain.
- The loss of friends, family spouses and life partners.

The strategies that you develop to manage the stress of practicing law should prove valuable in managing the stresses that you encounter once you stop.

Get more sleep. Our brains need sleep to recharge. Having our sleep cycle severely disrupted for even a brief period of several days to a week can have a significant negative impact on our brain's ability to function. I have worked with lawyers getting ready for large, complex trials who have suddenly been unable to get to sleep or stay asleep. Some of them have become so impaired that their cases had to be set over. Starting in middle age (between 45 and 60) not only does the amount of sleep per night start to decrease, but the character of sleep also changes. At this age, you spend less time in the stage of sleep associated with dreaming and more time in the lighter stages. During the lighter stages of sleep, you can be awakened more easily, and then spend time in bed in a twilight zone, feeling neither quite awake nor quite asleep. Several studies have shown that if you are sleep-deprived you will have more trouble than usual taking in new information and retrieving information you learned previously.[13]

I believe that employing the essential components of self-care that we have discussed, exercise, balanced nutrition and stress management help assure that our sleep is of the quality that our brains need to recharge and continue to function optimally. In my lawyer assistance role, however, I have had the opportunity to meet and work with lawyers whose sole means for managing their stress and getting to sleep has been to use alcohol, marijuana, and prescriptive drugs.

Aging and alcohol don't mix. Alcohol is the drug of choice for older adults, and the most damaging to the human body. Over time, alcohol affects virtually every organ system. And if you're curious how much damage alcohol and drugs can do to someone in their middle years, I suggest you get a copy of *Aging and Addiction* by Carol Colleran and Debra Jay.

Here are just a few eye-opening facts:

- One third of older alcoholics suffer from late onset alcoholism. Even if you never had problems with alcohol or other drugs before age 55 or 60, alcoholism can be triggered late in life, precipitated by increased drinking. And even if your level of consumption remains the same, your aging body reacts as if you were drinking more!

- Long-term heavy drinking causes damage to the cerebral cortex, the area of the brain responsible for abstract thinking and problem solving, verbal skills and memory, and fine and gross motor skills. A University of Maryland study found that 10 percent of patients aged 60 and over who were diagnosed with Alzheimer's disease were actually suffering from brain damage or toxicity caused by alcoholic drinking.
- A new study has found that consuming more than two beers or 10 ounces of wine per day was a greater risk factor for coronary artery disease than smoking.
- Half the medicines prescribed to treat illnesses caused by alcoholism interact badly with alcohol, causing even more health problems. And when it comes to long-term abuse of prescription drugs, there's no question that there is a cumulative effect, reducing your life expectancy by about 15 years.

Stay in charge of your life. One of the reasons I decided to become a lawyer was the belief that I could exert more control over my work life. As it turned out, nothing was further from the truth. And in my counseling work, I see that this lack of control is true for most other lawyers, too. Many lawyers report a sense of impotence in their attempts to achieve a reasonable or acceptable balance between their work lives and their personal and family lives. I knew the problem was serious, but what I didn't fully appreciate is that taking control of one's life and destiny is a major contributor to maintaining good brain function.

Dr. Marilyn Albert, director of the Gerontology Research Unit at Massachusetts General Hospital, and the Harvard-Mahoney Neuroscience Institute, has tested thousands of older individuals over two decades. Her research not only confirms the importance and benefit of continuous mental activity and physical activity for healthy brain aging. But she also identified a third factor that enhanced brain function. She calls it *self-efficacy*, the taking control of one's life and destiny.

In a companion study, Dr. Albert and her husband, Dr. Guy McKhann, who is director of the Zanvyl Krieger Mind/Brain Institute at John Hopkins,

---

Go to www.LawyerAvenue.com for a national roster of residential treatment centers. Click on Self & Family.

together studied some 3,000 individuals between the ages of 70 and 80. In their book, *Keep Your Brain Young: The Complete Guide to Physical and Emotional Health and Longevity*, they report that, "We believe that people who maintain their sense of effectiveness (into their 70's and 80's) are individuals who know how to adapt to life's challenges, rather than becoming overwhelmed by stressful situations. They maintain some degree of control in their daily lives, and are not overly dependent on others."

Health Insurance, Medicare & Long-Term Care

As we noted earlier, 62 percent of lawyers who participated in the Oregon Lawyer Retirement Survey identified concerns regarding health insurance, Medicare, and long-term care insurance as the most significant financial concerns they had about retirement. Their concerns are well-justified. The cost of health care and maintaining health insurance continues to outpace the overall rate of inflation. Three insurance specialists with decades of broad health insurance expertise have joined with us to distill the most salient information for you to be aware of regarding these three interrelated topics:

• Health insurance options if you are planning to retire prior to age 65;
• Medicare and Medicare Supplementary Insurance; and
• Long-Term Care Insurance.

If you're planning to retire before age 65. You have the right under Federal Law (COBRA) to continue having the same benefits as your group plan for 18 months by paying your former employer your monthly premiums. This allows you to maintain your current coverage during a period of transition.

If your spouse remains employed, you may be able to maintain coverage through him/her. You also should investigate group coverage through other organizations.

If you are unable to access a group insurance plan, you may have to convert to an individual plan for a period of time until you are 65 and Medicare begins. Some lawyers choose individual plans with high deductibles and limited medical coverage that cover catastrophic illnesses. For reasonably healthy individuals, this option can cut monthly premiums by half or more.

If you continue to practice after attaining age 65 and are covered by group health insurance through your employer or Bar association, you may decide to continue this coverage and postpone enrolling in Medicare.

Federal Law considers COBRA coverage to be individual health insurance coverage, not group health insurance coverage. This could become an issue when you apply for a Medicare supplement or Medicare Advantage plan to enhance your Medicare coverage. Currently, if you are leaving group (not COBRA) health insurance to enroll in Medicare, there is no health statement required for any supplemental coverage, so you are guaranteed the coverage that you want. But, if you are leaving individual coverage, some insurance companies may deny coverage if you have a preexisting condition.

Eventually for most of us, Medicare is going to become a very important component of our health insurance plan.

Health savings accounts. Health Savings Accounts (HSA's) were created by the Medicare Prescription Drug, Improvement and Modernization Act of 2003. An HSA is a tax-advantaged savings account much like an IRA. Deposits can be used to pay for qualified medical expenses. And if funds happen to be withdrawn but not used for a qualified medical expense, they're subject to income tax and a 10 percent penalty. Individuals 65 or disabled can withdraw funds from an HSA for any reason without penalty (but would still be subject to income tax). To open an HSA, you must be under age 65 and enrolled in a "high-deductible health plan" (HDHP), and have no other health insurance coverage as a spouse or dependent. The IRS establishes the minimum annual deductible and maximum annual out-of-pocket expenses for a health insurance plan to qualify as an HDHP. Contributions to an HSA can be made in three ways:

- An individual or family can make tax-deductible contributions to the HSA even if they do not itemize deductions.
- An individual's employer can make contributions that are not taxed to either the employer or the employee.
- Employers sponsoring cafeteria plans can allow employees to contribute untaxed salary through salary reductions.

All contributions to an HSA belong to the account holder immediately. For tax year 2007, the annual maximum deposit to a HSA is $2,850 for an individual and $5,650 for a family. For participants 55 and older, the IRS allows an extra catch-up contribution of $800. As earlier noted, to establish a HSA you must be enrolled in a high-deductible health plan. For additional details and updates, go to *kiplingers.com* or to the Treasury Department's web site (*ustreas.gov*).

Medicare. Medicare is the federal health insurance program for individuals age 65 and older, individuals under age 65 with certain disabilities, and individuals of any age with End-Stage Renal Disease (permanent kidney failure requiring dialysis or a kidney transplant). Medicare now has four component parts:

Part A. Pays for inpatient hospital care, skilled nursing when following a three-day hospitalization, some home health care costs and hospice. If you have worked 40 or more quarters of FICA-covered employment there is no cost for Medicare Part A.

Part B. Covers Medicare-eligible physician services, outpatient hospital services, certain home health services and durable medical equipment. There is a monthly premium for Part B coverage, which is optional. If you don't enroll in Part B when you are first eligible and are not participating in group insurance, the cost of Part B will go up 10 percent for each full 12 months that you could have had Part B but didn't sign up for it. There is a deductible each year before Medicare starts to pay for Part B coverage. Enrollment in Part B of Medicare triggers an open enrollment period for Medicare supplement insurance in which no health statement may be required. This open enrollment period begins three months prior to your 65th birthday, the month of your 65th birthday, and for three months following.

Part C. Medicare Part C (previously called *Medicare + Choice*) refers to Medicare Advantage Plans, which are primarily HMO- or PPO-type plans run by private insurance companies approved by Medicare. In Part C, Medicare pays an amount of money for your care every month to these private health plans, whether or not you use their services. Medicare Advantage Plans provide all your Part A and Part B coverage and must cover medically-necessary services. Some of these plans include Part D Prescription Drug Plans, some do not. These plans usually cover additional services that are not included in Medicare or Medicare supplement coverage. Some of these plans require that you use only the providers contracted with the plan, while some allow you to use non-plan providers.

Part D. Refers to Medicare's new prescription drug coverage. This coverage may help lower your prescription drug costs and help protect against higher costs in the future. Medicare prescription drug plans are run by insurance companies and other private companies approved by Medicare. If you join a Medicare drug plan, you will usually pay a monthly premium. Part D is optional coverage. However, if you decide not to enroll in a Medicare drug plan when you're first eligible, you may pay a penalty if you choose to join later.

What Medicare covers and doesn't cover. Medicare pays for most but not all of our hospital and doctor bills. Items and services not covered by Medicare Part A & B include:

- Deductibles, coinsurance or co-payments.
- Dental care and dentures.
- Routine eye exams and glasses.
- Hearing aids and hearing exams for the purpose of fitting a hearing aid.
- Routine or yearly physical exams.
- Many screening and laboratory tests.
- Vaccinations.
- Alternative health care, like acupuncture and chiropractic care.
- Custodial/long-term care.
- Health care you receive while traveling outside of the United States.

Physicians and medical providers in general cannot be required to accept Medicare coverage, so it is important to research whether it is accepted by your physician and medical providers.

Assignment under Medicare refers to an agreement between you as the person covered by Medicare, doctors, or other health care providers and Medicare. A doctor or health care provider that accepts assignment, (a) agrees to be paid directly by Medicare, and (b) agrees to receive only the amount Medicare approves for their services as payment in full…and can only charge you, or other insurance you have, the Medicare deductible or the coinsurance amount. If a physician or health care provider does not agree to accept assignment, they may charge you more than the Medicare-approved amount for their services. You may have to pay the entire charge for their services at the time of service. Medicare will then send you a payment for the share of the charge that Medicare will cover when the claim is processed. For a comprehensive explanation of assignment, please see the Medicare booklet, *Does Your Doctor or Supplier Accept Assignment?* at *Medicare.gov*.

Medicare enrollment. Approximately 90 days before your 65th birthday, you should receive a letter from Medicare stating that your Part A coverage is to begin the first day of the month in which you turn 65 (unless your birthday is the first of the month, at which time you will be eligible for Medicare on the first of the month prior to your birthday). This letter will also ask you if you want to enroll in Part B of Medicare. Waiving Part B coverage is recommended only if you are continuing on group coverage as an employee or as the spouse of an employee with group health insurance. If you do not receive this letter, please contact your local Social Security office or go online to to enroll in Medicare prior to your 65th birthday.

Medicare supplementary insurance. Once you enroll in Medicare, it becomes your primary health insurance. As previously noted, a gap exists between what hospitals and doctors charge patients and what Medicare will pay those providers for the services they provide. Supplementary insurance, also referred to as *Medigap* policies, are available, and the federal government has standardized the policies that are available through insurance carriers. There are many plans available to supplement or replace your Medicare coverage. All of them have minimum benefits mandated by Federal Medicare Law. Medicare supplements pay secondary to Medicare, and may cover part or all of your medical costs not covered by Medicare after Medicare has paid its portion. Some of these plans include coverage for prescription drugs. You may also buy an independent or free-standing Prescription Drug Plan to cover your drug costs.

You may enroll in a Medicare supplement or Medicare Advantage plan when you first turn 65. After that initial enrollment, there is an open enrollment period that begins November 15th of each year for new coverage beginning the following January 1st. This open enrollment period allows you to change or modify your coverage. There are additional special enrollment periods that may be triggered if you move outside of your plans service area and for other reasons.

Other things you should know:

- Medicare law and regulations change often, but the program's website (*Medicare.gov* is an excellent source of information and is updated frequently).
- Each state has different Medicare laws so check your coverage if you move.
- Independent health insurance agents specializing in Medicare-related products can help chose which plan is right for you, and generally they do not charge for their services. They can also help you with any claims or service issues that may arise with your insurance company.

Long-Term Care Insurance

Traditional health insurance, as well as Medicare, and Medicare supplemental insurance policies, usually do not cover either long-term nursing care, home health care, or adult day care.

If you are hospitalized for three or more days for a medical condition—for example, a stroke or hip replacement—and you are discharged from the hospital to a nursing home for short-term skilled nursing care and rehabilitation, traditional health insurance, Medicare, and some Medigap policies will cover a portion of the cost of the nursing or home health care expenses. If, however, you need to enter a nursing home or require home health care *indefinitely* because you can no longer perform all of what are referred to as *"activities of daily living"* (bathing, eating, dressing, toileting, or moving into and out of a bed, chair or wheelchair) due to age, accident, illness or cognitive decline, traditional health insurance, Medicare and Medigap policies *do not* cover these expenses.

What does nursing or home health care cost? In 2006, the national average daily rate for a private room in a nursing home was $206, or $75,190/year, and the national average daily rate for a semi-private room was $183 or $66,795/year. The national average hourly rate for home health care was $19/hour. Author's note: My own mother, now 89, has been living in assisted living for the past 13 years. She currently pays about $3,600/month or $43,200/year for a one-bedroom apartment and for supplemental care for medication management and assistance. If she were to require transfer to a private room in the nursing care component of her complex, it would cost $248/day or $90,520/year.

▶ If you have accumulated significant wealth, you should be able to absorb the expense of long-term care. If you are a middle-income attorney and either you or your spouse/partner has a family history of Alzheimer's or another catastrophic illness, consider long-term care insurance.

Should you get long-term care insurance? If you have accumulated significant wealth, you should be able to absorb the expense of long-term care. If you have suffered financial setbacks and will be relying on Social Security and a minimum in savings and investments in retirement, you can anticipate that Medicaid will be available to cover your long-term care needs. Your nursing or home health care options under Medicaid, however, may be limited in your geographic area. In my experience, most attorneys find themselves in the middle of the economic and wealth spectrum. And if they or their spouse or partner suffered a catastrophic illness requiring long-term care, their ability to maintain their standard of living in retirement—and absorb the expense of long-term care—would be severely tested. If you are a middle-income attorney and either you, your spouse or partner has a family history of Alzheimer's or another catastrophic illness, you most certainly would want to consider purchasing long-term care insurance.

How much will long-term care insurance cost? The cost of purchasing long-term care insurance depends on several factors, including your age at the time of purchase and the level of benefits you decide to purchase. Premium rates and the possibility of being declined increase with age. The policy benefits you must consider are:

Benefit amount. The range may be $100 to $300/day. You will need to research the nursing care and home health care costs in your geographic area to determine your potential expenses.

Waiting/elimination period. A longer waiting period before benefits begin will translate into a lower premium.

Benefit period. You may contract for benefits to be paid for a specific number of months or years, or for the lifetime of the insured. The longer the benefit, the higher the premium.

Inflation protection. A benefit of $200/day may be generous today but woefully insufficient in 15 or 20 years when you need it. Purchasing inflation protection can protect against the erosive impact of inflation.

Other issues:

- How does the policy decide when you are eligible for benefits?
- Are the benefits triggered when the insured needs help with two or more of the six assistance issues?
- Does the triggering of benefits require prior hospitalization or the certification of a physician?
- Is the policy guaranteed renewable?
- Is the policy tax-qualified for income tax purposes?
- Does the policy cover both nursing care and home health care?
- Are there any restrictions on where care is provided and by whom?
- Are pre-existing conditions excluded?
- Does the policy cover care due to Alzheimer's or other dementia-type disorders?
- Does the policy contain a non-forfeiture benefit if you stop paying your premiums?
- Does the policy provide for pooled benefits between spouses or life partners?
- What is the rating of the insurance company offering the policy?

CHAPTER 6

The Estate Planner

"Only 45 percent of the adults in the US have a will, only 41 percent have living wills, and only 38 percent have health-care proxies."

—A RESEARCH STUDY BY MARTINDALE-HUBBELL

My wife and I met in college and married after we both graduated. Soon after, I was in law school and my wife began working toward her MBA. Even though our marital estate didn't include much (a '63 Volkswagen Bug, a '77 Chevy Vega, and $25,000 in student loans), my wife suggested we have our wills prepared. I agreed, and promised to do it myself after I passed the bar. Well, I passed the California bar on my first attempt, but somehow our wills never got done. In time, we bought a starter house…two daughters were born…we moved to a larger house…and swapped the Chevy for a Honda. Occasionally, my wife would ask about the wills, but I continued to make my clients' needs and many other activities of daily living a higher priority. Finally, just shy of being exiled from the marital bedroom to a futon in the family room, a lawyer friend helped us prepare our wills and health directives. In retrospect, I feel lucky I can joke about my procrastination, and that my family did not suffer the consequences if either my wife or I had died without wills.

I know that I'm not the only lawyer in the country whose own estate planning fell victim to procrastination. But why is that? Why do so many high-functioning lawyers put off this critical function even though they know better? Perhaps our procrastination just might be motivated by a) the difficulty of facing up to our own mortality, and b) that estate-planning issues can cause family discomfort, even dissension.

We have plenty of time, don't we? According to an AARP survey, more than one third of Americans over 50 lack a will, living trust, or power of attorney. If you have put off creating an estate plan (or updating an existing plan), I hope you'll take advantage of some of the estate-planning tools discussed in this chapter. I don't need to remind you of the potential costs—in taxes, legal fees, emotional anguish, and family divisiveness—that could result from failing to complete and execute this planning task. As for lawyers in private practice, especially sole practitioners, there is an even greater urgency: you must develop a contingency plan in case you should become physically or mentally disabled and be temporarily or permanently unable to practice law. This plan must include developing a relationship/s with another lawyer/s that you can designate as assisting, caretaker or surrogate attorneys, to step in and protect your clients and your practice if you should become disabled. See Chapter 8 for help in developing a contingency plan.

Tools & Techniques

Basically, there are two ways to provide for the planned transfer of all or parts of your estate:

- While you are living, through gifts, sales of your assets and possessions, a partial sale and gift, and trust agreements; and
- At death, through your will (either the one you write or the one your state writes for you), and through contracts such as life insurance, buy-sell agreements, pension benefits, deferred income options, pre-marital agreements, joint tenancy of property, testamentary trust(s), charitable transfers or marital transfers.

Wills. A valid will is basic to effective estate-planning. It controls the distribution of property interests you solely own, and allows you to nominate the fiduciaries that will administer your estate. It's a great gift for them because it's a proactive tool to head-off problems for which your survivors may be unprepared. In addition to distributing your property, a will can be the most effective means of assuring that your final wishes are carried out, including matters of guardianship, providing for professional management of funds and special bequests.

Most of your assets can be passed to another by your will. Some exceptions:

- *Property subject to creditor's claims.* If property is subject to a creditor's claim and the will makes no provision for the payment of those claims, the property will automatically pass to the creditors.
- *Joint interests with the right of survivorship.* If property is owned jointly under a right of survivorship arrangement, the survivor will automatically inherit the property. This will result regardless of any will and what such a will might specify. In community property states, assets acquired during the marriage will pass to the surviving spouse.
- *Insurance, pension and other contracts with named beneficiaries.* Any named

beneficiary of an insurance policy, your pension, a trust, or a special account will also receive the proceeds involved regardless of the will's provisions.

Far too many of us who have prepared wills fail to update them as needed. We'll share two examples of unintended consequences that resulted from such failures:

- The managing partner of a small law firm and his wife get divorced. As part of the settlement, the husband takes out a million-dollar life insurance policy payable to his two daughters. From time to time, the ex-wife suggests he update his will, making the proceeds of the policy payable to a testamentary trust for the daughters. Unfortunately, the lawyer dies without updating his will…with predictable results. When the oldest daughter turns 18, she demands—and gets—half the inheritance, and blows it all within a year. Soon after, the second daughter turns 18, and she goes on a spree of her own, depleting within two years what's left of the inheritance.
- Husband and wife are both in their early 70's. Husband is diagnosed with Alzheimer's and a second degenerative disease, and has a life expectancy of less than nine months. The wife—herself in good health—and the couple's lawyer assist the husband in updating his will. The lawyer advises the wife to update her own at the same time. She demurs. "I'll take care of it after my husband passes away," she says. "I don't have time to deal with it now." Sadly, the wife predeceases her husband by a month. His will is updated; hers is not…and they had joint property. The probate was a mess.

Life events that should trigger you to review and possibly update your will:

- The birth, adoption, or death of a child.
- The marriage, divorce, or separation of anyone named in the will.
- After a significant change in your financial status or that of a beneficiary.
- After any major change or revision of the tax code.
- Upon any major change in the needs or circumstances of you, your spouse or partner, or your beneficiaries.
- Absent such intervening life events, every 10 years.

So, if you don't have a will, or if it hasn't been updated in a long while, don't procrastinate. Pay a colleague who drafts wills as a regular part of his/her practice to draft one for you.

> ► If you don't have a will, or if it hasn't been updated it in a long while, don't procrastinate. Pay a colleague who drafts wills as a regular part of his/her practice to draft one for you.

What if you die without a will? As you're well aware, if a person dies without a valid will and has estate property, the probate court will appoint an administrator for the estate, and in the event there is no surviving spouse, appoint a guardian for any minor children. The assets of the estate will then be distributed as specified by the state law where such property is located, regardless of the situation of each dependent or relative. In some states, a spouse with children may receive only one-third of the estate and a spouse without children must divide the estate with the decedent's parents. If a person leaves no heir or next of kin, his or her property will forfeit to the state.

Gifts. The federal gift tax was created to prevent individuals from avoiding paying estate taxes by gifting their property prior to their death. The general rule is that any gift is subject to the federal gift tax. However, there are many exceptions to the general rule. Generally, the following gifts are not taxable to the donor:

- Tuition or medical expenses you pay for someone else.
- Gifts to a spouse can be made at any time and in any amount without being a taxable event.
- Gifts to a political organization for its use.
- Gifts to qualified charities.
- Gifts whose value does not exceed the annual gift tax exclusion for the calendar year ($12,000 for 2008). Note: parents can give a child up to $24,000/year (up to $12,000 from each parent) by a process known as *gift-splitting.*

These lifetime transfers, especially over multiple years and to a variety of family members or others, can reduce the size of an estate, avoid gift taxes, and shift the income on income-producing property to the recipients. Making gifts to minors through the Uniform Gift to Minors Act (UGMA), or the Uniform Transfer to Minors Act (UTMA), can shift income tax liability to a minor's lower tax bracket. Most financial institutions will provide information on the advantages and disadvantages of such transfers, as well as the mechanics of how to make them. Gifts of appreciated assets carry the gain in their value over to the recipient, whereas, a *gift at death* or bequest erases the gain so the heir receives the asset at the fair market value. Sale of property to family members, a business partner, or others can provide another way of transferring appreciating property, especially when there is a desire to control the size of an estate.

Living trusts. A living trust provides an effective way for you to manage your property or to appoint a manager (trustee) to oversee it without it having to go through probate. A properly drafted living trust avoids probate, and can also designate management in the event of incapacity and preserve privacy. The initial costs to living trusts are the time required to prepare the trust documents or to have another lawyer prepare them, as well as, the time required to re-title assets to the trust. To be effective, the appropriate assets must be re-titled to the trust before the trust is fully funded.

Life insurance. Probably the most common contract provision effective at death is the payment of life insurance proceeds to a beneficiary. This transfer is normally tax-free and distributed only days after the insurance company has received proper documentation of the insured's death. Consequently, it is very important that beneficiaries are reviewed periodically, especially when family changes occur.

Pensions and retirement accounts. Retirement benefits and deferred accounts (i.e., IRA, 401(k) are also contracts that have beneficiary designations. Normally such accounts pass outside the probate process at death, but they normally have both estate and income tax ramifications for non-spouse beneficiaries. For this reason, these assets should be the first choice if you wish to make a charitable contribution on death.

Joint tenancy. Holding assets in joint tenancy is an effective and frequently used technique to transfer property, whether real or personal, directly to the survivor without the time and expense of the probate court. However, with large estates (above $2 million in 2006-2008), joint tenancy may cause increased estate taxes. Owning property jointly with your children has some pitfalls since the creditors of your children have access to the property. Sometimes a child who holds joint property with the parents fails to share the property with siblings at the parents' death.

> ▶ Holding assets in joint tenancy is an effective technique to transfer property, real or personal, without the time and expense of probate court. However, with large estates (above $2 million in 2006-2008), joint tenancy may cause increased estate taxes.

Testamentary trusts. These are set up through a person's will to begin at the person's death. The trust document describes the purpose of the trust, names the trustee (manager of the assets) and the trust beneficiaries, and often specifies the length of the trust and the ways to distribute assets at the trust's end. Such trusts are often used to provide for dependent children in case of premature death.

Charitable transfers. If you have achieved a sense of financial security, you may want to consider sharing part of your estate with your alma mater, a community program, your church, or some other public or private charity. Although you may not be able to afford outright gifts, you may be able to make charitable remainder gifts or participate in pooled income funds administered by the charity. In these situations, the charity will provide a life estate or funds to you while you are living, but claim the remaining assets at your death. In addition to the philanthropic value of such gifts, you may also benefit from tax deductions available for these charitable transfers. Most charitable organizations offer assistance with such giving. Unlimited marital transfers and charitable transfers of assets are available for lifetime gifts as well as testamentary transfers.

Power of attorney. A *springing* durable power of attorney may be one of the most important parts of your estate plan. As the name implies, it *springs up* when needed, giving someone you designate the power to make financial decisions for you if you're incapacitated.

Health care directives. Many people dread the thought of living their last days hooked up to medical equipment that prolongs their suffering and drains their family's assets. To lessen the chances of this happening to you, create an advanced medical directive that states your wishes about your medical care. With a Durable Power of Attorney for Health Care, you name a person called your health-care agent who is authorized to make medical decisions for you. A *springing* durable power of attorney for health care gives your agent decision-making power only after the doctors have determined you are incapacitated. You may want to name one or more alternates in case your first choice isn't available when a decision has to be made.

Get independent help planning your estate. Sad but true, the attorney who represents himself has a fool for a client. One national estate and financial planning author would add that, "*do-it-yourself estate and financial planning is the closest thing to do-it-yourself brain surgery.*" These two propositions support the suggestion that you would be well served by recruiting a team of professionals to assist you in developing your estate plan and reviewing your financial needs, objectives and current status on a regular basis. Depending on your circumstances, your team might include a lawyer specializing in estate planning or elder law, a CPA, an insurance agent, a trust officer and other certified financial services professionals.

Who Knows About Your Estate Plan?

If your estate plan has been created, and you have already taken all the steps necessary to implement it, we congratulate you. Now, forgive us for asking…but do the individuals and/or organizations directly impacted by your estate plan actually *know* about your plan...do they have the information needed to implement it...have you clearly communicated the existence of your plan to your spouse/life partner and your family...and does your spouse/partner, family or named personal representative have the following:

- The location of the original copy of your current will?
- A copy of your current will or access to it?
- A clear understanding of your current financial status and access to all your financial records?
- If your financial records are all on your personal computer, have you communicated that, and do they have your password and know how to access the records?

Here's a real-life example of what can happen when the details of your estate plan haven't been communicated with significant others:

A law firm partner we know had practiced for 40 years, and was busy making plans to retire at the end of the year. As the date approached, he and his wife were busy making plans to tour Europe, visit their children, grandchildren, and spend lots of time at their vacation home. Just before he retired, the lawyer suffered a heart attack and died. His wife was devastated...not just with grief, but at the prospect of understanding their financial affairs and putting them in order. No small task, because from the time the couple was married, it was her husband who managed the family's finances. Over time, and with the help of an adult son, the widow did take control of the estate. But progress was hampered by a lack of knowledge of the husband's estate plan and their personal finances. In fact, she discovered that, although her husband and his law partners did have a buyout plan of his partnership interest using life insurance, his personal will and estate planning were outdated. This error in judgement triggered unnecessary probate costs and estate taxes.

▶ Congratulations if you have created an estate plan and have taken steps to implement it. But have you communicated the existence of your plan to your spouse/partner and to your family?

In a related matter, your estate could be further complicated if you are a solo practitioner. Who, for example, would close your practice if you died before retiring? The wife of a Connecticut business lawyer had to do just that after her husband's death from cancer a few years ago. Her story—"*Closing a Spouse's Practice: What I Wish My Husband Told Me*"—was published by GP Solo Magazine in December 2006. The story has been reprinted in full in Chapter 8.

How Estate Taxes Work

Even though recent tax revisions have phased out federal estate taxes for all but a very small percentage of the population, you should know that the following tax liabilities are possibilities:

- The federal government levies an estate tax on certain transfers of wealth between individuals.
- Some states also levy a death tax or an inheritance tax payable by the recipient of the inheritance. In many cases, the exemption for state death taxes is smaller than the federal exemption.
- If you receive a cash inheritance, the amount received is not subject to federal income taxes.
- If you invest your inheritance, income from the investment is taxable as is profit from the sale of an investment.
- If you receive property as an inheritance such as stocks or a building, you receive it on a *stepped-up basis* or its present market value. If you sell the property, any gain you realize can be taxable as income.

Revisions to the federal estate and gift tax laws were enacted in 1977, 1982, 1997 and 2000. Any wills, trusts, or other forms of estate planning that were completed before these dates should be reviewed and adjusted where appropriate. In addition, the area of federal estate and gift taxes is highly technical and may require the assistance of a tax attorney or advisor for specific details in your situation.

Here is a simplified version of how these taxes work:

The federal estate tax is levied on so-called *taxable transfers*, money or property that one has passed along, either in the form of trusts and gifts while alive, or through estate distribution after death. If you make gifts in excess of the tax-exempt allowances, the excess will be considered as a taxable transfer and may be subject to tax.

An estate is valued as of the time of death, or upon election, six months after death. The total estate generally consists of all that the individual owned, plus all that was owed to him or her. This can include a home, investments, proceeds of life insurance policies owned by the decedent, personal property, money due under pension and profit sharing plans, and business interests. Jointly owned property may still be included in the total estate under certain conditions.

From the total estate are subtracted the debts of the decedent, as well as expenses such as funeral and burial costs, charitable bequests, and the costs of administering the estate; the remainder is known as the taxable estate. The amount of the taxable estate can be further reduced by the marital deduction, which is that portion of the estate that is left, in proper legal fashion, to the surviving spouse.

In calculating the amount of estate tax, use the following table:

FEDERAL ESTATE TAX AND GIFT RATES

Year	Estate Tax Applicable Exclusion Amount	Gift Tax Applicable Exclusion Amount
2006-2008	$2,000,000	$1,000,000
2009	$3,500,000	$1,000,000
2010	Repealed	$1,000,000
2011 & after	$1,000,000	$1,000,000

Example. *In 2006, John's total estate upon his death consisted of cash and property worth $2.9 million. His allowable expenses were $50,000. Subtracting $50,000 from the total estate, a taxable estate of $2.85 million remains. Let's see how some tax planning could result in neither John nor his wife paying any federal estate tax:*

Knowing that their estate is more than $2 million, John and his wife are advised by their attorney to set up credit shelter trusts and split the ownership of the assets between them, each owning approximately $1,450,000 or half of the assets. In the event of the first death, the assets of the deceased spouse are placed into the trust with the proceeds or earnings from the trust's assets going to the living spouse. At the passing of the second spouse, the assets in the trust are distributed per his/her estate plan. In this example, each spouse was able to take advantage of the $2,000,000 applicable exclusion or higher, depending on the year of death, with this result—no federal estate tax.

Sound estate tax planning requires that you focus on both possible taxes— husband's and wife's. Your tax attorney can help you work out alternatives to minimize, or totally eliminate taxes on the combined estates.

Special Problems of Estate Planning

Estate planning is not all wills, trusts, and taxes. There are a number of other special considerations that fall within the overall concept of estate planning.

Consider:

Spousal impoverishment. Too often, a spouse enters a nursing facility, and leaves the spouse remaining at home in a difficult financial situation. The *Spousal Impoverishment Law* changed the MEDICAID eligibility requirement for the spouse needing care so that the spouse at home can protect a portion of the family's income and resources. Generally, the healthy spouse will keep the home and its contents, one automobile, one burial plot, a funeral plan, a share of property and income. State regulation differs on the share, but a portion of the couple's combined monthly income and their combined cash assets can be kept by the spouse at home.

Death of a spouse. The grief and confusion at the death of a spouse can cloud the common sense of the surviving partner, which can interfere with their financial well-being. Quite often a non-attorney widow, or a widow who has not been involved with managing the family finances, is faced with the need to manage a fairly large sum of money, and she may not always be up to the task (see Mary Silverberg's poignant essay in Ch. 8). Statistics indicate that the average widow spends the proceeds of her husband's life insurance in about two years. The main reason is that the average amount of life insurance carried is equal to only about two years of income. Still, prudent management of the insurance proceeds should stretch it out over a longer period. Many widows or widowers are victims of their own lack of financial experience. In many families, the wife may be in charge of the day-to-day budget, but the husband assumes responsibility for the family investments, so the wife is ignorant of important financial matters. Surviving partners are vulnerable to the army of con artists and financial scams that prey on their grief and confusion. The best protection is to take a very conservative position in financial matters for a year or two. Take time to regain full control and do some homework on how to make the money work best. During the cooling off period, the spouse should be wary of financial appeals, and opt instead for federally insured savings plans or money market funds.

▶ Grief and confusion at the death of a spouse can cloud the common sense of the surviving partner, which can interfere with their financial well-being. During this time, the spouse should be wary of financial appeals, and opt for federally insured savings plans or money market funds.

Rights of spouses. Although children can be disinherited, a spouse has a legal right to a share of a deceased spouse's property, even if the will makes no such provision. If, however, one has been abandoned by one's spouse, or has signed a valid prenuptial agreement, then a spouse may be disinherited. In many states, the law entitles a spouse to use of one-third of the deceased's real estate. In a number of states, a spouse has a legal right to renounce the will and claim the share which would have been received if there had not been a will. In some states, community property laws give the spouse one-half interest in property acquired during the marriage.

Getting remarried. Perhaps the most common problem encountered when one makes a second marriage is the attitude of children. What appears on the surface to be personal resentment on the part of the children may actually be masking a more vexing concern: *"Who's going to get whose money?"* Two things can help prevent problems before they start: first, there should be open and frank communications between the parent and his or her children about the prospect of remarriage. Second, consider a prenuptial agreement, which spells out clearly who will get what and when.

Caring for the elderly. A major portion of overall estate planning is geared to assure significant others a continuity of security while you are still alive. But continuity can be severely tested...even disrupted...by the unanticipated responsibility of caring for elderly parents (see Appendix 4 for helpful Web links). If you can anticipate your parent's possible reliance on you, you can plan accordingly and minimize any disruptions to your own life and financial well-being. If you have brothers or sisters who would also be expected to share the responsibility for dependent parents, you should discuss the matter frankly with them soon. If you supply more than half of the cost of your parents' support in a given year, you are entitled to claim the appropriate number of tax exemptions and head of household status. Parents do not have to live with you for you to claim them as dependents, nor does where they live impact your filing status.

Selling your practice. If you live in a state that allows a lawyer to sell his/her practice, the money you expect from the sale of your practice may be an important factor in your estate planning (see Ch. 8 for a helpful essay on this subject). The transfer of a professional practice, whether to partners or strangers, must be timed carefully. There is a peak period during which you should begin to make your move. Your objective is to get the best possible selling price and retain the maximum amount of income for as long as you remain involved. To formulate your plans most efficiently, you may need the help of another lawyer and your accountant. As with all the other planning concerns, the time to get some advice is now.

▶ How much of your estate do you want to provide now...and later...to your children? How much can you afford to provide without cutting into your own comfort and security? The shape of your estate plan can have an effect on the shape of your children's lives, and on their subsequent estate plans as well.

Downsizing your residence. The single largest

asset for some families is the equity in their home. Consider the advisability of selling your home if it has outgrown your needs and moving to one that is more compact and energy efficient. Sentimental elements may enter into such a decision, but the practicality of downsizing has proved rewarding for attorneys in their 60's and early 70's. By downsizing, a part of this equity may be freed and invested to supplement income for the retirement years. As discussed in Chapter 3, instead of selling your residence, you may want to investigate a *reverse mortgage*.

Preparing your children and grandchildren. The shape of your estate plan can have an effect on the shape of your children's lives and on their subsequent estate plans as well. How much do you want to provide for them now and in the future? How much can you afford to provide without cutting into your own comforts and security? You should answer these questions in your own heart and mind, and then communicate your thinking to your children. Children who anticipated an inheritance that never materialized, or who did not expect one that did materialize, may have shaped their lives differently had they known what to expect. For example, a child who anticipates an inheritance might easily develop wasteful spending habits. He or she could then face financial disaster when the inheritance does not materialize. On the other hand, a child who does not expect an inheritance might needlessly sacrifice what you would have wanted him or her to have, such as a proper education for a talented grandchild. To the extent that you can help shape your children's lives for the better, the subject of your estate deserves frank discussion with them.

Larger estates. It's been estimated that six out of ten affluent families will lose the family fortune by the end of the second generation, and, nine out of ten affluent families will have depleted the family wealth by the end of the third generation. This follows an ancient Chinese adage that *wealth never survives three generations*. So what can be done by those who are fortunate to accumulate wealth? Wise families pass on values as well as valuables to successive generations. It won't be easy, but some wealthy families have been very successful in passing-on constructive wealth management as part of their family legacy. A few suggestions:

- Don't spare your children the hard work that contributed to your own financial success. Let family members learn things the hard way, doing without and making sacrifices sometimes.
- Discuss money and the strategies for not only making it but keeping it.
- Family council meetings and family retreats can foster better communications.

- Encourage philanthropy with children and grandchildren.
- Where a family member handles money unwisely, a trust, perhaps administered by an outside party, may be a good option to consider.

Preparing for your demise. As uncomfortable as it may be, preparing for your death is an important part of a total estate plan. You can make careful and unhurried decisions when you make your own funeral arrangements, particularly if you think about the cost and the discomfort of your survivors. There are various plans available through funeral homes (check to see if they have the sustaining assets to be around a long time), cemeteries, church groups or cremation societies. You can also put money away in a special account designed for this purpose after writing down your wishes and making them known to your heirs. AARP publishes several reports on this topic. These special aspects of estate planning may seem to be outside of the familiar scope of legalities and taxation normally associated with the task. A prudent estate plan can't afford to ignore these elements, lest the whole structure be severely weakened. The sooner you prepare your plan, the more secure you will be.

CHAPTER 7

The Midlife Career Planner

"When you turn 60, you say to yourself, 'OK, I've got about 20 good years left. How many of those do I want to spend practicing law?' It doesn't make sense to spend that time in a stressful environment." —Ed, a former BigLaw partner

Over the last 15 years, I've had the good fortune to assist nearly 1,200 lawyers on job and career issues, and facilitate close to 100 lawyer career workshops. And the work continues; I currently co-facilitate a weekly Lawyers In Transition support group.

But whether it's senior litigators or new admittees, solos or big firm partners, in-house counsel or public sector lawyers, or trial and appellate judges, I've come to understand that in law there is a fairly predictable career arc. In the early stage, most of us are highly motivated to establish and prove our legal competence. In the next stage, we spend a decade or two making our way up the (steep) legal learning curve getting established. And then—somewhere around midlife; late 40's, early 50's—we seem to pass through an invisible door and discover that our practice doesn't provide the same motivational energy or generate the same satisfaction it once did. Or, as Bill, the former Navy flyer-turned-lawyer put it at the start of Chapter One, the *"novelty of law"* wears thin after a lifetime of practice.

This is why, if you're a lawyer (or judge) at midlife, it's important to take a step back now and reassess where you are in your career:

- Are you still enjoying your practice enough to stay the course?
- Should you alter your practice or professional position in some way to increase the satisfaction and meaning you derive from your work?
- Or, is it time to make a significant or radical job or career transition?

As we noted earlier, today's midlife lawyers report that they intend to remain active in the workplace throughout their 60's and into their 70's. If that's so, then making the time in midlife to reassess your life and career aspirations will increase the probability that the work you do in the second half—or, as the ABA puts it, *the second season of service*—will be satisfying and meaningful. A little later in this chapter, I will share the stories of several lawyers who did just that. For now though, ponder these two questions:

Who am I now?
What do I want at this stage of my life and career?

Who Am I Now?

Trust me, this is not the beginning of some frivolous exercise on The Meaning of Life. On the contrary, this deceptively simple question goes to the heart of your midlife career search, and it demands a rigorous investigation of your personal strengths and preferences in five areas:

- Interests
- Skills
- Values
- People contact
- Work environment

Interests. Interests are subjects to which you are drawn, topics about which you read and inquire, and activities and areas of knowledge that are intriguing. Some people are generalists with broad interests that frequently change; others are specialists who like to focus on one subject or field. Our interests often change over time, and typically are different at midlife than when we were younger.

Skills. Skills are your natural abilities and those you have developed through experience. Behavioral research confirms that we enjoy jobs that call upon our natural aptitudes (those skills that come most readily to us), and that we dislike work that asks us to rely on skills we find difficult. Likewise, many studies prove what we know instinctively: that the tasks that come easily are the ones we do best. So, identifying the skills that you enjoy using the most and finding or creating opportunities that utilize these skills is one of the keys to satisfying work in the second half of life.

Values. Values are the intangible guiding principles and goals that bring meaning to your work and motivate your involvement and commitment. Some values shift as you mature and grow, but most guide your choices throughout a lifetime. If your work clashes with your values, you may produce easily enough, but you won't feel good about it. You'll experience a gut conflict, an unsettling doubt about whether you're doing the right thing. If your work is consistent with your values, however, you'll feel motivated to do more, even if the work itself is difficult. You'll want to accomplish your goals in order to express that value.

People contact. Your preferences in this category are all the ways you like to interact with coworkers and clients. Here you need to define the personality traits and cultural backgrounds of the people you prefer as colleagues and clients. Consider also whether you prefer to work alone, with a handful of others, or with larger groups. At least one lawyer in any group of 10 prefers an isolated environment for introspective, analytical work. Others prefer a team approach, working together with a compatible group toward a common goal. There are also those who prefer to have many and varied personal interactions in their workday.

Work environment. Environmental preferences involve the physical and intangible aspects of the workplace itself: the office atmosphere, the work schedule, the aesthetics of the physical setting, the degree of flexibility in office management, even the dress code. Some of you feel uncomfortable the moment you dress up for the office and would much rather throw on a pair of denims and a sweatshirt. Others hate "dress down" Fridays. Some of you might feel claustrophobic in an office without windows that open, while your colleague down the hall loves his corner office in a gleaming glass-and-steel tower.

Whether you work on this alone or with a career counselor, it will be important to explore and clarify your preferences in all five areas as you reassess who you are at midlife. Incidentally, one reliable way to identify your preferences is to analyze your past experiences—good and bad—and define the qualities that tie them together. This type of analysis is often more accurate and revealing than what you've learned about yourself from family and friends, or from experiences in past employment. We will be offering some exercises that will help you do this later in this chapter.

What Do I Want at This Stage of My Life & Career?

Effective career self-assessment—whether it's in your 20's, 30's, 40's, or at midlife—asks you to consider the practical and measurable. But it's only after you also give yourself permission to begin examining the fantastic and illogical that you make your way to a more satisfying future. "If I had to come up with one issue that makes working with attorneys such a challenge," says San Francisco career counselor Lesah Beckhusen, "It is their almost exclusively

FINDING WORK THAT MATTERS IN THE SECOND HALF OF LIFE

Marc Freedman, founder and CEO of Civic Ventures, a San Francisco nonprofit focused on expanding the contributions of older Americans, has emerged as a leading voice in discussions about the changing face of retirement. In his newest book—*Encore*—he explains why people in their 50's and beyond still need "productive relationships"—joining with others in pursuit of a larger goal.

In this excerpted interview with the Wall Street Journal, Freedman discusses what he calls "encore careers":

"…(They) take place in the second half of life, after the end of a midlife career. (They) involve some type of pay or benefits. And at their core is the search for new meaning, and a deep desire to contribute to the greater good. A prime example would be someone who—after spending 30 years in a profession—decides in his or her 60s to become a math teacher or to launch a second career with an environmental organization."

Asked how that differs from "working in retirement", Freedman said, "A retirement job is a bridge, a transition, a way to make ends meet between the end of one's working life and the beginning of full retirement. An 'encore career' is a goal in and of itself. For many people, it's the opportunity to do what they've always wanted to do." ●

left-brained thinking about how the world works." Lawyers, she says, are trained to rely upon rational, linear, organized thought. But down deep, all of us are motivated by what we want, not by what is logical or practical. Beckhusen advises lawyers to trust their right-brained intuition and feelings for a vision of what they want…and then let their left-brain skills get them there.

▶ What do you want to do now? Effective self-assessment asks us to consider the practical and measurable. But it's only after you give yourself permission to examine the fantastic and illogical that you will find your way to a more satisfying future.

Writer Ray Bradbury put it best when he said, "Listen to your stomach and not your head. Your head will only rationalize you into a job you shouldn't have."

But acknowledging one's occupational dreams can be a little unnerving if—like so many lawyers—you've spent most of your working life focused on the expectations and needs of others. And yet one of the gifts of midlife is the opportunity to reassess future occupational pursuits according to the *meaning and personal satisfaction* they will provide. So, you might begin thinking what you want by monitoring how you currently spend your time when you're not working.

Lawyer Nancy Ashley, a veteran practitioner who moved from private practice to human services consulting, described what she did: "For years, I had done volunteer work in human services—child advocacy issues, food banks, starting a domestic violence shelter. If only I had looked at how I used my time when it was my own choice, I could have saved years of trying to figure out a new direction for myself. It just took me a while to recognize the signals that everyone else could see."

In the past 15 years, I've had the privilege of witnessing other midlife lawyers who stepped back and asked themselves, *"What do I want at this stage in my life and career?"*

Here are capsule profiles of 10 lawyers who did just that:

Dick. Throughout the 23 years that Dick spent as a corporate lawyer in a large firm, he and his wife had been passionate about protecting and preserving the environment. At the age of 53, he decided to leave his firm to start the Northwest Earth Institute (*nwei.org*), a nonprofit that has since earned national recognition for its innovative environmental education programs. More recently, Dick started a second nonprofit, Center for Earth Leadership (*earthleaders.org*), which trains and motivates citizens to assume a leadership role in forging a sustainable culture.

Nancy. During the many years Nancy practiced as an employment lawyer, her passion was international travel. At midlife, she began to focus her travel on hiking in southern France and developed an intimate familiarity with this region. Friends and acquaintances began to ask her to lead them on hiking tours of France. She ultimately closed her law practice, and now operates a business leading hiking tours through France and selling rugs she imports from Turkey.

Bill. As I mentioned in Chapter 2, Bill's first love was aviation. A Navy fighter pilot in his 20s, he continued to fly—and instruct others—even while practicing law. Two years ago, at the age of 62, the conditions were right for Bill to close his law practice and return to aviation full-time as a flight instructor. He and his wife were debt-free and enjoyed a modest lifestyle, and she had a secure, lucrative job that she enjoyed and planned to continue to work at for the foreseeable future. Since then, Bill has partnered with the owner of a flight school, and they have purchased a state-of-the-art flight simulator. They plan to purchase a high-performance plane and launch a flight instruction business with a historical twist—challenging student pilots to map and fly the route of 19th

Go to www.LawyerAvenue.com for more career resources. Click on Careers.

Century explorers Lewis and Clark through Montana, Idaho, and Oregon. As of mid-2008, Bill is back flying full-time, and his "encore" career will be taking off soon. He's also rekindled his love of playing the piano!

> ▶ A few years before his firm's mandated retirement policy kicked in, Ed retired as managing partner and launched a mediation practice. Four months later, he had lost 20 pounds and reduced his blood pressure by 10 points.

Ed. Four years before his firm's mandated retirement policy kicked in, Ed retired as managing partner and launched a mediation practice that brings him into the office about two days a week. "When you turn 60," he said, "You say to yourself, 'OK, I've got about 20 good years left. How many of those do I want to spend practicing law?' It just doesn't make sense to spend that time in a stressful environment." Just four months after retiring, Ed had lost 20 pounds and reduced his blood pressure by 10 points.

Michael. Michael was very successful in a midsized civil litigation firm. But after two decades, he yearned for a different life. Fortunately, he had the financial resources to resign from his firm and move to California's Lake Tahoe, where he became a partner in a small business, and spent winters skiing and summers traveling in Europe. After four years, he decided to return to work, and participated in a career workshop and intensive self-assessment. Ultimately, Michael decided to get into human resource management. So, he enrolled in a state university program, and earned an HR management certificate. Soon after, he landed a job as a labor relations manager with the state. Now, he draws upon his legal experience to counsel agencies, negotiate contracts and offer presentations on employment law issues. Michael has the financial resources to re-retire anytime he wants; but after a decade, he continues to derive great satisfaction from his encore career.

Susan. Susan reached "the door of midlife" after nearly 20 successful years in business law. She, too, decided to engage in a period of self assessment. Soon after, she left law for nursing school, and became a psychiatric nurse practitioner. After working at a community mental health agency and opening her own private practice, Susan and her husband adopted a beautiful infant daughter. Her midlife dream continues to evolve.

Stan. Stan spent most of his 31-year career as in-house counsel to a major corporation. As a result of good financial planning, he decided to leave his full time practice in his late 50's ...and enroll in a career workshop. Six weeks later,

Stan had a plan: keep his hand in, and take on work as a contract lawyer. In no time, he was getting referrals from his old colleagues. And those referrals led to others, which led to others. The last time Stan and I spoke he had almost more work than he would like! In fact, some months his work-load is almost what he carried before he "retired"…with one big difference. Now, his schedule is his own. And as long as he completes the projects in the time promised, he can do the work when he wants. So, he works evenings or weekends if he has other things he wants to do during the weekdays. He also typically turns down last-minute projects without fear of losing clients. Now 64, and financially stable, Stan says he's not interested in returning to work as an employee. "Right now, I can pretty much schedule my own life, and I would not be willing to give that up," he said. For the foreseeable future, Stan intends to be a part-time solo as long as he is enjoys it.

Dennis. Dennis chose a different course at midlife. After a first career in the wood products industry, he got a law degree, and grew into becoming a county counsel. When that second career began to pale, Dennis found a way to bring together his legal background and his knowledge of natural resources. He moved to Central and South America and became an international environmental consultant. In time, Dennis was ready for yet a third career…in immigration law. By now fluent in Spanish, he moved back to rural Oregon, and opened a solo practice. Even though he hadn't practiced for almost 20 years, other immigration lawyers in the area welcomed him, and helped him get up to speed in this new practice area.

Steve's midlife passage took him from a big firm tax law practice to university director of planned giving. **David** went from estate planning solo to executive director of the local YMCA. And **Mary** went from private practice and working for a national bank to general counsel for a nonprofit that provides international relief and innovative programming in developing countries.

But enough with the story-telling. Time to roll up your sleeves and begin to explore who you are now and what you want.

What Do You Want to Do Now with Your Law Degree?

One of the resources I have used in guiding lawyers through career self-assessment is Deborah Arron's career workbook classic, *What Can You Do With a Law Degree?* In the material that follows, we have included a series of self-assessment exercises first introduced by Deborah that lawyers have found particularly helpful in starting to answer the questions: *Who Am I ?* and *What do I want?*

Today's assignments

Assignment #1. List the achievements and accomplishments of your life; the things for which you have bragging rights. Begin with childhood and work your way to the present. For each citation, describe the highlights about your involvement, the nature of the project, and the results achieved. Note: These achievements or accomplishments need not have been acknowledged by others. List any activity in which you took a leadership role, or in which you helped to create a product, or in which you wrote, spoke, taught, researched, coordinated or constructed, no matter how insignificant that contribution might seem now. When you finish gathering the information, organize your list chronologically to serve as a data bank for future résumé writing.

> ▶ Imagine you've won a $200,000 lottery annuity. Describe how it would change your daily existence.

Assignment #2.

a. Describe what you learned about money and work from your parents.

b. Describe what you'd like to do if your life expectancy was just a matter of months.

c. Finish the following sentences in detail:
   - I don't like to admit it, but I really need...
   - I feel happiest when I'm...
   - If money and education were not a consideration, the work I prefer would be...
   - When I was a child, I always wanted to be a...
   - Time passes most quickly for me when I'm...
   - One thing I've always done well is...

d. For one week, take a few minutes every day to jot a few key thoughts about your ideal work place. Describe your ideal work place in detail. If others are there, who are they and what are they doing?

e. For a full month, make notes on a desk calendar (or computer or PDA) of which daily activities you enjoyed the most and the least. At the end of the month, summarize and categorize your preferences.

f. For a full month, take a few minutes every day to visualize your ideal day. Describe it even if it has nothing to do with work.

g. In 10 minutes of continuous writing (without removing your pen from the paper or your fingers from the keyboard), describe what you enjoy doing when you're not working.

Go to www.LawyerAvenue.com for more career resources. Click on Careers.

h. Write a description of yourself. Describe your interests and define your personal style, including the way you like to dress, live, and interact with others. Be certain to list those skills at which you excel, and those you enjoy using, whether or not they have anything to do with work.

i. Describe what you know of your long-range career goals, and identify what contributions you would like to make to yourself, to your family, to your community, and to the world. At the end of this assignment, summarize in writing any themes, patterns, or contradictions.

j. Imagine you've won a $200,000 lottery annuity. Describe how it would change your daily existence.

Assignment #3. Describe up to 50 of the most enjoyable events of your life. Focus on experiences you remember as fun or fulfilling, and when time seem to pass without notice. Choose events you enjoyed as they were unfolding, not because of any outcome or positive feedback. Be sure to include at least a dozen experiences from childhood. Get in touch with experiences that lifted your spirits and that you would gladly repeat. Afterward, compile a list of 10 awful experience—when time dragged or was filled with frustration, dread or fear. Again, consider only the process and not the result. When both lists are complete, spend some time answering the following questions:

• How often were you alone and how often with others? What were you doing when you were alone? How did those activities differ from your activities with others?

• How many others were with you? What was the nature of your interaction with them? Were you conversing or participating with them, or quietly working alongside them? Were you engaged in group activity? What kind?

• What were the characteristics of the people around you? Up-beat? Analytical? Daring? Supportive? Competitive? Challenging? Smart? Artistic? Athletic?

• What were you doing? Was it physical, mental or both? Were you passive or active, moving around or staying in one place; conveying or receiving information?

• What was the purpose of your participation in each event? Personal growth, building something, enjoyment, making change, helping others, competition?

• In what environments did you find yourself? Indoors or outside, sunny, rainy, dark, bright, crowded, spacious, formal, informal?

• Were you relating emotionally, intellectually, physically or spiritually to your surroundings?

- Were your activities internalized-that is, thoughtful or meditative—or external to yourself—for example, teaching, advising, coaching, viewing entertainment?
- What was the tempo of each event? Fast-paced, relaxed?

Note that the answers to these questions may be contradictory. You may enjoy being alone and being with others, or engaging in high-energy activities and sitting peacefully outside in the sunshine. Include these observations in your answers to the questions.

Assignment #4. Imagine learning you have three years to live. How would you spend the time if money and energy were not a factor? In this exercise, answer three questions: What would you devote yourself to in the remaining time… how might others be impacted by your legacy… and what might others say about you and your legacy after your passing?

Assignment #5. Imagine yourself working at your fantasy job, and describe a day-in-the-life in this role. Be as specific and detailed as you like, and imagine yourself from your first cup of coffee to the end of the day:

Where are you?
What are your surroundings?
What activities are underway around you?
Who, if anyone, are you working with?
What are the others doing, and what are you doing in relation to them? If no one else is around, what are you doing?

Assignment #6. This assignment asks that you project yourself through time— 1, 5, 10, even 20 years—and describe what your life might look like if you remained on your present course. Describe your life in terms of opportunities, relationships, and your emotional and physical well-being.

The Dream Planner

Most of us minimize daydreams as the work of idle minds or children. Which is unfortunate, because daydreams could reveal the key to what life could become after the practice of law. Which brings us to the next exercise; we call it The Dream Planner. To do it, you need to find time (today, this week) to shut your office door, and switch off your phone, your computer, your BlackBerry, and commit to paper the answer to this simple statement:

"I've always wanted to..."

Everyone has a dream tucked away. Some of us act on them, others are reluctant, and still others won't even share them with family, friends or partners to avoid appearing foolish (or delusional). Well, here's your chance to explore the fantasy and/or reality of your dream...whether it's becoming an angel investor, going into politics or mediation, writing legal thrillers or starting a winery, climbing Everest or sailing the world in a catamaran. Hopefully, the self-assessment assignments we suggested earlier have already helped bring your dream(s) to the surface. And if you worked through the financial planning tasks in Chapters 3 and 4, you have a clearer idea of your current financial position and resources.

> ▶ Everyone has a dream tucked away. Some of us act on them, others are reluctant, and still others won't even share them to avoid appearing foolish (or delusional).

Now, before you tackle your own dream-planning exercise, read about how one lawyer couple began thinking through their own dream:

At 58, Bill has had a successful law practice for 26 years. He and his wife, Mary, have raised and educated two children, who now live on their own. Bill nets about $150,000 a year from his practice along with the firm's contribution's to his 401(k) plan. Both want to reduce the stress from Bill's work and their ever-challenging social life. Their dream is to move to the San Juan Islands off the Washington State coast, and start an upscale bed-and-breakfast. Recently, they found a waterfront property with an appropriately zoned, five-bedroom house with a price tag of $750,000.

The Reality. The delayed maintenance on the house is of some concern to them since the repairs and build-out is estimated as $225,000, and would require nearly six months to complete. And either Bill or Mary would have to be on-site to supervise the renovation. The reality is that carrying out such a dream would present a radical lifestyle change for both, not to mention putting at risk the financial security they both have worked to establish.

INCOME. $150,000/year from Bill's law practice; $28,000/year from the firm's pension (at age 60); estimate $25,000 from Social Security (age 67).

ASSETS. Money Market Account—$75,000; Bill's 401(k)—$750,000; Mary's IRA—$32,000; joint brokerage account—$250,000; checking—$15,000; home equity—$425,000.

LOANS. Home mortgage—$125,000; vehicles—$12,000.

The Plan. Realizing the island property won't remain on the market for long, they feel pressed for a decision, so Bill and Mary begin by studying their present and future finances.

If they empty their brokerage account, take the equity from their home, and start taking a four percent withdrawal from Bill's 401(k), they will still need to borrow an additional quarter-million dollars to buy and update the property, and they would need considerable cash for moving expenses. B&Bs, especially in remote locations, come with considerable risk and take time to grow into profitability (sometimes up to five years). Selling their residence and cashing out the brokerage account could be problematic, too.

An alternative would be for Bill to continue in his legal practice another two years. Delaying his departure would allow ample time to inform his partners, qualify for a $28,000 pension, allow him to build his 401(k) account, pay down the mortgage on their home, and grow his after-tax brokerage and cash accounts. In considering the lifestyle change, neither Bill nor Mary have ever worked in a "service environment" where they are always serving their customer's needs. If they delay the decision for a couple of years, Mary could work in a B&B near their home as a test and to gain experience. And the wait would give both of them time to prepare for the change. For Bill, just knowing that there is a change in the near future from his stressful law practice, could produce positive results.

Now, with the format used in the example above, grab a legal pad and start working on your dream:

Your Dream. . .

The Reality. . .

The Plan. . .

Every Dream Has its Twists and Turns

Embracing a period of honest and rigorous self-assessment is an important first step in clarifying both who you are now and what you want in the second half of life. But self-assessment and your imagination can only take you so far. At some point you just have to put your toes in the water and try on a new role, or decide to shift your practice in some way. Only then will you know whether the reality of this new course will provide you with the increased satisfaction and purpose you are striving to create.

But every dream has its twists and turns.

- Our co-author Pat Funk retired in her 40's from her first career at IBM, and moved to Vail, Colorado. When a great property came on the market, she decided to buy it and start a B&B. It was profitable, it was fun, but after a few years she was weary of the day-to-day realities of running a hostelry. So, she leased her business to a British company that flies in Brit's during the ski season. Smart move; Pat earns more with this arrangement than she did when she was running the B&B herself!

- In Chapter Two, we introduced you to Frank, who retired from his Philadelphia firm to begin a new career as an alcohol-and-drug counselor. Eighteen months later, Frank had an epiphany: he had brought to the new career the same intense work ethnic and work style that had made the practice of law difficult. "Perhaps my Type A personality contributed to that," Frank told me. "I couldn't leave at the end of the day until I had all of my jobs in proper shape, and until I was 100 percent ready for the next day's business. I had no energy to do anything but work. I would come home at the end of the day like I did when I was practicing law. The bottom line is that I really burned out after about a year-and-a-half." So, Frank resigned, with no plans other than to take some time off and explore other opportunities. A short time later, he saw an ad for a position in the Labor and Employment section of the state Department of Justice. "It just seemed designed for me, so I applied. As I went through the interview process, almost everything I learned about the position was attractive to me. The job involved a minimal amount of litigation in court, which was the worst part of my prior practice. It did involve trying arbitration and administrative agency cases, which I always loved to do. It paid about 25 percent of what I was earning in private practice in Philadelphia, but that was okay because it paid enough to support our current lifestyle. At this point the money is not important anymore. With my kids educated, I don't need to generate as much as I did before."

Frank was offered the position and he accepted. In his first year, he accepted an offer to become attorney in charge of the labor and employment department. In that first year, Frank was also diagnosed and successfully treated for prostate cancer. As he approached his 61st birthday, Frank reported that he was happily finally living his dream of public service.

…And Every Transition Has its Hurdles

The first hurdle—and it is no small consideration—may be the loss of one's lawyer identity.

Those of you who consider yourselves "successful lawyers" may have to give up the external rewards associated with your position—the status, prestige, self-esteem, and financial resources. And if you never found success in the law, leaving the profession can be especially traumatic. Because even though you know you would be more suited in another profession, your professional identity—the ability to introduce yourself as a lawyer or a law school graduate —may be your greatest sense of pride. If you renounce even this accomplishment, what do you have left to offer? In a study done by two Minnesota career services offices, many lawyers considering leaving the profession were especially concerned that their colleagues would look down on their new careers as having less prestige. The anxiety didn't last long, though. Once they'd made the move, they didn't look back. And they appreciated the improvement in their quality of life, the greater independence, flexibility and family time, and the reduction in stress!

Other hurdles you may encounter include:

The conflict between money and meaning. Despite all the evidence that money does not buy happiness, the conflict between money and meaning is doubtless the most difficult for lawyers to resolve. Those of you who are experienced practitioners might now be earning good money, but perhaps you're no longer satisfied with your work. To find fulfillment, you may have to trade the assurance of a comfortable, or even regular, income for the risk and invigoration of a meaningful change. Others of you—especially solo practitioners, small town lawyers, or public interest lawyers—might be earning too little money. It could be that you place a higher priority on the meaning you derive from your work—whether contribution to society or to your individual clients—or on your lack of pretentiousness, than on the money you earn. You're afraid that if you move into better paying work, you'll sacrifice your integrity. You might also envy those in lucrative practices or those receiving regular salaries in private industry or government, but you can't overcome what you believe is your inadequacy to find that type of work. You may be placing a higher priority on autonomy, self-direction, and control than on the income you generate.

The conflict between work and personal life. Some of you may love your work but wish you could spend more time with family and friends. Still others never find the time to explore personal interests or simply relax. You may all believe that your families are your highest priorities. But think a moment: if you work long, hard hours for a good income but seldom see your families, you might be placing a higher priority on the needs of your clients or coworkers, or on supporting your family's lifestyle, than on actually spending time with your family. If you don't have time for yourself, you may be acting quite consistently with your priority of spending time with your family, or you might be placing an even higher priority on your work, with time for self coming last. None of these choices are wrong per se, but refusing to acknowledge that all your priorities cannot be weighted equally can cause frustration and guilt.

An example:

> Gordon, with nearly 20 years of law practice behind him, hated his work. But at a group career workshop he confided that something was preventing him from leaving the law. He had promised to put his sons through college, and the only way he could meet that commitment was to keep practicing law. When someone in the workshop asked whether he had shared the dilemma with his sons, Gordon looked shocked. *"I can't do that,"* he said. He had given his word, and that was that. And yet at the next meeting, he arrived looking 10 years younger and 100 times happier. He had told his eldest son about his career conflict and was astonished by his son's response. The young man urged him to quit. He said he admired his father for putting himself through college and wanted to enjoy the same opportunity to prove himself. More importantly, he missed the supportive, fun-loving father he had before Gordon's depression set in. So, Gordon chose to leave his law partnership and began driving a city bus, teaching in a paralegal program, dabbling at writing fiction, and handling a little bit of legal work out of his house. You might not make the same choice, but it worked for him.

None of these hurdles, or conflicts, require all-or-nothing solutions. You don't have to give up money to find meaning in your work. You don't have to drive a bus just to find quality time to be with your family. And you don't have to go bankrupt to achieve career satisfaction. *You simply need to clarify your values, and make the compromises that bring your priorities and the realities of your life into alignment.* Until you identify a next-step and engage in some personal research, you can't know how much you're going to have to give up or whether the sacrifice will be worthwhile. The point is to begin your introspection and analysis and deal with this last issue when required. You won't have to make decisions about household expenses and outside obligations until you choose a direction and confirm the sacrifices it will require. By then, you'll know whether the loss will be worth the reward.

Career Crossroads for Senior Lawyers

We are fortunate to conclude this chapter with the perspectives of two professionals with decades of experience assisting lawyers and law firms:

Carol Kanarek, a New York career counselor with extensive experience guiding lawyers through job and career changes, offers her perspective and suggestions for senior lawyers who wish to continue to practice after retiring from their firms. And *Stephen Gallagher*, an executive coach and former Practice Management Advisor for the New York State Bar, makes the case for why law firms today need to head-off the expertise and experience drain they would suffer if Boomer lawyers reaching the traditional age of retirement were to leave their firms.

I'm Leaving My Law Firm, But I'm Not Ready to Retire
Career-Planning Strategies for Midlife & Senior Lawyers
by Carol M. Kanarek, JD/MSW

For many senior lawyers this book may be the catalyst for a self-guided journey to a satisfying retirement. Some may want or need to make a transition from their current place of employment but don't want to stop practicing law...others may wish to explore law-related or non-legal employment options...and there are still others with work-centered lives who may need some assistance in making the basic decision of whether or not to continue to focus your energies around your career. Any of these options could be daunting if the last time you gave them serious thought was 20, 30, even 40 years ago.

So, where can you turn for some help? Let's start with the first category: lawyers who are leaving their current jobs but who want to continue practicing law. This group is rapidly growing, in part because of the prevalence of mandatory retirement policies in big law firms, and in part also because of the desire of many senior lawyers to move to "lower stress" practice settings. Take note, though: before you take steps to make a job change, find out what impact, if any, your continued practice of law will have on your eligibility to receive retirement benefits from your current employer. To determine this, you may need to consult an employment lawyer.

Search firms: the reality. After you've done the legal legwork, what's next? Many lawyers-in-transition assume that executive search firms or legal "headhunters" are the best resources to use to find a new position. This is an understandable misconception, given that there are hundreds of legal search firms in the US. In reality, though, legal search firms are responsible for placing only a small percentage of senior lawyers.

There are a few reasons for this:

- Most large law firms and major companies seek mid-level associates, or more senior lawyers, with large books of portable business, and/or very specific skills, who they cannot easily recruit through advertising, word-of-mouth, and/or unsolicited resumes (more about that later).
- Most employers of lawyers—small law firms, many companies, and virtually all governmental agencies, academic institutions and non-profit agencies—don't hire search firms because of the expense, which ranges from 20 to 33 percent of the initial annual compensation of any lawyer placed with that employer.
- Most legal search firms place lawyers only at large law firms (or branch offices or small firm "spin-offs" of large law firms). The vast majority of legal employers in suburban or rural areas—other than branch offices of large national law firms—do not use search firms. Companies that do use search firms to hire lawyers are generally located in major metropolitan areas, and are usually publicly traded. States with significant numbers of legal employers that use search firms include California, Connecticut, the District of Columbia, Florida, Georgia, Illinois, Maryland, Massachusetts, Michigan, New Jersey, New York, North Carolina, Ohio, Pennsylvania, Tennessee and Texas. Note: if you're seeking to relocate to another geographic area, you will generally get the best results by working with a search firm in the state or region in which you wish to practice.

Search firms are used by employers to find "square pegs for square holes". Consequently, if you are seeking a non-legal position or wish to change to a new area of practice, a legal search firm will rarely be of help. Non-legal search firms in other business sectors that interest you may provide information about the overall availability of jobs in those sectors, as well as insights regarding the skills and experience employers in that sector are seeking. As a general rule, however, they will not be able to assist you in finding your first position in a non-legal career.

The most comprehensive national directory of legal search firms is published annually as a pull-out supplement to the January issue of the American Lawyer. Many other legal periodicals also publish lists of search firms or search firm advertisements on a regular basis. If you believe you may be an appropriate candidate for a search firm, draw on your own contacts first. This way, you will almost always get a more enthusiastic hearing—and a better financial arrangement—if you "place yourself". Afterward, seek out and speak with a few search firms that are both well-connected in your target market and experienced in placing senior lawyers. If respected search firms say they can't place you, listen to them. Don't look for an inexperienced search firm that will "paper the market" with your resume. You won't get interviews that way; in fact, you may close doors by having your credentials submitted along with a hefty price tag attached. Above all, don't be discouraged if you are among the 95 percent of senior lawyers who won't be placed by a search firm. It doesn't mean that you are unemployable; it simply means you need other strategies.

The ideal candidate. The ideal senior lawyer candidate usually has large law firm experience, as well as a current or prospective client base substantial enough to keep him/herself and a number of more junior lawyers busy at the billing rates in effect at large law firms. Some large law firms will use search firms to hire senior lawyers with specialized expertise, e.g., ERISA, insurance, mutual funds, Sarbanes-Oxley, and no client base, but that is rare. If you are senior and don't have significant portable business (usually defined as over $1,000,000 in annual revenues), you are much more likely to get your foot in the door if you approach law firms directly and help them avoid the "sticker shock" of a headhunter's fee. While large law firm experience is generally required, many corporations that use search firms to fill senior attorney or general counsel positions request candidates who have both large law firm and in-house counsel experience. Most jobs listed by corporations with search firms require corporate, securities, and/or regulatory experience, with the exception of litigation-intensive companies and financial services institutions, which may list positions with search firms for litigators with insurance, securities, employment or products liability experience.

Advertised job openings. In the Internet era, it is tempting to think you will find work by responding to online legal classifieds. And you may. After all, many law firms and corporations have online job boards. You'll find one at The Association of Corporate Counsel Web site (*acc.com*), and another at *TheLadders.com*, which posts legal jobs with annual salaries of $100,000 or more. So you may indeed find work online. But only if your credentials and experience are squarely on point with the posted job description. And be sure your resume highlights your relevant experience, and that you use your cover letter as an opportunity to explain how you are specifically qualified for the position rather than why you want it.

A large and growing percentage of advertised job listings for lawyers are project-based or temporary in nature. The majority of these positions are listed by an employment agency, which in most instances will be your "employer" for the duration of the work assignment. Most temporary assignments involve discovery for major litigations. The work is generally full-time, and can be very hours-intensive for the duration of the assignment. This kind of work can be a good option for someone who wants to take time off between assignments, or who may want to take part of the year off. Hourly wages are generally between $20 and $50/hour (plus overtime), although temporary positions in financial institutions or for corporate, tax or trusts and estates lawyers may pay up to $100/hour in major cities. Many of the legal temporary agencies are listed in the American Lawyer's Directory of Legal Search Firms.

Professional networking. The overwhelming majority of senior lawyers discover that professional networking is the most effective means for securing new employment. In this way, all sorts of possibilities open up: valuable tips about the market, and what approaches work best, from those who recently changed positions themselves…information from senior lawyers in other firms who may have work that might tie in with what you're doing or hope to develop…possible referrals to clients looking for in-house counsel…and, from business executives in the community, you might find companies that have emergent legal needs…perhaps even a position. Incidentally, don't assume that a company without a general counsel's office doesn't need a lawyer. In the process of networking, ask local business owners if they are satisfied with the price and quality of their legal services. Find out what their problem areas are, and then sell yourself as a solution to those problems. You may discover that some of these companies are paying a lot of money for expensive outside counsel, but haven't hired in-house counsel because they don't need someone on a full time basis.

Identifying such situations can be win-win for both you and the company; they save money, and you can reduce your work hours while continuing to practice law.

Of course, networking is not for everyone. So, you might want to explore what job-search or lawyer-in-transition programs are available through your local bar or through business networking organizations such as the Five O'Clock Club. Your local college or university may also offer continuing education programs on the various elements of the job search process. And don't overlook the career services office at local law schools, and the professional development professionals at local law firms. Both are often a good source of referrals to networking groups.

Once you have identified some general employment sectors that sound interesting to you, talk to as many people as possible who are actually employed in those jobs. Ascertain what they really do on a day to day basis, what the level of demand is in their fields, what compensation levels are, and what skills, training or licenses are prerequisites for entry-level employment. This so-called informational interviewing is important for two reasons. First, it is next to impossible to sell yourself for a non-legal position if you don't know what specific skills are required so that you can functionalize your legal credentials in a way that will make sense to a potential new employer.

Second is the "be careful-what-you wish-for" factor. Your due diligence will give you a reality check by gaining an insider's view of the pros and cons of a particular prospective job. You may discover that many people think YOUR current job sounds wonderful, and they secretly wish they could change places with you!

It is also especially helpful to see a resume of the person who holds the type of job that appeals to you, so that you can create a version of your own resume that uses the language of your desired new career. This will also help you to pinpoint key skills you may be lacking so that you can determine whether or not you will need additional training before you can pursue this line of work.

Are you thinking about going back to school? Admissions officers tend to paint a rosy picture because they are looking for your tuition dollars. So, seek out the school's career services office to get a realistic sense of the types of jobs and salaries obtained by new graduates, and what special challenges second-career students may face.

Finding work inside, outside & around the law. Although most self-help books tell you that career-change begins with personal introspection, this actually might be less helpful for a senior lawyer than a market analysis. By this, I mean identifying legal jobs for which demand in a particular employment sector exceeds the supply of those currently working in or trained for that field. The advantage is that potential employers are more willing to look "outside of the box" in terms of previous experience for new hires. How can you identify what areas are in demand? Look at the ads in your local newspaper, talk to human resource directors at local companies, and—most important—make professional networking a way of life. Whenever you meet someone new, ask him or her what is at the top of their employer's wish list in terms of skills needed for new employees.

There are a number of law-related jobs for experienced lawyers who want to make a career transition. They fall into five main categories—law school teaching, law school administration, law firm administration, legal search, and continuing legal education:

Teaching opportunities. Includes adjunct, clinical and legal writing or "lawyering" faculty positions at law schools. Compensation is low, but the work usually facilitates professional networking and practice development. Check out the Web site for the Association of American Law Schools (*aals.org*), the professional association of more than 160 law schools.

Law school administration. Opportunities include career services, admissions, alumni programs, fundraising/development and diversity initiatives. Most successful applicants for these positions are lawyers. Fund-raising and development, in particular, is a growing field.

Law firm administration. Includes law student recruiting, lateral recruiting, associate orientation and training, practice group assignments and/or administration, legal personnel (evaluation, diversity, outplacement), marketing, and pro bono coordination.

Legal search firms. In major metropolitan areas there are often many opportunities in legal search with both permanent and temporary placement firms, particularly when the economy is strong.

Continuing legal education. One of the biggest growth areas in recent years has been in lawyer training. If CLE's are mandated in your state, there are probably employment opportunities in bar associations, law firms and private training companies for lawyers who can provide training and/or organize training programs. To help identify other work opportunities for lawyers, I can recommend two resources—*What Can You Do With a Law Degree?* and *Changing Jobs: A Handbook for Lawyers.*

Using a career counselor. Career counselors have very little in common with legal search firms, yet many lawyers mistakenly believe that they are interchangeable. The most fundamental difference between them is that legal search firms represent the interests of employers (because they are paid by them), while a career counselor works for you. You can hire a career counselor to guide you through the process of career planning—including self-assessment and market assessment—and/or to assist you in the job search process by providing guidance in resume and cover letter writing, drafting a practice development plan, networking strategies, interviewing techniques, and negotiation of the terms of employment.

When you work with a career counselor, you are the client and you pay the fee. Consequently, you should perform the "due diligence" necessary to satisfy yourself that the counselor's approach is compatible with your particular needs and objectives. Just as in therapy, a good counselor can help you explore options and find answers...but they are not a placement agency. Indeed, be wary of companies that charge a hefty up-front fee (usually several thousand dollars), and imply that they will be able to find work for you "because they are so well-connected". Usually these companies are little more than very expensive mass-mailing services, and they have no secrets not known by more reasonably priced counselors. Look for a counselor who charges by the hour; this allows you to retain the option to spend as much time with that person as is useful to you.

It is important to select someone who has significant experience working with attorneys. Otherwise he or she may not have information on relevant resources, options and challenges. In a national roster of career counselors at *LawyerAvenue.com*, most of the individuals once practiced law themselves...and all have considerable experience working with lawyers in transition. You can find additional referrals from law school career services offices and local bar associations. Incidentally, if you have a spouse or partner, you may want to bring them to an early session with your career counselor so that they will gain a deeper understanding of the options that will be both satisfying and realistic for you. Some senior lawyers find couples counseling to be a useful addition to the job or career transition process, as many non-lawyers do not fully understand the stresses and realities of the legal profession.

Above all, at this time in your life, surround yourself with others who share your view of the change process as an opportunity for personal and professional fulfillment. For many lawyers, "retirement" opens doors to even greater success and satisfaction. It's a journey...enjoy it!

—Carol Kanarek, JD/MSW (kanarekandbrady.com), a New York career counselor and psychotherapist, has over 20 years of experience working with lawyers in transition.

Retaining Boomer Leadership and Expertise
by Stephen P. Gallagher, Esq.

Today, we are facing a shortage, not a surplus of talented lawyers, so law firms must begin to phase out "retirement" as we know it. As a replacement, law firms need to explore how a staged reduction in work hours and responsibilities ahead of full retirement might work. Could it be that the same senior lawyers that many law firms are now looking to sunset may become the untapped resources firms will need to lead the talent pool of the future?

The first of the boomer generation lawyers are approaching their early 60's. Due to the dominant size of this generation within the legal profession, law firms throughout the country are potentially facing a massive exodus of skilled senior lawyers. Many if not most of these firms face this potential exodus with traditional retirement policies and procedures that define retirement in terms of the removal or withdrawal of midlife and aging lawyers. In attempting to meet this challenge, law firms today must create meaningful and purposeful roles for lawyers between midlife and true old age.

Declining birth rates guarantee a recurrent shortage of talented young workers—a problem many law firms are experiencing at this time. In 2001, the American Productivity and Quality Center (APQC), a consortium that focused on identifying business best practices and innovative methods of transferring those methods, explored links between succession management and company leadership development process. The study pointed out that if economic growth continues at a modest two percent for the next decade and a half, this would result in the need for a third more senior leaders than there are today. Yet the supply of the age cohort that has traditionally filled the demand for new leadership (35- to 44-year-olds) is actually declining in the U.S. and will have dropped by 15 percent between 2000 and 2015 because of the differences in the size of the baby boom generation and the much smaller Generation X. So, law firm strategists will have to look for new approaches to attract and build leadership teams.

Flexible retirement for competitive advantage. Over the past 20 years, I have worked with dozens of sole practitioners and literally hundreds of senior attorneys in developing Exit or Retirement Plans. In my experience, senior lawyers or pre-retirees are clearly not looking to fade away. They want to find fulfilling activities. They want enriching endeavors. Certainly they want to leisure…at times, and they naturally want to have fun. But, contrary to the popular media view of retirement, the most important thing lawyers anticipating retirement are looking for is their own fulfillment…their own sense of purpose and meaning.

I have found that those firms that prize the interdependence and mutual responsibility among the multiple generations of firm lawyers are better prepared to help their pre-retirees through this period of transition. These firms are more inclined to encourage their senior lawyers to tackle fresh assignments designed to offer variety and challenge and to stimulate new skills development.

Senior lawyers in these law firms seem to approach retirement as a way of gaining renewed purpose in their lives. They want something new, something different, perhaps something novel, and certainly something interesting at deep personal levels. Law firms play an increasingly important role in creating a firm culture that will allow this transition to take place.

In a recent book on the approaching talent shortage, *Workforce Crisis: How to Beat the Coming Shortage of Skills and Talent*, Ken Dychtwald and coauthors Tamara J. Erickson and Robert Morison, recommend that employers look to phasing as a variation on the traditional retirement model. They describe flexible retirement, as an approach that encompasses flexible roles and work styles, attracting work assignments suited to one's experience and inclination, and reduced hours, flexible schedules, and more control over one's time—before and after the point of official "retirement."

The idea of a more flexible retirement option, would allow not only partial retirement, so that senior lawyers can enjoy other pursuits, but also active retirement, wherein seniors can remain productively and socially engaged in the workplace. Going to a more flexible retirement option will demonstrate a fundamental shift in the way lawyers of all ages live their lives.

Redefining value and profitability. Before law firms can begin looking at retaining midlife and aging lawyers through flexible retirement options, law firms will have to re-examine how they have been determining value throughout the whole organization. Many firms determine partner value based almost exclusively on billable hours. As more partners begin reaching senior status, it should be anticipated that more of your senior people will find it increasingly more difficult in keeping-up with targeted hours.

When lawyers define themselves primarily by hourly rates and billable hours, one hour is not distinguishable from that of a competitor's, so clients will begin thinking of you—and the services you offer—as commodities. If you believe that all you can offer your clients is time, and you behave as if logging hours on a time-sheet is more important than actually servicing the needs of clients by delivering results, you might want to take a step back and consider exploring new ways to create client value. Unless law firms are able to create value in new ways, senior lawyers will be the first group to suffer. Law firms need to take a serious look at changing their cultures to allow this transition to take place.

Many law firms remain mired in the notion that the only way to create wealth is by leveraging people and hours; that the two main drivers of profitability are leverage (number of associates or paralegals per partner) and the hourly rate utilization achieved by each team member. The thinking has been that if a firm wants to add to its revenue base, partners have two choices: work its people more hours or hire more people.

Confronted with new forms of competitive and market challenges, the practice of law is long past due for a new way of looking at profitability in law firms. It is also long past due for a new way of looking at its lawyers—including senior lawyers. It's time for a new business model that will attract individuals who are fully engaged, physically energized, emotionally connected, mentally focused, and spiritually aligned with a purpose beyond immediate self-interests.

To imagine what this new business model might look like, let's start by agreeing that clients are not interested in buying time. They are interested in buying: results, expectations, good feelings, hope, dreams, a preferred vision of the future, and solutions to problems. Today, a lawyer's ability to create wealth ultimately depends on the firm's capacity to create, disseminate, innovate, and leverage intellectual capital, so firms must begin pricing their intellectual capital based upon the value to the client, not the internal labor cost of its human capital; or the profit desires of its owners, and certainly not the labor hours involved in creating it. Keep in mind that intellectual capital in most law firms resides with the most experienced practitioners—your senior lawyers.

With the emergence of a new business model for private legal practice, the success factors of the past will increasingly becomes less relevant. Billable hours will become less meaningful to clients, and the criteria for success in the future have yet to be established. This new law firm culture will create the framework for setting new performance expectations and the ways in which people relate to one another. I suspect that law firms will find creative ways of "quantifying senior lawyers continuing involvement."

Changes in law firm culture. Because lawyers have so much discretion and autonomy in a law firm setting, firm culture is the dominant force in determining how lawyers in any firm actually behave towards one another and towards their clients, so one of the first challenges that law firms will face in the years ahead will be finding ways of changing the firm culture to ensure an adequate supply of qualified lawyers. Two aspects of a new law firm culture that young people are now demanding include: a strong performance orientation and an open, trusting environment. It logically follows that, law firms whose culture supports both a performance orientation (which includes inspiring mission, stretch goals, accountability for results, and tight performance systems) and an open, trusting environment will have a much greater chance of attracting and retaining talented people. Senior lawyers share the same interests in a strong performance orientation and an open, trusting environment.

Law firm retirement/exit planning. William Bridges, author of *Managing Transition: Making the Most of Change,* defines Transition as the inner process through which people come to terms with a change. The process takes place over a period of time as they let go of the way things used to be and reorient themselves to the way that things are now. Transition management is based on the idea that the best way to get people through transition is to affirm their experience and to help them to deal with it. In a law firm setting, managing transition means helping people to make that difficult process less painful and disruptive. Many law firms have been following the mistaken idea that the best way to get people through a transition is to deny that they are even in a transition.

Once a senior lawyer begins winding down a full-time law practice, he/she may need time and possibly support as he/she moves away from the external, material, achievement definition of self, toward the more personal, intimate and, for many, the spiritual definition of self. The journey from full-time work to full-time retirement in its traditional sense may take a number of years to accomplish. Attaining a particular age does not miraculously give anyone the requisite tools, competencies, knowledge, and attitudinal shifts to ensure that retirement will proceed smoothly.

In order for law firms to help senior lawyers through this transition/renewal stage of life, they need an adequate change management plan in place. They should determine where senior lawyers are in the transition process, and they will need to develop strategies for helping people let go of the old way of doing things.

It is important to keep in mind that every person approaching their first retirement transition needs exactly the same process of self-analysis and sound consultation that they would receive from a competent career consultant if they were going through a job change. Time to work on such a plan is very hard to do with other responsibilities in a busy law practice. As job changers need to generate their career options in a clear and understandable way, so too, pre-retirees need the same "options generation" process but with slightly different content, slightly different goals, and an entirely different purpose. That's exactly what persons approaching retirement at any age need... they need options.

Increasingly, professional service firms are turning to retirement coaches or mentors to help senior partners set retirement goals and exit strategies. As a general rule, these retirement or exit plans include both long-term goals (e.g., to continue working three-days a week for two more years) and the more immediate performance goals that move lawyers toward the long-term goals (e.g., to transition 10 of my clients to younger partners in the next 30 days). This form of transition planning allows senior lawyers to learn new skills and competencies well before they begin any type of retirement.

One of the frequently forgotten benefits law firms receive in helping senior lawyers manage transition/retirement planning is the impact this has on younger partners. Young people are now demanding strong performance orientation and an open, trusting environment. What better way of demonstrating a commitment to each other than assisting the people who built the firm in preparing for the next stage of their lives.

—STEPHEN P. GALLAGHER, ESQ. (*LEADERSHIPCOACH.US*)—AN EXECUTIVE COACHING FIRM THAT WORKS WITH ATTORNEYS, PRACTICE GROUP LEADERS, AND "HIGH POTENTIAL" INDIVIDUALS TO DEVELOP EXIT STRATEGIES AND RETIREMENT PLANS.

CHAPTER 8

Closing a Practice

"…A lawyer's duty of competent representation includes arranging to safeguard the clients' interests in the event of the lawyer's death, disability, impairment, or incapacity."

—Barbara Fishleder, Oregon State Bar Professional Liability Fund

We opened Chapter One by reporting that a significant percentage of the lawyers we surveyed planned to continue to practice into their 70's, with as many as 10 percent saying they don't plan to retire at all. However, all of us will one day be faced with the task of leaving the law and closing our practice. And depending on one's practice setting—midsize/big firm vs. solo/small firm—the checklist of tasks, questions, and concerns will vary but fall into certain key areas:

- Determining whether your practice has marketable value and whether you plan to sell it?
- Notifying clients
- Retention/destruction of client files
- Retention/destruction of attorney trust account records
- Withdrawal from active cases
- Malpractice insurance tail coverage
- Determining your ongoing bar membership status (active, inactive, resigned)

Of course, every lawyer wants the chance to decide for themselves when to leave their practice, and the opportunity to work at their own pace with all the associated (and required) tasks. Unfortunately, we won't all have that luxury. Death and unexpected disability trump career assumptions and expectations every time, a reality that took a very real turn in my own work.

Just as this book was being completed, I was asked to help close a practice for a respected plaintiff's lawyer dying from cancer.

At the time of the man's diagnosis, he was concerned his practice would be negatively impacted if word got out. So, he did his best to keep the diagnosis to himself, and despite huge demands—mental, physical, financial—this extraordinary lawyer continued to practice. When he had at last exhausted all treatment alternatives and his condition deteriorated, a long-term colleague suspended any new cases to help him, and she called in a practice management advisor and myself for assistance and guidance regarding the transfer of cases and the closing of the man's practice. A week before the man died, he used whatever little energy he had left to tie off legal loose ends—even while receiving hospice care at home. It was a noble effort, but I know the man's wife and adult daughter would have preferred to have more of his energy and attention those last few months. My point is that for lawyers generally, and for sole practitioners specifically, it is crucial that you develop a relationship and understanding with a colleague who is prepared to step in and assist in times of unexpected disability.

> ▶ Every lawyer wants the chance to decide when to leave their practice. Unfortunately, we don't all have that luxury. Death and unexpected disability trump career assumptions and expectations every time.

Some years ago, the Oregon State Bar Professional Liability Fund (PLF), and Barbara Fishleder, director of the PLF'S Personal and Practice Management Assistance Program, developed the nation's first handbook to guide lawyers in planning for such unexpected disruptions in their ability to practice. Called *Planning Ahead: A Guide To Protecting Your Clients' Interests In The Event Of Your Disability or Death*, the book is a comprehensive resource that includes numerous downloadable forms that might be necessary in this situation and the closing of one's practice generally. Since its publication, other jurisdictions have developed similar guides. If your jurisdiction has not yet developed such a resource, Planning Ahead is available to non-Oregon lawyers for $15 (*osbplf.org*).

In the meantime, this chapter will offer some expert guidance in a few key areas:

- We begin with an excerpt from *Planning Ahead*, which provides an overview of the issues, tasks and decisions you need to proactively address in order to prepare for unexpected disruptions to your ability to practice.
- We provide a checklist for closing your practice at the end of the chapter.
- We are fortunate to present the works of a nationally recognized expert on buying and selling a law practice, and an insurance professional who discusses malpractice insurance tail coverage.
- We conclude with an essay written by the widow of a sole practitioner:

Closing a Spouse's Practice: What I Wish My Husband Had Told Me, which poignantly captures the essence of this chapter.

Planning Ahead
By Barbara S. Fishleder

It is hard to think about events that could render you unable to continue practicing law. Unfortunately, accidents, unexpected illnesses, and untimely death do occur. If any of these events happen to you, your clients' interests may be unprotected.

For this reason, a lawyer's duty of competent representation *includes* arranging to safeguard the clients' interests in the event of the lawyer's death, disability, impairment, or incapacity. Most commercial malpractice carriers require the lawyers they insure to make arrangements for office closure in the event of death or disability.

The first step in the planning process is for you to find someone—preferably an *"assisting attorney"*— to close your practice in the event of your death, disability, impairment, or incapacity.

The arrangements you make for closure of your office should include a signed consent form authorizing the Assisting Attorney to contact your clients for instructions on transferring their files, authorization to obtain extensions of time in litigation matters when needed, and authorization to provide all relevant people with notice of closure of your law practice.

The agreement could also include provisions that give the Assisting Attorney authority to wind down your financial affairs, provide your clients with a final accounting and statement, collect fees on your behalf, and liquidate or sell your practice. Arrangements for payment by you or your estate to the Assisting Attorney for services rendered can also be included in the agreement.

At the beginning of your relationship, it is crucial for you and the Assisting Attorney to establish the scope of the Assisting Attorney's duty to you and your clients. If the Assisting Attorney represents you as *your* attorney, he or she may be prohibited from representing your clients on some, or possibly *all*, matters. Under this arrangement, the Assisting Attorney would owe his or her fiduciary obligations to you. For example, the Assisting Attorney could inform your clients of your legal malpractice or ethical violations only if you consented. However, if the Assisting Attorney is not *your* attorney, he or she may have an ethical obligation to inform your clients of your errors.

Whether or not the Assisting Attorney is representing you, that person must be aware of conflict-of-interest issues and must check for conflicts if he or she (1) is providing legal services to your clients or (2) must review confidential file information to assist with transferring clients' files.

In addition to arranging for an Assisting Attorney, you may also want to arrange for an *"Authorized Signer"* on your trust account. It is best to choose someone other than your Assisting Attorney to act as the Authorized Signer on your trust account. This provides for checks and balances, since two people will have access to your records and information. It also avoids the potential for any conflicting fiduciary duties that may arise if the trust account does not balance.

Planning ahead to protect your clients' interests in the event of your disability or death involves some difficult decisions, including the type of access your Assisting Attorney and/or Authorized Signer will have, the conditions under which they will have access, and who will determine when those conditions are met. These decisions are the hardest part of planning ahead.

If you are incapacitated, for example, you may not be able to give consent to someone to assist you. Under what circumstances do you want someone to step in? How will it be determined that you are incapacitated, and who do you want to make this decision?

One approach is to give the Assisting Attorney and/or Authorized Signer access only during a specific time period or after a specific event and to allow the Assisting Attorney and/or Authorized Signer to determine whether the contingency has occurred. Another approach is to have someone else (such as a spouse, trusted friend, or family member) keep the applicable documents (such as a limited power of attorney for the Assisting Attorney and/or the Authorized Signer) until he or she determines that the specific event has occurred. A third approach is to provide the Assisting Attorney and/or Authorized Signer with access to records and accounts at all times.

If you want the Assisting Attorney and/or Authorized Signer to have access to your accounts contingent on a specific event or during a particular time period, you have to decide how you are going to document the agreement. Depending on where you live and the bank you use, some approaches may work better than others. Some banks require only a letter signed by both parties granting authorization to sign on the account. However, you and the Assisting Attorney and/or the Authorized Signer may also want to sign a limited power of attorney. Most banks prefer a power of attorney. Signing a separate limited power of attorney increases the likelihood that the bank will honor the agreement. It also provides you and the Assisting Attorney and/or the Authorized Signer with a document limited to bank business that can be given to the bank. (The bank does not need to know all the terms and conditions of the agreement between you and the Assisting Attorney and/or the Authorized Signer.)

If you choose this approach, consult the manager of your bank. When you do, be aware that power of attorney forms *provided by the bank* are generally unconditional authorizations to sign on your account and may include an agreement to indemnify the bank. Get written confirmation that the bank will honor *your* limited power of attorney or other written agreement. Otherwise, you may think you have taken all necessary steps to allow access to your accounts, yet when the time comes the bank may not allow the access you intended.

If the access is going to be contingent, you may want to have someone (such as your spouse, family member, personal representative, or trusted friend) hold the power of attorney until the contingency occurs. This can be documented in a letter of understanding, signed by you and the trusted friend or family member. When the event occurs, the trusted friend or family member provides the Assisting Attorney and/or the Authorized Signer with the power of attorney.

If the authorization will be contingent on an event or for a limited duration, the terms must be specific and the agreement should state how to determine whether the event has taken place.

• For example, is the Assisting Attorney and/or the Authorized Signer authorized to sign on your accounts only after obtaining a letter from a physician that you are disabled or incapacitated?
• Is it when the Assisting Attorney and/or the Authorized Signer, based on reasonable belief, says so?
• Is it for a specific period of time, for example, a period during which you are on vacation?

You and the Assisting Attorney and/or Authorized Signer must review the specific terms and be comfortable with them. These same issues apply if you choose to have a family member or friend hold a general power of attorney until the event or contingency occurs. All parties need to know what to do and when to do it. Likewise, to avoid problems with the bank, the terms should be specific, and it must be easy for the bank to determine whether the terms are met.

Another approach is to allow the Assisting Attorney and/or Authorized Signer access at all times. With respect to your bank accounts, this approach requires going to the bank and having the Assisting Attorney and/or Authorized Signer sign the appropriate cards and paperwork. When the Assisting Attorney and/or Authorized Signer is authorized to sign on your account, he or she has complete access to the account. This is an easy approach that allows the Assisting Attorney and/or Authorized Signer to carry out office business even if you are just unexpectedly delayed returning from vacation. Adding someone as a signer on your accounts allows him or her to write checks, withdraw money, or close the account at any time, even if you are not dead, disabled, impaired, or otherwise unable to conduct your business affairs. Under this arrangement, you cannot control the signer's access. These risks make it an extremely important decision. If you choose to give another person full access to your accounts, your choice of signer is crucial to the protection of your clients' interests, as well as your own.

Access to the trust account. As mentioned above, when arranging to have someone take over or wind down your financial affairs, you should also consider whether you want someone to have access to your trust account. If you do not make arrangements to allow someone access to the trust account, your clients' money will remain in the trust account until a court orders access. For example, if you become physically, mentally, or emotionally unable to conduct your law practice and no access arrangements were made, your clients' money will most likely remain in your trust account until the court takes jurisdiction over your practice and your accounts. In many instances, the client needs the money he or she has on deposit in the lawyer's trust account to hire a new lawyer, and a delay puts the client in a difficult position. This is likely to prompt ethics complaints, malpractice complaints, or other civil suits.

On the other hand, as emphasized above, allowing access to your trust account is a serious matter. You must give careful consideration to whom you give access and under what circumstances. If someone has access to your trust account and that person misappropriates money, your clients will suffer damages. In addition, you may be held responsible.

There are no easy solutions to this problem, and there is no way to know absolutely whether you are making the right choice. There are many important decisions to make. Each person must look at the options available to him or her, weigh the relative risks, and make the best choices he or she can.

Adding an Assisting Attorney or Authorized Signer to your general or lawyer trust account is permitted regardless of the form of entity you use for practicing law.

Client notification. Once you have made arrangements with an Assisting Attorney and/or Authorized Signer, the next step is to provide your clients with information about your plan. The easiest way to do this is to include the information in your retainer agreements and engagement letters. This provides clients with information about your arrangement and gives them an opportunity to object. Your client's signature on a retainer agreement provides written authorization for the Assisting Attorney to proceed on the client's behalf, if necessary.

Other steps that pay off. You can take a number of steps while you are still practicing to make the process of closing your office smooth and inexpensive. These steps include (1) making sure that your office procedures manual explains how to produce a list of client names and addresses for open files, (2) keeping all deadlines and follow-up dates on your calendaring system, (3) thoroughly documenting client files, (4) keeping your time and billing records up-to-date, (5) familiarizing your Assisting Attorney and/or Authorized Signer with your office systems, (6) renewing your written agreement with the Assisting Attorney and/or Authorized Signer each year, and (7) making sure you do not keep clients' original documents, such as wills or other estate plans.

If your office is in good order, the Assisting Attorney will not have to charge more than a minimum of fees for closing the practice. Your law office will then be an asset that can be sold and the proceeds remitted to you or your estate. An organized law practice is a valuable asset. In contrast, a disorganized practice requires a large investment of time and money and is less marketable.

Death of a sole practitioner: special considerations. If you authorize another lawyer to administer your practice in the event of death, disability, impairment, or incapacity, that authority terminates when you die. The personal representative of your estate has the legal authority to administer your practice. He or she must be told about your arrangement with the Assisting Attorney and/or Authorized Signer and about your desire to have the Assisting Attorney and/or Authorized Signer carry out the duties of your agreement. The personal representative can then authorize the Assisting Attorney and/or Authorized Signer to proceed.

It is imperative that you have an up-to-date will nominating a personal representative (and alternates if the first nominee cannot or will not serve) so that probate proceedings can begin promptly and the personal representative can be appointed without delay. If you have no will, there may be a dispute among family members and others as to who should be appointed as personal representative. A will can provide that the personal representative shall serve without bond. Absent such a provision, a relatively expensive fiduciary bond will have to be obtained before the personal representative is authorized to act.

For many sole practitioners, the law practice will be the only asset subject to probate. Other property will likely pass outside probate to a surviving joint tenant, usually the spouse. This means that unless you keep enough cash in your law practice bank account, there may not be adequate funds to retain the

Assisting Attorney and/or Authorized Signer or to continue to pay your clerical staff, rent, and other expenses during the transition period. It will take some time to generate statements for your legal services and to collect the accounts receivable. Your accounts receivable may not be an adequate source of cash during the time it takes to close your practice. Your Assisting Attorney and/or Authorized Signer may be unable to advance expenses or may be unwilling to serve without pay. One solution to this problem is to maintain a small insurance policy, with your estate as the beneficiary. Alternately, your surviving spouse or other family members can be named as beneficiary, with instructions to lend the funds to the estate, if needed.

Most states give broad powers to a personal representative to continue a decedent's business to preserve its value, to sell or wind down the business, and to hire professionals to help administer the estate. However, for the personal representative's protection, you may want to include language in your will that expressly authorizes that person to arrange for closure of your law practice. The appropriate language will depend on the nature of the practice and the arrangements you make ahead of time. For an instructive and detailed will for a sole practitioner, see Thomas G. Bousquet, *Retirement of a Sole Practitioner's Law Practice, 29 Law Economics & Management* 428 (1989).

It is important to allocate sufficient funds to pay an Assisting Attorney and/or Authorized Signer and necessary secretarial staff in the event of disability, incapacity, or impairment. To provide funds for these services, consider maintaining a disability insurance policy in an amount sufficient to cover these projected office closure expenses.

Start now. We encourage you to select an attorney to assist you; follow the procedures outlined in *Planning Ahead* or your jurisdiction's version. This is something you can do *now*, at little or no expense, to plan for your future and protect your assets. Don't put it off—start the process today.

—EXCERPTED FROM *PLANNING AHEAD: A GUIDE TO PROTECTING YOUR CLIENTS' INTERESTS IN THE EVENT OF YOUR DISABILITY OR DEATH*, PUBLISHED BY THE OREGON STATE BAR'S PERSONAL AND PRACTICE MANAGEMENT ASSISTANCE PROGRAM. REPRINTED WITH PERMISSION.

New Opportunities for Buying and Selling Law Practices
By Edward Poll, Esq.

Selling a law practice has been prohibited for decades. Times are changing! California has permitted such sales since 1989. The American Bar Association altered its opposition in 1991. Since then, other states have changed their prohibitions. The legal profession is taking one more step toward recognizing the economic realities of modern professional life.

Some attorneys in larger firms have bemoaned the commercialization of the legal profession. Yet, these very same attorneys have always had mechanisms in place that provided them and their heirs with funding for the value of their interests in the larger firm. Allowing small firms and sole practitioners, and their heirs, the opportunity to reap the rewards of years of effort in building a valued reputation from delivery of quality legal services levels the economic playing field in considerations for retirement and estate planning. Now that all attorneys can sell their practices, the true value of the practice, by reference to the marketplace, can be determined.

Slowly, the mechanisms for selling the law practice from one attorney to another attorney are developing. Larger firms are accustomed to the process of buying and selling a practice. The process is called "merger" or "retirement" or "breakup," among other headings. An increasing number of sole practitioners and small firm partners are thinking about getting out of the practice of law and doing something else. What else? That is less clear. But, many attorneys have left the practice of law, just closing their office doors one day and never returning. By doing this, the attorney forsakes "cashing in" on a valuable asset that has taken many years to build. That no longer has to happen.

And, what about the situation where the attorney dies suddenly and leaves his/her spouse to "mop up." Is there anything of value that can be sold? Yes, the books in the library, the computer equipment, the office furniture, and the like. There are also accounts receivable. But, there are also client files and good-will; this goodwill and the clients' files have value. And that value can now be recognized as a result of the change in the Rules of Professional Conduct.

Value vs. price. The right and ability to sell a practice says nothing about the value or price to be paid/received for the sale of the practice. These are separate issues. An attorney should realize that his/her practice is valuable and that the value (not the practice) can be passed on to the heirs of the attorney at time of death or otherwise become part of the attorney's estate if the practice is sold before death.

Is every practice saleable? Maybe not. Some practices are so small and so personal in nature that without a continuing involvement of the first attorney, a second attorney would not succeed in keeping the clients. However, even the smallest and most personal practices might be saleable for the right price and under the right terms. If the buying attorney were assured that he/she would receive that which was negotiated…a law practice of a certain volume of revenue or a certain client base that remained with the buying attorney for a designated period of time…a sale would be highly likely even for the smallest firm.

Then, the question every attorney wants answered is: "How much can I get for my practice?" At this point, "valuation" issues are out the door and the "bottom line" question is asked. The price to be paid may be estimated by reference to financial data and certain market place guidelines. But, no amount of analysis will determine the precise price a willing buyer and a willing seller will accept. That figure is subject to many different factors including terms of payment, geography, nature of the practice, history of client retention by the selling firm and size of the practice. But, whatever the price, a key issue for the buyer is whether the buyer will retain the practice being sold. In order to assure the buyer, an earn-out or pay-out based on collections may be created. This will assure the buyer that payments will be made only for designated revenues received. The selling attorney then has an incentive to help the buying attorney in his/her efforts to keep the clients of the practice.

Additional information on how to value a law practice and specific tips concerning the negotiation of the price to be paid may be obtained from (1996).

Who would buy a practice? We can imagine the seller, the attorney who has been in practice for a number of years and wants to retire, the attorney whose dreams of what the practice might be like just haven't been fulfilled, the attorney who has been elected or appointed to a judgeship, the attorney whose family has decided to relocate to another geographic area, etc.

> ▶ Even the smallest and most personal practices might be saleable for the right price and under the right terms.

But, who's buying law practices? First there are the lawyers practicing in larger firms who want to go out on their own. Some law firms have grown so large that the individual lawyer feels lost or out of step with the new culture of the large firm. Operating your own practice is a way of retrieving the personal touch and total involvement in the practice of law. Another segment of potential buyers is the larger firms' faithful servants who fail to make the grade on the "partner track." Another group of prospective buyers is attorneys who failed to develop a personal client following and were terminated. As more attorneys find the partnership track in larger firms unattractive or unattainable, as larger firms "down-size" or "right-size," the importance of law firm acquisition choices grows. Sole and small firm practitioners make excellent buyer-candidates.

Yet another group of potential law practice buyers is law school graduates, especially those in the bottom 90 percent of their class who are finding that jobs are not so easy to find as in the 1980s. After spending three or more years in law school and many thousands of dollars on an education, frequently with large student loans to repay, these new lawyers are not willing to shift careers without a gallant effort to succeed on their own. They are going to hang out the shingle one way or another and succeed by sheer determination. While the number of prospective buyers in this category remains small, the number is growing. Stories appear more frequently in the legal press about one success story after another of recent entrants to the practice buying an existing practice. We have many successful examples in other professions. Why should the legal profession be different? Many lawyers are ready—either by themselves or with others—to start their own practices. Many are opting to do what is common in other professions: Buy an existing practice rather than start a practice "from scratch."

How do you let it be known you want to buy/sell a law practice? Business opportunities brokers, law firm management consultants, accountants, valuation firms and appraisers are excellent resources to spread the word that you are looking to buy a law firm practice or that you are looking to sell a practice. Another source, not yet used for this purpose, but not to be discounted, is the Internet and law-related Web sites. In the future, electronic means of spreading the word may be the most effective and least expensive method of communicating this information.

Rules of professional conduct. In business, it frequently is easier to buy an ongoing operation rather than start a new one. In an existing business, there is a history of sales, of revenue, that can be counted on as a continuing base. Customers tend to continue their purchasing habits if they like the product or service in spite of new ownership. Costs of operations are known, merely by looking at previous records; little or no guessing is necessary. The buyer can visualize where savings can be implemented by making changes.

The same rationale applies to the purchase and sale of a law practice. The differences between other business enterprises and a law practice are primarily in the areas of:

- Ethics (especially dealing with the rights of clients and the transition process).
- Negotiations (attorneys tend to negotiate their own deals rather than involve third party experts such as brokers).
- Pricing protection (lawyers-buyers usually want more security that they're receiving what they bargained for than buyers of other enterprises).

The Rules of Professional Conduct set forth requirements for transferring one's interest in a law firm. For example, fees charged clients cannot be increased solely because of the sale and the selling attorney must give written notice to clients no less than ninety days before the transfer that clients have the right to their files and to retain other counsel. In other industries, the transfer of ownership is seldom announced en masse because of the desire not to disturb existing relationships. The state bar has gone overboard to assure clients have the knowledge that they can leave for new counsel. Despite this, however, most clients remain with the new attorney, especially where the selling attorney participates in the transition and assures clients that the new attorney is very well-qualified. The Rules of Professional Conduct raise additional issues that can be answered only by reference to the Rules of each jurisdiction. For example:

> ▶ Most clients remain with the new attorney, especially where the selling attorney participates in the transition and assures clients that the new attorney is well-qualified.

- Can an attorney break off and sell or buy only a portion of a practice? Assume a rural or suburban sole practitioner who has a general practice and who has developed a sub-specialty in pensions and profit-sharing; the attorney now wants to retire and sell the practice. It may be impossible to find a single buyer who would be willing to come into the community and practice general law and who is also competent to handle the technical pension and profit-sharing work. Can the practice be split?
- Does client confidentiality prevent discussion about specific clients or their matters? If not, how can a buyer know the nature of the practice without some disclosures? Would a buyer be willing to purchase something, sight unseen?
- Is the sale of a law practice equivalent to a referral for a fee, something that is not allowed in many jurisdictions?
- Does an attorney's existing errors and omissions insurance policy cover the new cases acquired from the selling attorney?
- Does an attorney's existing errors and omissions insurance policy cover the selling attorney for allegations of negligence made after the transfer of the case and matter files? What about the client who doesn't realize until after the transfer that the alleged negligence occurred? Is the selling attorney protected when the claim for the alleged negligence is filed after the expiration of the policy in effect at the time of the transfer? The alleged malpractice might come from the attorney's own negligence that occurred before the sale of the law practice, but not known to the client until after

the sale, or the alleged negligence might have been committed by the buying attorney and the client is trying to use a large net to ensnare anyone who might have "deep pockets." What protection is there for the selling attorney? What are his/her choices?

Conflicts of interest. The conflicts check will be the last element before the actual transfer. In smaller communities, the possibility of conflicts of interest increases substantially. Has a conflicts check been done by both attorneys? The parties may want to consider, in advance, whether they want to negotiate a modification in the price or terms in the event a conflict of interest does arise in one or more matters that would prevent the buying attorney from taking on that/those matters.

The ethics issues can be resolved. State and local bar associations are becoming more sensitive to the needs and economic realities facing sole and small firm practitioners that do not face larger firm attorneys. Balancing these realities against the legitimate concerns for client protection can result in benefit for both clients and attorneys (and the estates of deceased attorneys).

Some negotiating issues. Who should do the negotiating? Would you negotiate the purchase or sale of your own residence? Probably not. Traditionally, buyers and sellers of real estate act through agents, or real estate brokers. Would you negotiate the purchase of a new car? Probably. What is the difference? One difference is the size of the transaction. Another difference is the personal stake in the outcome. If we can't buy the car we want because the seller is obstinate, we'll walk away, not having our ego bruised. But, if we can't get the house we want, our vision of the future and our stature in the community is somehow impacted. To reduce the possibility of this happening, we retain an independent third party to help us. Another difference is that sellers often talk themselves out of a transaction after the deal has been negotiated, but before the papers have been finalized. To reduce the chances of this occurrence, third party experts are engaged.

The nature of the practice of law is very personal. The lawyers must know that their respective "cultures" or approach to the practice are complementary and not too dissimilar. But, until the financial aspects of the transaction are agreed upon, at least in their broad parameters, it is advisable to keep the principals' contact with one another to a minimum. The attorneys will not be practicing together; one will be the buyer and one will be the seller. Therefore, as in the residence example, the less contact between the two, the less the egos of either will become involved.

Conclusion. The practice of law is an honorable profession. The practice of law is also a business. And the efforts and hard work of attorneys over years of toil does have value and can be transferred to the benefit of all concerned.

—ED POLL, ESQ. (*EDPOLL.COM*)—POLL, A FORMER CORPORATE GENERAL COUNSEL, GOVERNMENT PROSECUTOR, SOLE PRACTITIONER, PARTNER, AND LAW FIRM CHIEF OPERATING OFFICER, HAS COACHED LAWYERS AND LAW FIRMS IN STRATEGIC PLANNING, PROFITABILITY ANALYSIS, AND PRACTICE DEVELOPMENT FOR MORE THAN 20 YEARS. AUTHOR OF *LAW FIRM FEES & COMPENSATION* (2008), A FELLOW OF THE COLLEGE OF LAW PRACTICE MANAGEMENT.

Understanding Tail Coverage

Mark Bassingthwaighte, Esq.

Rule 1.3 of the ABA Model Rules of Professional Conduct addresses diligence. The Rule reads, "*A lawyer shall act with reasonable diligence and promptness in representing a client.*"

Most, if not all, attorneys are well aware of this rule. They are to act with commitment, dedication, and zealous advocacy. Workloads are to be reasonable so that all matters can be resolved competently. Procrastination is an enemy to be avoided at all costs, for it can and does lead to malpractice claims when clients are harmed. In the end, all attorneys should strive to deliver their services in a professional, competent and timely fashion. Do these obligations end here? Under this Rule, they do not. Attorneys should also try to prevent the neglect of a client matter post attorney death or disability. In 2002, the comments to Rule 1.3 were amended to address this very issue:

Comment 5 now states, "*To prevent neglect of client matters in the event of a sole practitioner's death or disability, the duty of diligence may require that each sole practitioner prepare a plan, in conformity with applicable rules, that designates another competent lawyer to review client files, notify each client of the lawyer's death or disability, and determine if there is a need for immediate protective action.*"

Malpractice liability can outlive the lifetime of an attorney, as applicable statute of limitations do not become a nullity upon an attorney's death. Claims can be and, in fact, have been brought against the estates of deceased attorneys. Heaven forbid that even years after an attorney's death, his or her heirs may have to use their inheritance to pay for the defense and/or loss of a malpractice claim. For this reason alone, retirement planning should include consideration of how to protect client interests post attorney death or disability. One solution that can appropriately address this concern would be the purchase of adequate tail coverage upon retirement. Before beginning a discussion of the intricacies of tail coverage, it is important to set the stage:

When lawyer's professional liability (LPL) insurance first came to market, it did so as an occurrence-based product. This meant that an attorney was covered for any act, error or omission that occurred during the period in which any given policy was in force and in effect. This created a problem for the insurance industry, however, as the discovery of an error and the filing of a claim might occur years later. There was no way for an insurance company to appropriately calculate premium because the risk was too much of an unknown. As a result, all LPL insurance companies now only offer claims-made products.

> Malpractice liability can outlive the lifetime of an attorney, as applicable statute of limitations do not become a nullity upon an attorney's death. For this reason, retirement planning should include consideration of how to protect client interests post attorney death or disability. The purchase of adequate tail coverage upon retirement is one solution.

Under this type of policy, an attorney is afforded coverage for claims made and reported to the insurance company while a policy is in force and effect and the act, error or omission occurred after the policy's retroactive date. Further, LPL policies provide coverage for one year and in order for an attorney to have coverage in force at all times a policy must be purchased (or renewed) every year. Finally, a policy may only be purchased or renewed while an attorney is actively practicing law. This shift to claims-made products created a problem for any attorney who wished to go into retirement. Retiring attorneys were unable to purchase LPL coverage because they no longer actively practiced law yet the exposure to a professional liability claim remained. One solution to this dilemma has been for the retiring attorney to purchase tail coverage. Consideration of the purchase of a "tail" must begin with an understanding of what tail coverage is and what it is not.

The insurance industry defines the word "tail" as an extended reporting period. The purchase of tail coverage adds an endorsement to an existing policy that extends the period of time in which a claim may be reported to the insurance carrier. Stated another way, the purchased endorsement (the "tail") provides an attorney the right to report claims to the insurer after a policy has expired or been cancelled. Further, the right to report a claim afforded under the purchased endorsement is not unlimited. The only claims that would be covered under such an endorsement would be limited to those that arose as a result of professional services provided by the attorney after the policy's retroactive date and on or before the policy was cancelled or non-renewed.

It is important to note that under most tail provisions, the purchase of the endorsement is not one of additional coverage or of a separate and distinct policy. Thus, a "tail" does not provide coverage for any professional services provided by the attorney after the effective date of the tail coverage. In other words, there would be no coverage for a wrongful act that took place during the "tail" itself. This is why insurance companies will require that the attorney close or transfer all active files to another attorney prior to the issuance of the "tail." Also, note that any and all claims reported under the "tail" would be subject to the available remaining limits of the existing policy. For this reason alone, a decision to lower policy limits in the later years of one's practice may not be a good idea. Insurance companies will not allow an attorney to purchase significantly higher limits of coverage on the policy that is to be in force on the eve of retirement. An attorney can't bump up coverage limits upon retirement hoping to make certain that an adequate amount of coverage will be in place throughout the retirement years. This can be one of the downsides of semi-retiring and purchasing a part-time policy with reduced limits.

Q: Is tail coverage available to all who wish it?
A: Unfortunately, it is not. Most insurers prohibit any insured from purchasing tail coverage when an existing policy has been canceled for nonpayment of premium, or if the insured fails to reimburse the insurance company for deductible amounts paid on previous claims. Other reasons tail coverage would likely not be available may include an attorney's failure to comply with the terms and conditions of the policy, and the suspension and/or revocation of the insured's license to practice law. This reality underscores the importance of timely reporting changes within a firm as well as circumstances that could reasonably be expected to lead to a claim.

An insured's right to purchase tail coverage varies from carrier to carrier. Read your policy and, when comparing coverage between two insurance companies, understand the differences when it comes to the ability to purchase tail coverage. In general, there are two approaches to tail coverage: the first is a one-way "tail" provision, which permits the insured to purchase a "tail" only if the policy is cancelled or non-renewed by the insurer. A two-way "tail" provision permits the insured to purchase a "tail" when the policy is cancelled or non-renewed by either the insurer or the insured. This is an important distinction and one worth knowing about in advance.

An attorney's practice setting is relevant as well. For the retiring solo practitioner, insurers frequently provide tail coverage at no additional cost to the insured if the attorney has been continuously insured with the same insurer for a stated number of years. For this reason, it may not be a good idea to shop for the cheapest insurance rates year after year, particularly in the later years of one's practice, given that tail coverage can be quite expensive.

For the attorney who retires from a multi-member firm the situation is a bit more complex. Not all insurance companies provide an opportunity for the retiring attorney in this setting to purchase tail coverage due to policy provisions. The reason is that the named insured (the firm) will continue to have its attorneys actively practicing law. In other words, the existing policy is not expiring or about to be canceled. All is not lost, however. The retiring attorney may be able to rely on "former attorney" language under the definition of "Insured." This language varies among insurers and should be reviewed with the firm's insurance representative well in advance of a planned retirement.

▶ Tail coverage is often provided at no additional cost if an attorney has been continuously insured with the same insurer for a stated number of years. For this reason, it may not be a good idea to shop for the cheapest insurance rates year after year, particularly in the later years of one's practice, given that tail coverage can be quite expensive.

If tail coverage is not available to the attorney retiring from a multi-member firm, one option might be to try to contractually bind the firm to maintain LPL coverage for a period of years. While not a perfect solution, this option can provide some peace of mind for the retiring attorney. Another possibility may be that tail coverage could be available to the retired attorney should the firm eventually dissolve several years post retirement. For this reason, it is always prudent for any retiring attorney to request that the firm notify him or her in advance that the firm's insurance policy is going to expire or be canceled. The retired attorney should then immediately review the situation with the insurance representative to discuss whether tail coverage is available and if it should be purchased at that time.

The window of opportunity in which to purchase tail coverage is not unlimited. Most policies allow either a 10-day or a 30-day window for the insured to purchase the "tail" and this window will begin to run on the effective date of the expiration or cancellation of the existing policy. However, be aware that there are a few very restrictive policies that will require the insured to exercise the option to purchase tail coverage on the date of cancellation or non-renewal. Clearly, the most beneficial time for attorneys to review relevant policy language concerning the provisions and options regarding the purchase of tail coverage is at the time of policy purchase. The opportunity to purchase tail coverage comes just once and is an opportunity that any attorney cannot afford to miss.

The duration of tail coverage and the associated costs can vary greatly between insurance companies. Thus, the available options and costs should be one of the considerations in making the decision to purchase any given policy. The duration of the "tail," or more accurately the extended length of time under which a claim may be reported commonly varies from fixed or renewable one, two and three year reporting periods to unlimited reporting periods. The unlimited reporting period would be the most desirable tail coverage, if available. This would be particularly true for practitioners who may face long periods of professional liability such as those attorneys who have written wills during their later years of practice.

The premium charge for tail coverage is usually specified in the policy language. Often tail coverage costs are a fixed percentage of the expiring policy's premium, and can range from 100 percent to 300 percent, depending on the duration of the tail coverage that is purchased. For renewable "tails," the premium-based percentage will reduce each year at renewal. An advantage of renewable tail coverage is that the costs associated with the "tail" can be spread out over time making extended coverage more affordable.

There are several take-away points worth highlighting:

• All files and/or cases must be closed or transferred prior to the purchase of tail coverage. If the Extended Reporting Period provisions outlined in your policy language were not reviewed prior to purchasing the policy, review these provisions now.

• When nearing retirement contact the insurance representative well in advance in order to discuss the provision for tail coverage and the options that are available.

• Finally, should the unexpected happen—such as the untimely death of an attorney still in practice—tail coverage can be obtained in the name of the deceased attorney's estate if timely pursued in accordance with policy provisions. Setting forth instructions in this regard as to who to call, and within what time frame for use by the personal representative or the attorney named to administer the winding up of the practice, would be a very practical, prudent, and yes, diligent step to take in accordance with Rule 1.3.

—MARK BASSINGTHWAIGHTE, ESQ. SERVES AS RISK MANAGEMENT COORDINATOR OF ALPS LAWYERS'
PROFESSIONAL LIABILITY INSURANCE AND RISK MANAGEMENT RESOURCES

Closing a Spouse's Practice:
What I Wish My Husband Had Told Me
By Mary Silverberg

Editor's note: Mary Silverberg's husband, Steve, was a solo practitioner in West Hartford, CT, specializing in commercial collections. After a long battle with cancer, he died in 2004, after which Ms. Silverberg wrote this essay for the ABA's GP/Solo Magazine:

If your spouse is not used to asking questions about your practice, the two of you may want to rethink this position. Too many lawyers' spouses, female or male, are fond of saying they are not attorneys and don't need to know about the practice. They sometimes assume that because the lawyer has an assistant, he or she will know what to do in the event the lawyer dies or becomes unable to handle professional duties. Unfortunately, the underlying reason for this attitude is often simple denial: "I don't want to face the fact that my spouse might die before I do."

This is an intimidating prospect for any couple. Yet with the ethics and practice responsibilities that cover lawyers' code of confidentiality, case transfers, and even file storage and the like, it is essential to face such a scenario and develop a plan that your spouse, your children, or your colleagues can follow to cover the many complexities involved in closing down a legal practice, particularly a solo practice. Why? You worked diligently over a lifetime to establish a financially viable practice and gain the respect of clients and the legal community. As a couple, you developed a way to provide for your family while helping others. But just as a law practice and its clients must be protected while the lawyer is alive, the need to protect them becomes an even greater mandate after the lawyer's death.

Consider this question: where do you want the benefits of all this hard work to go?

I spent many years with my lawyer-husband, Steve, without caring very much about the nuts and bolts of his practice. But when a friend of mine was caught totally off guard by her husband's dropping dead of a heart attack at the courtroom in the middle of a trial, I was deeply affected. So, after much urging on my part, Steve and I began to put a plan in place. Remember: when the business of your practice needs to be settled, your spouse will still be grieving your loss—and in an extremely emotional and vulnerable state even without the burden of correctly closing the business.

> ▶ Too many spouses are fond of saying they are not attorneys and don't need to know about the practice. But who will take care of things if the lawyer dies or becomes unable to handle professional duties?

Letting go. Initially, I would like to ask all lawyers to reflect on the factors that led you into solo or small firm practice in the first place. Be honest; it's likely that one of them was that you wanted your business conducted in a certain way—yours. But when you make the calls for everything important, how do you admit to yourself, I can no longer do this? If you are given the gift of knowing that you will die soon, and the necessary time to prepare for that journey, you will at some point need to say to yourself and your spouse, I'm done, and literally walk away from your desk.

The last few months of his life, Steve had worked very hard to settle cases and tie up loose ends as much as he could. Closing his practice was one of the most difficult decisions I'd ever seen him make. He could not let go. Finally, an attorney friend and I, full of intensity and pain, asked him one afternoon: "*Is this how you want to spend your last few weeks of life?*" He thought for a moment, took off his glasses, and wheeled his wheelchair out of the room. He then got on with the process of dying—and from then on, displayed as much courage and dignity as he had shown in life.

As I stated earlier, if you are fortunate enough to have a prognosis for the time you have left, you will be able to see the people you need to see and say the things that need to be said. If you are not granted this gift of time, you will surely need to have data accessible and procedures prearranged and in place, including full names and phone numbers for everyone and anyone those closing your practice may need to contact. I cannot stress this last point enough: names and phone numbers!

Planning as a couple. Do you have a Will and do you and your spouse know its location?—If you are incapacitated for a time until your death, does your spouse have power of attorney? For specific or general purposes? Do you have a medical directive in place? Do you have a DNR (Do Not Resuscitate) order, or have you left it to chance—remember the story of the shoemaker and his barefoot children? In maintaining your practice, you likely became used to calling the shots and planning things the way you wanted them. Your spouse is likely used to this mind-set. During my husband's last two weeks in hospice, we agreed that I would make his funeral arrangements. Which leads me into one of my favorite "lawyer stories.":

The funeral director and I reviewed the arrangements. Though I understood the itemized paperwork, it all seemed so…permanent. As a well-trained lawyer's wife, I asked about the three-day recession period pertaining to signing a contract. The mortician smiled and stated, gently, "*This doesn't often come up in my business.*" When I shared the story with Steve, he found it quite amusing and assured me I had done well in planning his funeral according to his wishes.

Questions you should consider:

• Does your spouse have access to the names and numbers of individuals at your local bar association or ABA office to use as resources?
• Is your spouse familiar with the terms and provisions of your professional

liability insurance? Is it up to date? When is the premium due? I recall speaking with Steve's malpractice insurance carrier during the last weeks of his life. As it turned out, he died on the very day his insurance expired. Had he lived even one more day, I would have had to continue the policy for another six months or one year. As it was, the agent and I discussed the need for a "tail" to cover past work but no future work. Does your spouse have your agents' name(s) and phone number(s) and your policy information?

- Do you have a backup attorney(s) to help you with court appearances or filings that you cannot handle yourself? If you're in a small firm or partnership, you likely already have back-up. But if you are a solo, you should make such an arrangement with one or two trusted colleagues.

- Do you have plans regarding your assistant; that is, a plan your assistant should follow in the event of your incapacitation as well as a plan for his or her own future? As you already know, while your spouse is with you outside the office, your trusted assistant is with you for the entire workweek. Such assistants know you well. They keep your schedule and may even pay your bills. They know which courts you need to be in and when. They know your clients, other attorneys, and their secretaries. They are familiar with your files, with what is stated in them and what is not. Be sure that your spouse understands that your assistant is one of your (and your spouse's) strongest allies. Also remember that your assistant, too, has suffered a loss and will want to help your family as much as possible to ease the transition. Also remember—especially if your assistant has been with you for a long time—that your assistant will be wondering, 'What will happen to me now?' Will you give a bonus, regular salary, some form of severance pay, or other compensation for staying on through the transition? Who will supervise your assistant? Who will write the paychecks? Is your spouse familiar with your assistant's salary and benefits? Who will continue to oversee employment records?

- Who among your most trusted, personal, lawyer-friends will make themselves available to your spouse? Remember, your spouse always had his or her own personal attorney. Now that attorney is gone. This is something I truly miss—my own "in-house" attorney. Some tasks will require immediate attention, for example: will you need to go through probate (which will depend on your situation and the rules in your state)?

Planning as a business. While the living are in the middle of funeral arrangements and mourning, many others—clients, law firms with pending cases, the courts—all need to be notified. Continuances for court appearances must be obtained. Clients must be formally informed of your passing, and of who now handles the file so that they can decide whether to remain with that attorney, or to request the file be sent to a different attorney, or to end the relationship altogether and pick up the file themselves.

So, who will notify your clients that you can no longer practice or that you have passed on?

> ▶ Who will notify your clients, the courts, and the firms with whom you have pending cases, that you can no longer practice or that you have passed on?

Files, files, files! First of all, does your filing system look like Fibber McGee's closet, or does it have a Martha Stewart-like precision and organization?

Which files are open or closed? How will someone know unless you have in place a system with forms clearly indicating the status of each case? Which files are "inactive" and in storage? Are they labeled and dated for when they can be shredded? Who will do this? When we went through this process, I was grateful that my husband had been so organized and methodical. During his last month of life, from his wheelchair, he personally supervised the sorting and shredding process. And he arranged for another local commercial collection attorney to take a large group of open cases.

During the last two weeks of Steve's life, I spent several late evenings sorting and labeling files. I found myself just shifting into auto-pilot and doing what I had to do, all the while being well aware that the files represented events in people's lives, the outcomes for which my spouse was still legally and ethically liable. At that point I also knew that the rest of my husband's files would soon be assigned to a court-appointed trustee who would then take on responsibility for them. The last few weeks of completing this process felt tremendously burdensome (and this was with planning).

More issues:

Are your client fund accounts in order? They had better be perfectly in order. The attorney handling your cases will disburse monies as required. Determine the fee arrangements for cases the attorney will settle after your passing. Are other non-client business accounts in your name only? Be certain your spouse or assistant has access to and can pay any outstanding bills, and plan how the remaining money will be disbursed.

Do you rent office space or own your building? If you rent, does your spouse or assistant know where the lease is, what the rent is, and how to resolve any special conditions in the lease? The name and number of the building manager or leasing agent? If you own your building, do you need to go through probate?

Who has the deed to the property? Will decisions need to be made regarding future use or sale of the property? Do you have tenants? Can they remain in the building? If yes, are any of them prepared to purchase the building? Do you have a trusted real estate agent who can handle this part of your estate? Again, have you left names and contact information for all these people?

What are your plans for your office equipment? What about items such as photocopiers or telephone systems that may be leased? What are the terms? What about computers, printers, scanners, and other digital equipment? Should they be sold or donated to a nonprofit or a local school system? Or are they too old to rank as gifts? What about the information on your cellphone, BlackBerry, PDA?

Will you need commercial storage space or a self-contained portable locker? Professional/commercial storage is expensive. Also, it won't be any easier for your spouse and friends to sort through the belongings in your office than through those at home. My husband had many mementos of his life at his office: family pictures, a wide variety of artwork, photographs, awards, and gifts given to him through the years. These items will need special attention.

What about professional resources and subscriptions? Does your assistant have the information necessary to discontinue Lexis/Westlaw service, ABA and other legal reading materials, professional memberships, etc.?

If you own your building, have you planned for real estate taxes? Local or state attorney property taxes? Who has access to your IRS records, including several precious years' tax returns and quarterly IRS and Social Security payments for you and any of your employees? Does your spouse or assistant have your accountant's contact information? Your spouse most probably will spend quite a bit of time with attorneys and accountants in the first year after you are gone; planning may help shorten these sessions.

Is state and federal tax information about your assistant and other employees readily available? Your spouse will need to provide the information for your accountant to prepare all W-2s for the following year. Be ready.

Do your spouse and assistant know how to access all of your password-protected electronic means of communication, including all mobile devices? Are the passwords up to date? Locating information and compiling and printing out lists for client files, clients' fund accounts, office accounts, etc., are extremely important but exceedingly time-consuming.

What do you want done with your professional wardrobe? This is another intimate, vulnerable area to deal with, one we also don't like to think about it. Because my husband had a large wardrobe of courtroom clothing, I wanted it to go somewhere it would be needed, appreciated, and put to use. After much detective work, I found a local nonprofit organization called Clothes Make the Man, which collects and distributes work attire that is in style and in excellent condition to men referred by agencies who are returning to the workforce. Many come from halfway houses or prisons, go through a training program, and then select a complete suit of clothing for their job interviews. After one year of employment, they may return for a second suit. A very appreciative director personally came to my home to pick up suits, sport jackets, dress pants, business shirts, ties, belts, shoes—even dress hats and an overcoat. I received a tax deduction, but even better was the satisfaction of doing something positive even within my grief. Your local YWCA may also participate in its similar Working Wardrobe program for women returning to the workforce. After your passing, your spouse and family members will be receiving many cards, letters, and e-mails that offer condolences, make charitable contributions in your memory, and share reminiscences about you. Your spouse may receive heartwarming notes from people you might never have thought to hear from—other attorneys, law school professors, judges and courthouse staff—all of whom took the time to share their memories and thoughts about you with your spouse. We never can be certain of how we've touched another's life. Though your spouse may shed many tears, he or she will welcome the tributes and treasure them. I certainly did.

—MARY SILVERBERG IS A SPEECH/LANGUAGE PATHOLOGIST WORKING IN THE CONNECTICUT PUBLIC SCHOOLS SYSTEM. REPRINTED WITH PERMISSION.

CHECKLIST FOR CLOSING YOUR OFFICE

1. Finalize as many active files as possible.

2. Write to clients with active files, advising them that you are unable to continue representing them and that they need to retain new counsel. Your letter should inform them about time limitations and time frames important to their cases. The letter should explain how and where they can pick up copies of their files and should give a time deadline for doing this. (See sample *Letter Advising That Lawyer Is Closing His/Her Office* available at *osbplf.org*).

3. For cases with pending court dates, depositions, or hearings, discuss with the clients how to proceed. When appropriate, request extensions, continuances, and resetting of hearing dates. Send written confirmations of these extensions, continuances, and resets to opposing counsel and your client.

4. For cases before administrative bodies and courts, obtain the clients' permission to submit a motion and order to withdraw as attorney of record.

5. If the client is obtaining a new attorney, be certain that a Substitution of Attorney is filed.

6. Pick an appropriate date to check whether all cases either have a motion and order allowing your withdrawal as attorney of record or have a Substitution of Attorney filed with the court.

7. Make copies of files for clients. Retain your original files. All clients should either pick up their files (and sign a receipt acknowledging that they received them) or sign an authorization for you to release the files to their new attorneys. (See sample *Acknowledgment of Receipt of File and Authorization for Transfer of Client File* available at *osbplf.org*). If a client is picking up the file, return original documents to the client and keep copies in your file.

8. Tell all clients where their closed files will be stored and whom they should contact to retrieve them. Obtain all clients' permission to destroy the files after approximately 10 years. The Oregon Professional Liability Fund recommends that closed files be kept for 0 years or longer. (See File Retention and Destruction available at *osbplf.org*). If a closed file is to be stored by another attorney, get the client's permission to allow the attorney to store the file for you and provide the client with the attorney's name, address, and phone number.

9. Send the name, address, and phone number of the person who will be retaining your closed files to the appropriate authority in your particular jurisdiction. Also send them your name, current address, and phone number.

10. If you are a sole practitioner, ask the telephone company for a new phone number to be given out when your disconnected phone number is called. This eliminates the problem created when clients call your phone number, get a recording stating that the number is disconnected, and do not know where else to turn for information.

The PLF handbook, *Planning Ahead: A Guide to Protecting Your Clients' Interests in the Event of Your Disability or Death* is available online at *osbplf.org*. ●

In a Class By Herself

This book has been enriched by the stories of lawyers who embraced change in midlife and flourished. So, we are fortunate to conclude with the story of one pioneering lawyer who did embrace change, and challenged the status quo as a way of life. Her irrepressible spirit rejected attempts by others to impose artificial limits upon her life choices, and at midlife she chose to channel her energies into continued service and engagement in the legal profession.

Betty's story:

Betty was a college freshman when she met her future husband, and they married the following summer. She decided to not return to school; instead, she moved to her husband's home state of Oregon, and, over the next 10 years they had four children. In 1955, at the age of 32, Betty decided—against her husband's wishes—to return to college. She earned her bachelor's degree, and decided—again, against her husband's wishes—to pursue teaching. The couple divorced, but for the next four years Betty pursued teaching, worked toward a Masters in political science during summers, and along the way was elected to the local school board.

> "… After my Masters, I went to the chair of the political science department to discuss pursuing a Ph.D. He said, 'Betty, I can't let you do that. You're 39 now, and when you get your doctorate you'll be 45, and you will only have 20 years to repay the taxpayers of Oregon.' You see, there had never been a woman Ph.D candidate in the Political Science department up to that time, and—if he had anything to say about it—I wasn't going to be the first!"

Betty had friends in Oregon's Democratic Party, though, and they urged her to do something she never considered—to get a law degree. "Why not?" she thought, and so she enrolled in the evening program at the local law school.

> "My grades dropped in law school, and that didn't surprise me. I had three of my four children still at home with me; I was teaching full-time, and going to school in the evenings. In my third year of law school, I ran for the state legislature and was elected as

a state representative. You put all that together and it's no wonder I didn't pass the bar exam the first time."

Betty passed the bar on the second try, though, and was licensed to practice law at the age of 46.

Over the years, Betty served as a state representative and state senator; she was also a Democratic candidate for governor, a Democratic candidate for the U.S. Senate, the first woman appointed to the Oregon State Court of Appeals, and in 1982, became the first woman appointed to the Oregon Supreme Court. Four years later, Betty stepped down from the Court, and put her energies into mediation and arbitration.

When I met Betty, she was writing her memoirs, working her way back from knee-replacement surgery and anxious to get back out on the golf course. At the age of 84, she was still passionately enthusiastic about using the legal skills she had worked so hard to acquire and develop. She was still actively engaged in her community, in the legal profession as an arbitrator and mediator, and—by the way—she was not considering retiring any time soon.

The Oregon Lawyer Retirement Survey

As noted in the Preface, the Oregon Attorney Assistance Program (OAAP) has offered retirement planning workshops for Oregon lawyers since 2001. In developing the workshops, I reviewed several national and regional retirement surveys and studies that had been taken of the general, non-lawyer population:

- AARP's 1998 study entitled, *Baby Boomer's Envision Their Retirement* & 2004 *Baby Boomers Envision Retirement II: Survey of Baby Boomers Expectations for Retirement;*
- The *Cornell Retirement and Well-Being Study* (2000);
- The *Reinventing Aging: Baby Boomers and Civic Engagement* survey that had been done in 2004 by the Harvard School of Public Health and MetLife Foundation Initiative in Retirement and Civic Engagement; and
- The Employee Benefit Research Institute ("EBRI") *Retirement Confidence Surveys.*

I was unable to locate a reported survey that had been conducted to identify the retirement hopes, dreams and concerns of lawyers. So, to better access the retirement-planning needs of Oregon lawyers, I developed a survey of our own. The survey borrowed some elements from the earlier national and regional retirement surveys that had been conducted of the general population, and incorporated them into a survey specifically tailored to lawyers.

In June, 2006, the OAAP sent a broadcast email to 6,000 active and inactive members of the Oregon State Bar (OSB) age 50 and older, inviting them to complete our lawyer retirement survey ("retirement survey"). Some 930 lawyers completed the 50-and-older survey. Two months later, a second broadcast email was sent to nearly 1,900 OSB members born between 1957 and 1964 (younger boomers), inviting them to take our survey. Some 171 lawyers in their 40's completed this second round of the retirement survey.

Initially, we surveyed lawyers 50 and older; it was they who largely attended our retirement workshops. Only a small percentage of lawyers attending was younger. Later, we chose to survey boomer lawyers in their 40's to find out if their perspective of retirement was different than older colleagues who were either already retired or who would be reaching retirement age ahead of them.

The survey response:

- 76 percent of the lawyers surveyed were 50-64 years old; 15 percent were 40-49; and 9 percent were 65 or older.
- A majority of the lawyer respondents were practicing full-time in private practice as sole practitioners or in small firms. Of the lawyers practicing full-time in private practice, 25 percent were practicing in firms of 21 or more lawyers; about 25 percent of the lawyers surveyed were working in the public sector as judges, government lawyers, or in government positions.
- In the survey of the older lawyers, only 11 percent reported being retired. Since the vehicle used for the survey was broadcast email, it seems likely that the survey did not get to a percentage of lawyers in this age group that had actually retired because email was not the most effective means to contact them.
- 70 percent of the lawyers surveyed were male, 30 percent female. However, the following breakdown by age reflects the increasing participation of women lawyers in the legal profession with each succeeding decade:

Age	% of Women Lawyers
70+	0%
60–69	14%
50–59	32%
40–49	53%

Envisioning retirement. The Employee Benefit Research Institute (EBRI) reported in its 2004 Retirement confidence Survey that 68 percent of workers it surveyed said that they plan to work for pay in retirement. Our survey indicates that a large percentage of lawyers also plan to continue working for pay into their retirement years:

- 11 percent of the lawyers surveyed do not plan to ever retire. They plan to continue to practice full-time or part-time until they die or are no longer capable of practicing.
- 30 percent plan to continue practicing law part-time after age 65 mainly for the stimulation, sense of purpose, and satisfaction it provides.
- 11 percent plan to continue practicing law part-time after age 65 primarily for the income it will provide.
- 18 percent plan to retire completely and no longer work for pay by age 65; almost 60 percent plan to do so by age 70; about 40 percent plan to continue to practice law or work after age 70.

Hopes and dreams. Almost half of the surveyed Oregon lawyers 50 and older report being *very optimistic* about retirement, and are very much looking forward to their retirement years. Thirty-nine percent report feeling *somewhat optimistic* about their retirement years, and are pretty much looking forward to them. About 15 percent of those surveyed are *not feeling too optimistic* about their retirement years, and are either not looking forward to them or are looking forward to them with mixed feelings.

The under-50 lawyers (40-49) surveyed reported less optimism toward retirement. Only 36 percent are *very optimistic* about their retirement years, and almost 25 percent are *not feeling too optimistic* about their retirement years, and are either not looking forward to them or are looking forward to them with mixed feelings. A significantly higher level of financial anxiety is reflected in the responses of the under-50 lawyers.

Seventy-one percent of lawyers envision retirement as a time to begin a new chapter in life by being active and involved, starting new activities and setting new goals, compared to 29 percent who envision retirement as a time to take it easy, take care of themselves, enjoy leisure activities and take a much-deserved rest from work and daily responsibilities.

Lawyers older than 50 who have not yet retired report looking forward most to the following opportunities:

- More time and opportunity to travel (81%);
- Time for community service, volunteering, hobbies, recreation or new educational opportunities (79%);
- More time for family and friends (72%);
- More time for exercising and fitness (64%);
- A slower pace (61%);
- Increased control over their schedule (46%); and
- A decrease in adversarial relationships (39%).

Lawyers over 50 who have retired report that they are actually enjoying the following opportunities most in retirement:

- More time and opportunity to travel (71%);
- Increased control over their schedule (71%);
- Time for community service, volunteering, hobbies, recreation, or new educational opportunities (65%);
- More time for family and friends (64%);
- A slower pace (64%);

- More time for exercising and fitness (60%); and
- The decrease in adversarial relationships (59%).

Primary concerns. The two most significant financial concerns lawyers hold as they look toward their retirement years are: (1) projecting their long-term financial needs, and (2) concerns regarding Medicare, health insurance and long-term care insurance. Here's what lawyers reported as their most significant financial concerns about retirement:

	Age: 60+	50–59	40–49
Projecting long term financial needs	73%	68%	74%
Concerns regarding Medicare, health insurance and long-term care insurance	50%	65%	58%
That you won't be able to afford to retire	20%	36%	52%
Knowing how to invest for and in retirement	26%	36%	47%
Living without a paycheck or monthly draw.	25%	29%	36%
That you will struggle to make ends meet	21%	32%	36%
Concerns regarding the continued existence/availability of Social Security	13%	31%	40%
Other	9%	7%	7%

Personal concerns. The most significant personal retirement concerns reported by lawyers were:

	Age: 60+	50–59	40–49
Loss of professional camaraderie and affiliations	44%	31%	30%
Loss of intellectual stimulation	40%	37%	31%
Loss of professional identity	38%	22%	9%
Loss of opportunities to use professional skills and experience	35%	29%	14%
Loss of social interactions/social isolation	33%	32%	30%
Loss of daily structure	31%	21%	17%
Concerns regarding how time will be spent	25%	24%	14%
Concerns regarding maintaining health and independence	23%	32%	37%
Other	13%	13%	13%

The responses to the survey by these different age groups of lawyers offers two possible interpretations:

- The primacy of the concerns of these different age cohorts of lawyers is different; or
- The primacy of these retirement-related concerns change as we get closer to retirement age.

The heightened financial concerns reported by the younger baby boom lawyers will be discussed further in the in the following section addressing this age group.

The "Number" (what lawyers believe they need to retire). Our survey of 50-and-older lawyers suggests that the amount of wealth believed to be needed in order to retire may depend in part on the size of firm one practices in.

- About 30 percent of lawyers practicing as sole practitioners or in two-lawyer firms believe they would need to accumulate over $1.5 million, and another 20 percent believe they would need to accumulate over $1 million. About 20 percent of lawyers practicing as solos or with one partner believe they would need to accumulate between $750,000–$1,000,000, and another 20 percent believe they would need less then $750,000.
- Almost 80 percent of lawyers practicing in firms with 50 or more lawyers believe they need to accumulate over $1.5 million, and another 11 percent believe they would need over $1 million in accumulated wealth to retire. Less than four percent of lawyers practicing in large firms believe that accumulated wealth of less than $1 million would be sufficient in retirement.
- Almost six out of ten male lawyers believe they would need more than $1 million in accumulated wealth. Four out of ten women lawyers believe they would need more than $1 million in accumulated wealth.
- At the time of the survey, almost 40 percent of male lawyers over 50 reported accumulated wealth of over $1 million; 25 percent reported accumulated wealth of $500,000–$1,000,000; 29 percent reported accumulated wealth of between $0-$500,000.
- At the time of the survey, 20 percent of women lawyers over 50 reported accumulated wealth of over $1 million; 25 percent reported accumulated wealth of $500,000–$1,000,000; 38 percent reported accumulated wealth of $0–$500,000.

- Male lawyers over 50 were almost three times more likely to have accumulated wealth of over $1.5 million (25%) than women lawyers (9%).

Only one-in-four lawyers reported that they had retained the services of a financial planner or advisor to help them develop a financial plan for retirement. Four-in-ten lawyers reported that they had developed a financial plan that included specific goals for retirement.

Women lawyers. The following breakdown of lawyers responding to the lawyer retirement survey reflects the increasing participation of women lawyers in the legal profession with each succeeding decade.

Age	Male	Female
70+	100%	0%
60–69	86%	14%
50–59	68%	32%
40–49	7%	53%

Employment settings: A higher percentage of women lawyers are working in the public and non-profit sectors than male lawyers.

Setting	Male 50+	Female 50+	Male 40–49	Female 40-49
Private practice	63%	40%	70%	41%
In-house counsel	6%	5%	5%	10%
Govt. law	14%	22%	10%	18%
Judge	4%	7%	4%	4%
Govt. non-law	1%	6%	1%	3%
Nonprofit	3%	5%	2%	9%
Private non-law	2%	0%	0%	3%
Own non-law business	1%	3%	5%	2%
Other	4%	11%	2%	9%

In retirement: Male and female lawyers 50 and older who had already retired reported enjoying most the following opportunities in retirement. It would seem that woman lawyers are enjoying themselves more.

	Males 50+	Females 50+
Increased control over my schedule	68%	87%
More time and opportunity to travel	68%	87%
More time for family and friends	62%	81%
A slower pace	62%	75%
Time for community service, volunteering, hobbies, recreation or new educational opportunities	62%	81%
More time for exercising and fitness	56%	81%
A decrease in adversarial relationships	55%	75%

Retirement concerns. Women lawyers 50 and older reported higher levels of retirement-related financial concerns.

	Males 50+	Females 50+
Projecting long-term financial needs	71%	64%
Concerns re Medicare, health insurance and long-term care insurance	57%	74%
Knowing how to invest for and in retirement	30%	39%
Concerns you won't be able to afford to retire	29%	39%
Living without a paycheck / monthly draw	27%	31%
Concerns that you will struggle to make ends meet	26%	36%
Concerns re continued existence of Social Security	23%	36%

New chapter. Almost 80 percent of women lawyers 50 and older described retirement as a time to begin a new chapter in life by being active and involved, starting new activities, and setting new goals compared to almost 70 percent of male lawyers who described retirement in this way.

Accumulated wealth. Male and female lawyers 50 and older did not differ dramatically in their beliefs of the amount of wealth they would need to accumulate for retirement, except the percentage of those who believed they needed to accumulate over $1.5 million (41% male, 23% women) and

	Males 50+	Females 50+
$100,000 or less	6%	8%
$100,001–$250,000	9%	11%
$250,001–$500,000	15%	23%
$500,001–$750,000	14%	17%
$750,001–$1,000.000	12%	13%
$1,000,001–$1,500,000	15%	12%
Over $1,500,000	26%	9%
Don't know	4%	7%

those that weren't sure how much they needed to accumulate (11% male, 25% women).

There were reported differences in the amount of wealth male and female lawyers 50 and older had actually accumulated for retirement.

Health care coverage. Women typically out-live men. Women lawyers 50 and older were much less confident than male lawyers 50 and older that health care coverage during retirement would adequately meet their needs.

Anticipate that health care coverage during retirement will adequately meet needs	Male	Female
Yes	43%	23%
No	13%	18%
Not sure	44%	59%

Protecting client's interests in case of disability. One cause for concern raised by the survey was that about 80 percent of sole practitioners report that they have not made any arrangements with another attorney to cover their practice if they are temporarily unable to practice due to disability or extended absence, or to close their practice due to permanent disability or death.

Who's Enjoying Practicing Law?

Over the past 20 years, much has been written about the high levels of dissatisfaction and distress amongst lawyers. Much less has been written about lawyers who enjoy the practice of law and the aspects of practice they find most satisfying.

As an attorney-counselor with the Oregon Attorney Assistance Program (OAAP), I must say that satisfied lawyers typically don't call and schedule appointments to confide how happy they are practicing law. Still, the OAAP wanted to get a sense of how satisfied Oregon lawyers are practicing law today, so we created a survey. In February, 2007, the OAAP sent a broadcast e-mail to all 9,625 active members of the Oregon State Bar, inviting them to complete a Lawyer Satisfaction Survey. Approximately 1,500 Oregon lawyers completed the survey over a two-week period, giving it a confidence level (the level of certainty that the survey results are within the margin of error) of 95%, +/−3%.

The following are some of the preliminary results:

- Almost 9 out of 10 who responded are working full-time, about two-thirds work in private practice, with about one-third practicing as sole practitioners or with one other lawyer. Almost 60 percent are male, and 40 percent are female. Over half are between the ages of 40 and 59 and well established in their careers.
- Two-thirds of the lawyers surveyed had not been exposed to what the day-to-day life of a lawyer was like before enrolling and attending law school. This finding confirms our experience as attorney-counselors that most lawyers don"t have realistic expectations for law practice when they enroll in law school and embark on a law career.

So what motivates lawyers to go to law school? The top three reasons lawyers cited are:

	% of respondents
Desire for intellectual stimulation	38%
Interest in the subject matter	38%
Desire to make a difference	32%

A majority of Oregon lawyers are satisfied. Seventy percent of Oregon lawyers surveyed report being either very satisfied (26 percent) or satisfied (44 percent) practicing law; 12 percent are neutral, 14 percent report being somewhat dissatisfied; and only five percent report being very dissatisfied practicing law. These satisfied and very satisfied Oregon lawyers report that what they enjoy the most about practicing law is:

The intellectual stimulation/challenge	81%
Counseling/advising clients	56%
Feeling that they are making a difference	54%
The subject matter of their practice area	50%

Most lawyers do highly value intellectual stimulation and intellectual challenge. This survey confirms that the thirst for intellectual stimulation is a primary motivator in the decision to go to law school, and that is the most frequently cited aspect of practicing law that lawyers report enjoying most.

In the Lawyer Retirement Survey conducted by the OAAP in 2006, the loss of intellectual stimulation was the personal concern that lawyers most frequently cited when contemplating retirement. The percentage of lawyers who reported being either very satisfied or satisfied practicing law did vary by employment setting:

Private practice	69%
Corporate counsel	72%
Government	75%
Judge/hearings officer	82%
Law school faculty	100%
Legal aid	88%
Non-legal	30%
Other	59%

Other findings from the survey:

• Eighty-seven percent of the lawyers surveyed agreed with the statement:
"The role I play and the work I do as a lawyer is consistent with my values, beliefs and who I am when I am not practicing law."

• Two-thirds of the lawyers reported that they were either very satisfied (22 percent) or somewhat satisfied (41 percent) with the income they were earning practicing law; 10 percent were neutral; 18 percent were somewhat dissatisfied; and 9 percent were very dissatisfied.

• The lawyers identified that what best helps them manage the stress of practicing law is:

Vacations/time away from the practice/hobbies	70%
Exercise, sports, and/or outdoor activities	66%
Relationships with and the support of family and friends	67%
Relationships with and the support of other lawyers	34%

The top three aspects of practicing law that lawyers find most dissatisfying are:

Time pressure/workload	54%
Concerns about making mistakes	48%
Adversarial nature of practice	42%

These three factors were the three most frequently cited sources of dissatisfaction amongst lawyers, although their rank ordering changed depending on such factors as age, gender, and practice setting. When asked, *"Knowing what you know now, if you had it to do over, would you become a lawyer?"*, 70 percent said they would, 30 percent said they would not.

One survey finding that is a continued cause for concern is that almost one-out-of-five lawyers reported that either alcohol (11 percent) or drugs prescribed by their physician (seven percent) best helped them manage the stress of practice. In addition, several lawyers indicated that marijuana was what best helped them manage the stress of practice. Practicing law continues to be a high-stress profession. Lawyers who rely on alcohol and/or drugs to manage that stress remain personally, medically and professionally at-risk.

One alarming finding of the survey is the confirmation of the dramatically increasing student debt load of lawyers graduating from law school over the past 15 years. The following table shows the total educational debt (unadjusted for inflation) that the different age groups of lawyers report carrying on graduating from law school:

	70 and older	60-69	50-59	40-49	30-39	20-29
$ 0	94%	47%	27%	11%	7%	5%
1-5000	6%	20%	11%	3%	1%	2%
5001-25,000		23%	41%	32%	8%	4%
25,001-50,000		9%	10%	24%	16%	9%
50,001-100,000		1%	10%	23%	48%	45%
100,001-150,000		1%	7%	17%	23%	
Over 150,000				3%	12%	

Not surprisingly, as student debt load increases, lawyer satisfaction decreases with the income they earn from practicing law. The Chicago Lawyers Study (Heinz,Nelson,Laumann, and Sadefur, 2005) found that, in the profession as a whole, the level of satisfaction is highly correlated with the lawyers' incomes. If this trend continues, lawyers carrying high debt loads are likely to experience decreased job satisfaction in practicing law.

Caring for Your Parents

When my parents were in their late 70's, I helped them move from their home to an assisted-living complex near my home. Even with some outside care-giving, my dad's declining health was exceeding my mom's capacity to provide the level of care that he needed at home. At the time that I helped my parents make this move and took on care-giving responsibilities for them, my two daughters were ages two and seven. Suddenly, at age 41, I had become a member of the *sandwich generation*, the generation simultaneously caring for dependent children and dependent parents or elderly family members. In the years leading up to…and including…our retirement years, many of us will be assuming care-giving responsibilities for an aging parent, family member, spouse or friend.

- Nearly one-in-four U.S. households and more than 50 million people in the U.S. provide care for a chronically ill, disabled or aged family member or friend in any given year.
- Forty percent of people age 55 and older, and about half of those age 55 to 64, spent time caring for family members in 2002.
- Thirty-five percent of care-givers are age 75 or older[1]
- Spouses account for 9 out of 10 primary care-givers of married adults with disabilities. Adult children (and children-in-law) account for nearly 8 out of 10 primary care-givers serving unmarried older people.
- The average length of time care-givers spent providing care for a family member over the age of 50 was about 8 years with approximately one third of care-givers providing care for 10 years or more.

Assuming a care-giver role can impact your attempt to plan for retirement and your experiences and choices in retirement, both financially and otherwise.

In an ideal world, each of us would be able to anticipate the care-giving needs of aging parents and family members, as well as our own, and proactively plan and make arrangements that protected everyone concerned. In my experience and those of others I have observed, one doesn't often have the opportunity to plan and prepare methodically before assuming care-giving

People who don't prepare to care for their sick and aging parents could fall victim to what economists call "negative inheritance." It's when costs for caring for their relatives outstrip any gifts or bequests they might receive in return. And where most Americans see a family obligation to care for aging parents, a growing number of financial advisors see lurking risks, analogous to those carried by an asset class like commodities futures, that can destroy their clients' financial plans. While advisers say planning far ahead can pre-empt much of the emotional and financial duress that caring for a sick and aging parent entails, the most crucial—and also most-elusive—ingredient is proactive family discussion. —*Wall Street Journal*

responsibilities. Typically, a loved one's need for assistance is triggered by an illness or life event resulting in a sudden decline. Some of us will directly assist a parent or family member with activities of daily living. Others will assist by arranging for professional care-giving assistance, assuming responsibilities for managing a parent or family member's financial affairs and/or providing financial assistance, or assisting with their transportation needs. And then there will be some of us who will face the additional challenge of attempting to assist with the care-giving needs of a parent or family member from a distance.

- Two-thirds of individuals providing care to an elderly family member also work.
- Forty-one percent of those providing care for an elderly family member have children under 18 at home they are also caring for.
- Juggling care-giving, parenting and professional responsibilities requires flexibility and support at work. You are not going to be able to perform at the same level or meet the same level of expectations that you would if you did not have these care-giving responsibilities.

If you decide to become the care-giver, plan from the beginning to take care of yourself:

- Learn about aging and the illnesses and impairments of the impaired care recipient.
- Base care-giving decisions on the realistic needs of everyone, not on emotions or guilt feelings.
- Deal with today and plan for tomorrow.
- Accept help. Tell others how they can help. Be honest, specific and appreciative.
- Accept your feelings without guilt.

- Forgive yourself for mistakes and outbursts, and forget them.
- Maintain your own friendships and activities.
- Take care of your health. To replenish your mind, body and spirit is not selfish.

Be prepared for the possibility that the need for care may exceed your most determined efforts. Alternative arrangements may become necessary. It is not uncaring, you have not failed. You may have simply advanced to another challenge.

Care-giving options. If a change in the living arrangement of the care recipient is required, several options are available depending on the care required.

Retirement complexes or communities. In retirement complexes, an aging parent or family member has their own apartment but is around others with similar interests and activity levels. These complexes may include facilities for group meals, transportation, and recreational activities. Retirement complexes are a safe alternative for those able to live independently. The cost of complexes vary depending on their location and amenities. Additional services can sometimes be added as needed with an increase in the monthly fee.

Assisted living facilities. In an assisted living facility, each resident has his/her own apartment or room with a bath and perhaps a small kitchen. Each facility offers a limited range of services for each resident. These services vary from place to place but can include dining rooms for resident meals and group activities, weekly laundry (which may or may not include personal items), house cleaning, transportation, and on-call staff to help in case of emergency. Additional services may be available for an additional fee, such as help with bathing, dressing and supervision and dispensing of medications. Rates for assisted living facilities vary greatly depending on location, amenities and services.

Adult foster homes. An alternative that should be considered if more supervision is required than can be provided in an assisted living facility. Adult foster homes are licensed by the state for no more than five residents and have round-the-clock trained personnel. Prospective residents of an adult foster home should be mobile, though some homes will accommodate wheel chairs. Nursing needs may be provided depending on the provider's skill and willingness to care for the resident with additional care-giving needs. Adult foster home care costs vary according to the area and services required, but usually cost about half the cost of a skilled nursing home and provide a more home-like environment.

Nursing homes/convalescent care centers. Skilled nursing homes and convalescent care centers offer the highest level of care for a care recipient. They may be needed as a temporary residential option when rehabilitation from an illness or injury is needed. They may also be needed as a permanent residence when an aging person's care needs require licensed nursing staff.

Guidelines for choosing a nursing home. Learn about the facilities in your area by calling your local Area Agency on Aging (AAA) or your State Long-term Care Ombudsman's office. Both of these offices have general information about each facility and your AAA may provide you with a list of facilities. Visit several facilities. Visit at mealtime to determine the quality of meals served, and in the evening and on the weekend to observe the staff-to-patient ratio. Make your first visit by appointment to interview the administrator and person in charge of resident care and to tour the facility. Make a follow-up visit, unannounced, to see if things look the same.

- Look for conditions such as the cleanliness of both the facility and the residents (glance at hair and nails), signs of activities for the residents, whether residents appear to be active and happy or asleep.
- Ask about the facility's policy regarding physical and chemical restraints.
- Ask about record keeping of nursing care and medications dispensed.
- Confirm the schedule of fees (what is included and what is not) in writing and ask to see the room where your loved one would live. Is it a pleasant room, perhaps with natural light? Can residents bring some of their own possessions?
- Listen to communication between staff and residents. Is kindness and compassion used?
- Look at the last survey of the facility.
- Talk to alert residents and family members visiting the facility.
- Ask to see the activities calendar for the month; even foster homes should have planned activities.
- Check the menus for the week; are they varied and interesting as well as nutritious? Are meals served promptly so the food is hot?
- Is the outside of the building nicely landscaped and well maintained?
- You will want to consider location. Is it close to family and friends so frequent visits can take place? What about visiting hours and parking?

In all of our planning, we sometimes forget to plan with the older person requiring care and not just for them. We forget the importance of dignity and independence. The importance of being treated with respect and dignity only increases as we get older and are experiencing some decline. We see that we are able to do less and less for ourselves and may have to depend more and more on others. Help preserve this dignity and as much independence as can safely be preserved for your elderly family member needing care and assistance.

Resources. Millions of Boomers find themselves hundreds—even thousands of miles—from their aging parents, and struggle to manage the geographic gap. Among executive and professional women, one in three are care-givers and voluntarily leave their careers for a period of time to care for their parents. Law firms are just beginning to recognize the problem, and are expanding their child-care provisions to help attorneys and staff torn between family emergencies and their jobs. But what can you do … now … to care for parents who are sick, injured, or alone? In this section, we've gathered some professional resources to help:

AARP (*aarp.org/families/caregiving*). The Tools section has several helpful articles and resources.

American Association of Daily Money Managers (*aadmm.com*). Maintains a state database of daily money managers who can pay a senior's bills, make deposits, process insurance claims, and handle other financial tasks.

CCRCdata (*CCRCdata.org*). Publishes the Complete Directory of Continuing Care Retirement Communities. Its 2006 edition listed more than 900 CCRC's. Electronic copies of the document available online for $10.

Clearinghouse For Caring From a Distance (*CFAD.org*). A private nonprofit linking caregivers with local service providers. Executive director is Nora Jean Levin, author of How to Care for Your Parents: A Practical Guide to Eldercare. Click on "Links" for an abundance of eldercare organizations.

ConsumerReports (*ConsumerReports.org*). CR's most recent investigations of assisted-living facilities and nursing homes were published in July 2005 and August 2006. According to their reports, choosing a good, safe, and affordable facility can be extremely difficult and has become problematic for seniors and their families. For more on CR's assisted-living investigation, go to their Web site and type assisted living facilities in the search box. For more on nursing homes, type in nursing home quality monitor. In both stories, take note of the state inspection survey (Form 2567), to see what it can tell you about the quality of a facility.

Eldercare Locator (*eldercare.gov*). The Eldercare Locator is the first step to finding essential services for older adults in any US community. Established in 1991, the Locator is a free service of the Administration on Aging (US Dept. of Health and Human Services). It is designed to help older adults, their families, and caregivers identify trustworthy local support resources, including meals, home care or transportation, or caregiver training.

Family Caregiver Alliance (*caregiver.org*). A San Francisco-based nonprofit that offers a range of information, including a downloadable "handbook for long-distance caregivers".

Faith in Action (*Fiavolunteers.org*). An interfaith volunteer caregiving initiative of the Robert Wood Johnson Foundation. Local FIA programs bring together volunteers from many faiths to help neighbors with long-term health needs, and who may need someone to run errands, get groceries, a ride to the doctor, or just a friendly visit. Users can search by state or zip code to find an FIA group in their area. The Robert Wood Johnston Foundation is the nation's largest philanthropic group devoted to health and health care.

HealthGrades (*HealthGrades.com*). Fee-based reports on nursing home quality. The findings are based on the same inspection data as the Medicare site, but HealthGrades' information goes back further and comes in easy-to-understand summaries.

Medicare (*medicare.gov/NHCompare/home.asp*). The most complete national resource on nursing home quality. In April, 2008, the federal agency that oversees Medicare announced plans to identify some of the most troubled nursing homes in an online database. Plans call for adding the identities of so-called Special Focus Facilities, the nursing homes that rank in the worst 5 to 10 percent for inspection results in a given state. The list will include some 130 facilities out of approximately 16,000 nursing homes in the US.

Member Of The Family (*MemberoftheFamily.net*). Offers color-coded ratings of nursing homes based on the latest federal nursing home data.

National Association for Home Care and Hospice (*nahc.org*). The NAHC is the nation's largest trade association representing the interests and concerns of home care agencies, hospices, home care aide organizations, and medical equipment suppliers. Click on "Agency Locator" for a list of home care and hospice agencies in your area.

National Association of Professional Geriatric Care Managers (*caremanager.org*). Geriatric care managers are health and human services specialists who help families care for older relatives. A PGCM may be trained in any of a number of fields related to long-term care, including, but not limited to, nursing, gerontology, social work, or psychology, with a specialized focus on issues related to aging and elder care. Click on "Find a Care Manager" to locate a care manager in your area.

National Association of Senior Move Managers (*nasmm.org*). Established in 2003,

NASMM is dedicated to assisting older adults and families with the physical and emotional demands of downsizing, relocating, or modifying their homes. The Web site provides a "Find a Senior Move Manager" in your area.

National Association of Social Workers (*socialworkers.org*). The NASW maintains a national database of licensed social workers. Click on "Find a Social Worker" on the home page. Note: Geriatric social workers help older adults navigate the continuum of care from independent living to skilled nursing care. They conduct assessments of physical, financial, social, and spiritual factors to guide older adults in determining the best living arrangements for this time in their lives. In addition to providing information and referral to local resources, social workers empower clients to access services, and monitor their progress to ensure they continue to receive the help they need.

National Center on Elder Abuse (*ncea.aoa.gov*). The National Center on Elder Abuse, a program of the U.S. Administration on Aging, serves as a national resource center for the prevention of elder mistreatment. The NCEA maintains a state resource directory of adult protective services.

National Family Caregivers Association (*thefamilycaregiver.org*). Tips and guides for family caregivers, and information on agencies and organizations that provide caregiver support.

SNAPforSeniors (*SNAPforSeniors.com*). A free online resource providing information and tools necessary to make informed decisions about senior housing. Founded in 2005, the site provides the most current database of all licensed senior housing in the U.S., as well as a growing number of independent living communities. The database lists some 65,000 licensed facilities and independent living communities. Users can search by city, state, or specific criteria such as budget and special needs.

US Government (*usa.gov/Citizen/Topics/Health/caregivers*). The federal government's database of elder care resource links.

Suggested Reading

Baby Boomers Guide to Nursing Home Care (Eric Carlson JD, Katharine Hsiao JD, 2006).

Caring For Yourself While Caring for Your Aging Parents (Berman, 2005).

Caregivers' Handbook: How to Care for Your Aging Parent Without Losing Yourself (Alexis Abramsom, 2004).

Coping With Your Difficult Older Parent: A Guide for Stressed Out Children (Lebow, 1999).

Doing the Right Thing: Taking Care of Your Elderly Parents Even if They Didn't Take Care of You (Roberta Satow, Ph.D., 2006).

Hard Questions for Adult Children and Their Aging Parents (Piver, 2004).

How to Care for Aging Parents (Morris/Butler, 2004).

Is Your Parent in Good Hands? Protecting Your Aging Parent from Financial Abuse and Neglect (Edward Carnot JD, 2003).

Taking Care of Parents Who Didn't Take Care of You: Making Peace With Aging Parents (Cade, 2002).

The Complete Elder Care Planner: Where to Start, Which Questions to Ask & How to Find Help (Loverde, 2000).

Twenty Common Nursing Home Problems, and How to Resolve Them (a 34-page booklet available online at the National Senior Citizens Law Center, *nsclc.org*).

Walking on Eggshells: Navigating the Delicate Relationship Between Adult Children and Parents (Jane Isay, 2007).

General Resources

The personal characteristics of boomer attorneys varies widely, but this much is true—they're healthier, living longer, and have no desire to slink into the sunset for a life of leisure. In fact, studies show that many plan to stay professionally active well into their 70's. Still, when boomers do begin retiring in a few years, what sort of retirement will it be? And are they doing enough to maximize their investment return? This section provides links to some of the best online calculators to explore the financial dimension of retirement.

AARP (*aarp.org*). Click on "Money" on the home page, and click again on Tools in the left-hand column. The retirement calculator might not be as fancy as some others but the results are just as productive.

CNN Money (*cnnmoney.com*). Plug in your age, your income, the amount you have, when you plan to retire, and other information. You get quick estimate of how large a nest egg you'll need and the odds of reaching it.

Employee Benefit Research Institute (*ChooseToSave.org*). This private, Washington DC-based economic research group offers Choose to Save, an online program dedicated to personal financial education. The site includes more than 100 separate online calculators, including nearly a dozen devoted to retirement.

Fidelity Investments (*fidelity.com*). Its asset-allocation feature can help you find the best mix of stocks and bonds for your retirement goals. Already retired? Use the Retirement Income Planner tool, which can reduce your chances of running out of money.

Immediate Annuities (*immediateannuities.com*). Online annuities broker Hersh Stern makes available a calculator that provides an estimate of how much an insurer will be willing to pay you (and/or your spouse) each month for the rest of your life. You supply your age, gender, and the amount you want to convert into a guaranteed stream, and the software does the rest.

Morningstar (*morningstar.com*). It can tell you whether you're eligible to contribute to a traditional IRA, a Roth IRA or both; help you decide which type to contribute to in a given year; and show you whether it makes sense to convert traditional IRA assets to a Roth.

T. Rowe Price (*troweprice.com*). Enter a few simple pieces of information and you'll get the odds that your portfolio will last throughout retirement. You can then see how tinkering with your withdrawls or investment mix might improve your chances.

Suggested Reading

How Much is Enough? Balancing Today's Needs With Tomorrow's Retirement Goals (McCurdy, 2005)

How Mutual Funds Work (Fredman and Wiles; 2nd ed., 1997)

How to Protect and Manage Your 401(k) (Elizabeth Opalka, JD/CPA; 2003)

Kiplinger's Money Smart Women: Everything You Need to Achieve a Lifetime of Financial Security (Bodner, 2006)

Kiplinger's Make Your Money Grow (Miller; 2007)

Mutual Funds for Dummies (Tyson, 3rd ed., 2006)

One Up on Wall Street: How to Use What You Already Know to Make Money in the Market (Peter Lynch, 2001)

Retirement Countdown: Take Action Now to Get the Life You Want (Shapiro, 2004)*Retire Worry Free: Money-Smart Ways to Build the Nest Egg You'll Need* (Kiplingers, 2005)

RINKS: Retired, Independent, No Kids (Mignone, 2006)

Smart and Simple Financial Strategies for Busy People (Jane Bryant Quinn, 2006)

Social Security Q&A Answer Book—Written by New York lawyer Stanley Tomkiel III, a former claims representative for the Social Security Administration. The contents are available online (*socialsecuritybenefitshandbook.com*).

Standard and Poor's Guide to Saving for Retirement (Morris, 2007).

Personal Health

American Academy of Family Physicians (*FamilyDoctor.org/men.xml*). The AAFP's consumer site allows users to search by symptoms for possible diagnosis, suggestions for self-care, and when it might be necessary to see a doctor. Offers help finding a family doctor by ZIP code.

American Heart Association (*AmericanHeart.org*). The site offers a short quiz to help determine your 10-year risk of heart attack. To find the calculator, go to the search box and type "heart attack risk assessment".

Association of Cancer Online Resources (*ACOR.org*). 159 online cancer groups work with researchers and inform patients of clinical trials, tissue banks and genetic studies.

Harvard Center for Cancer Prevention (*yourdiseaserisk.com*). According to the Wall Street Journal, the site is one of the best health-oriented sites on the Web. Users get customized information on their risk for developing 12 different cancers, as well as heart disease, stroke, diabetes, and osteoporosis. The site also generates a tailored action plan on ways to lower your risk for health problems.

HealthLine Networks (*healthline.com*). One of the top 10 health information destination sites with over 4.2 million monthly unique visitors.

Lawyers With Depression (*lawyerswithdepression.com*). Launched in 2007 by a managing partner struggling with depression, this site offers articles, podcasts, links and other resources on depression as they relate to the legal profession. Profiled in the ABA Journal (January 2008).

National Cancer Institute (*cancer.gov/bcrisktool*). Site includes a calculator that lets women calculate their risk for breast cancer.

Prostate Cancer Foundation (*prostatecancerfoundation.org*). The foundation, founded by former junk-bond king Michael Milken, funds research into prostate cancer, and provides comprehensive information on risk factors, detection and screening, diagnosis and treatment, questions to ask the doctor, and guidelines on how to live with the disease.

Revolution Health (*revolutionhealth.com/healthy-living/menshealth*). The site, a new ad-supported venture of AOL founder Steve Case, offers a home page for men that includes a treatment-rating service that lets users post their own ratings of treatments, drugs, and medical services. The Men's Health 101 section includes top men's screening tests.

TauMed (*TauMed.com*). A virtual health community where you can ask, share, interactively navigate, and search the most relevant personalized consumer health information available on the Web.

Executive Physicals. When it comes to your annual checkup, should you upgrade to first class? The answer is "yes" for more and more professionals. And they're spending a few thousand dollars for the kind of medical workup that used to be a perk mainly for CEOs. Although there's no Consumer Reports for executive health programs, the medical cognoscenti seem to agree that the institutions described here are state-of-the-art:

The West

Canyon Ranch Health Resorts (*canyonranch.com*). Locations in Tucson AZ and Lennox MA. The famed spa has had a health-and-healing component since 1979, and began offering annual physicals in 1988. It's Executive Health Program was launched in 2003, and includes a four-day agenda including consultations with doctors from the Cleveland Clinic.

Cooper Clinic (*cooperaerobics.com/clinic*).

Mayo Clinic (*mayoclinic.com*). For complete listing, see The Midwest.

Scripps Center for Executive Health (*scrippshealth.org*)—A not-for-profit, community-based health care network in San Diego that includes four acute-care hospitals on five campuses. In a single day, a multi-disciplinary team of Scripps physicians and degreed lifestyle specialists conduct a comprehensive WholePerson Examination. Test results in 24 hours, followed by a bound portfolio of test results, physicians' interpretations and recommendations, and educational materials.

Stanford (*execmd.com*).

Straub Clinic (*straubhealth.com*).

UC Los Angeles (*exec@mednet.ucla.edu*).

The Midwest

Cleveland Clinic (*clevelandclinic.org/executivehealth*).

Mayo Clinic (*mayoclinic.com*). The one-day Executive Examination program includes a comprehensive medical history and physical exam by a clinic specialist in internal medicine and referrals to sub-specialists; screening tests for early detection of cancer, heart disease and other serious problems; cardiovascular fitness evaluation; review and update of medications and immunizations; a lifestyle assessment regarding nutrition, stress management, alcohol, tobacco, personal safety and other indicators of disease risk. Test results on the day of the examination. Locations in Minnesota, Arizona, and Florida.

Northwestern Memorial Hospital (*centerforpartnershipmedicine.com*).

The Northeast

Canyon Ranch Health Resorts (*canyonranch.com*). For complete listing, see The West.

Johns Hopkins Executive Health (*hopkinsmedicine.org*). Comprehensive medical assessment and personalized preventive strategies for busy individuals. Located in Baltimore MD. Examinations, testing, and summation are conducted in a single day, with a possible second day if additional studies are required.

Lahey Clinic (*lahey.org/medical/executivehealth/index_exechealth.asp*).

The South

Duke University Executive Health Program (*dukeexechealth.org*). Located in Durham NC. Offers a comprehensive, one-day health assessment at the university's full-service medical facility with on-site labs and current technologies.

Emory (*executive.health@emoryhealthcare.org*).

Greenbrier Clinic (*greenbrierclinic.com*). Located at Greenbrier Resort in White Sulphur Springs WVA, the clinic has offered an executive health program since

1948. It has a CT scanner for diagnosing coronary disease, a dozen medical professionals with specialties from coronary care to gastroenterology, and its own lab to process tests.

Mayo Clinic (*mayoclinic.com*). For full listing, see The Midwest.

Guide to Doctors

American Academy of Family Physicians (*FamilyDoctor.org*). The AAFP's consumer site allows users to search by symptoms for possible diagnosis, suggestions for self-care, and when it might be necessary to see a doctor. Offers help finding a family doctor by zip code.

American Medical Association (*AMA-assn.org*). The AMA's DoctorFinder includes virtually every one the nearly 700,000 licensed physicians in the US. An alphabetical listing (Allergy to Urology) lets you search by state and/or zip code for a specialist near you. The same database provides professional information on each one of their members.

American Board of Medical Specialties (*ABMS.org*). The organization that assists 24 approved medical specialty boards in the development and use of standards in the ongoing evaluation and certification of physicians. Click on the link that asks, "*Is Your Doctor Certified?*" A quick registration lets users check whether a specialist is "board-certified". See accompanying article below.

Federation of State Medical Boards (*DocInfo.org*). From this site, the public can access disciplinary, education, licensure, and location information about physicians and physician assistants licensed in the US. Data from some 70 medical boards and the Department of Health/Human Services is updated at least monthly; sometimes daily and weekly. Whenever disciplinary information exists, the report identifies the state medical board or licensing agency that initiated the action, what type of disciplinary action was taken, and the date and basis or reason(s) for the action. The FSMB Physician Profile does not include information on medical malpractice settlements or claims. Registration required; $10 per doctor inquiry. To be included in the data bank, a disciplinary action must be a matter of public record or be legally releasable by state medical boards and other licensing authorities.

Guide to Hospitals

Health Grades (*healthgrades.com*). A private company that rates more than 5,000 hospitals on 32 conditions and procedures, from appendectomies to heart valve-replacement surgery. Much of the information is available at no cost, and searchable by state, procedure, and other criteria. More elaborate reports available for $18.

Hospital Compare (*hospitalcompare.hhs.gov*). According to the Wall Street Journal, Hospital Compare is the best-known source for hospital data. The site was jointly established by the federal Centers for Medicare and Medicaid Services, and hospitals and other groups. Users searching by city, state or other criteria, can look up a variety of statistics comparing more than 5,000 hospitals against one another, and to state and federal averages.

Joint Commission (*qualitycheck.org*). An independent nonprofit that accredits most of the hospitals in the US. Users can search by hospital, location or type of service, and get reports on hospital practices that draw on the commission's inspections of facilities it accredits.

Leapfrog Group (*leapfroggroup.org*). A not-for-profit consortium of big health-care buyers (e.g., General Motors) provides hospital ratings that are available to the public. The site collects some data of its own, and analyzes 30 different practices at about 1,300 hospitals.

Qualitycheck (*qualitycheck.org*). Established by the independent nonprofit group that accredits most US hospitals, this site lets you search by hospital, location, or type of service, and get reports on the hospital practices used for accreditation.

Futures & Options

As millions of people in their 50s and 60s leave the workplace, many will search for encore careers, resulting in a huge transformation in the public and nonprofit sectors. What's an encore career? It's when someone can earn income, find new meaning, and use accumulated experience in ways that have a positive impact on society. And it just may represent the best use of the accumulated experience of the baby-boom population. In this section, we've gathered a few ways you might be interested in a give-back career of your own:

AARP & ABA (*abanet.org/secondseason*). AARP's Legal Counsel for the Elderly has joined forces with the American Bar Association to recruit retired lawyers for pro bono activities around the country.

BoardAssist (*Boardassist.org*). Matches potential board members with non-profits in need, using a "personal approach similar to corporate recruiters".

BoardnetUSA (*BoardnetUSA.org*). A New York City-based nonprofit that allows users to search online through more than 2,000 nonprofits nationwide and sort them by area of interest and needed skills.

CivicVentures (*CivicVentures.org*). Founded in the late 1990s, Civic Ventures is about helping redefine the second half of life as a source of social and individual renewal. The organization has developed an Experience Corps, a national service program for Americans over 55 who want to tutor and mentor kids in under-served schools. Now in 14 cities. Their free guide to public service jobs (The Boomers' Guide to Good Work: An Introduction to Jobs That Make a Difference) is available online.

Dinosaur-Exchange (*dinosauer-exchange.com*). Short- and long-term job opportunities for what it calls "dinosauers" (retirees with experience), including consultant and management positions all over the world, some in developing countries.

ExecutiveCorps (*ExecutiveCorps.org*). Award-winning program engaging people over age 55 in meeting their community's greatest challenges. In nearly two dozen cities across the country, more than 2,000 members tutor and mentor elementary school students struggling to learn to read. Most members serve five to15 hours a week. Independent research shows that Experience Corps boosts student academic performance, helps schools and youth-serving organizations become more successful, and enhances the well-being of the older adults in the process.

Global Volunteers (*globalvolunteers.org*). A non-governmental organization that mobilizes approximately 150 service learning teams year-round to work in 18 countries.

National Pro Bono Opportunities Guide (*volunteerforprobono.org*). The online guide, co-sponsored by the ABA and Pro Bono Net, contains listings of more than 1,100 service organizations nationwide that need volunteer lawyers to represent individuals on various legal matters. Users can search the directory by region, practice area, and client base, as well as whether CLE credits are available for any aspect of particular assignments.

RetiredBrains (*RetiredBrains.com*). Connects retiring or retired workers with employers and provides information on charitable organizations and nonprofits looking for senior volunteers. Lists between 20,000 and 30,000 open positions that are refreshed several times a week.

Senior Corps (*seniorcorps.org*). Opportunities to represent neglected and abused children as a guardian ad litem.

Travel

Accommodation Search Engine (*ase.net*). A database with more than 150,000 hotels, motels, inns, B&B's, and holiday rentals worldwide. Established in 1995.

Home Away From Home (*homeaway.com*). Thousands of vacation rentals (cabins, cottages, castles, condos, and villas) in 90 countries. Users are put in direct contact with the property owner or agent to answer specific questions.

Leading Hotels of the World (*lhw.com*). A New York-based marketing group for luxury hotels maintains a network of 430 five-star hotels, resorts, and spas in 80 countries. As a reflection of how the Euro continues to inflate the cost of European vacations for Americans, LHW recently introduced guaranteed dollar rates at nearly 60 hotels throughout Europe. To get the rates, customers must call Leading Hotels at (800) 223-6800 and ask for discount code L09, and pay in full when booking.

LuxuryLink (*luxurylink.com*). Launched in 1997, LuxuryLink appeals to affluent travelers who have the option to bid on or immediately purchase world-class getaways. No membership fee. According to Conde Nast's Traveler Magazine, "Many travel sites claim to offer discounts on luxury hotels, but we've found that Luxury Link delivers the best values on the greatest array of upscale properties worldwide". Note: Travelers must be flexible about travel dates. You pick the dates from a limited range only after you pay.

WorldHotels (*worldhotels.com*). A marketing and distribution group for independent leisure and business hotels, is offering a "Stay in Europe, Pay in Dollars" deal at more than 50 of its hotels that allow travelers to pay the listed euro rate in dollars. Bookings must be made from the US by calling (800) 223-5652.

Air Ambulance/Medical Assist

Accessible Journey (*disabilitytravel.com*). For frail or disabled travelers. Offers organized group tours and cruises, concierge service, and companions for travel. Companion wages by the week plus travel expenses.

AIG Travel Guard (*travelguard.com*). It's annual MedEvac plan is designed for travelers but works for students, too. It includes both medical transportation and secondary medical insurance that pays costs not covered by members' primary health policy.

American Express (*americanexpress.com*). Platinum members have medical repatriation benefits; in 2007 the company upgraded its evacuation benefit to return members to a hospital near their home.

Air Ambulance Card (*airambulancecard.com*). If you are hospitalized while traveling anywhere in the world the company agrees to fly you home to the hospital of your choice as long as a physician agrees to admit you. Individual memberships; age limit 74.

Executive Care Service (*execcareservices.com*). Private duty nursing, concierge service, air transportation, ambulatory escort service. Types of nurses—RN. Daily fee plus travel expenses.

HTHWorldwide (*HTHWorldwide.com*). A US-based travel insurance company helping world travelers gain access to quality healthcare services around the globe. For about $4 to $6 a day, HTH Worldwide includes medical evacuation and cashless access to its worldwide network of 4,000 English-speaking doctors and 750 hospitals.

Inn-House Doctor (*inn-housedoctor.com*). Established in 1991, the company provides 24/7 physician services to hotel guests in Washington DC, Philadelphia, Boston, Chicago, Houston, Dallas, Phoenix, Las Vegas.

International Association for Medical Assistance (*iamat.org*). The New York-based nonprofit has a database of English-speaking physicians in 125 countries. The network includes general practitioners and specialists as well as hospitals and clinics. Check out the organization's Web site for useful medical information for travel.

International SOS (*internationalsos.com*). Offers a 10-day program that includes medical assistance, evacuation, short-term insurance, and access to its 28 global alarm centers. Annual memberships available.

Medjet Assist (*MedjetAssist.com*). Medical evacuation on demand from almost any U.S. or international destination at your request. Annual membership $225 (individual)/$350 (family). Slightly higher for individuals 75 or over. AARP discount available.

Trip Nurse (*tripnurse.com*). Provides private duty nursing, concierge service, and air transportation. Includes registered nurses, licensed practical nurses, and certified nursing assistants. Daily fee plus travel expenses.

World Access (*worldaccess.com*). A travel insurance company whose Annual Med Evac plan includes medical repatriation for three months, six months or 12 months.

Travel Reviews

Epinions (*Epinions.com*). Unbiased reviews (some cranky, most helpful) from real people. Go to the toolbar and click on Travel to find literally thousands of personal observations about hotels, resorts, cruises, airlines, ski resorts, parks, and tour operators. The huge database is broken out by state, region, and country.

Fodors (*Fodors.com*). The user-generated reviews (mostly hotels and restaurants) are generally more helpful than the Fodor's reviews.

Gusto (*Gusto.com*). This site covers hotels around the world, and has an audience that's 70 percent female with an average age of 39.

HotelShark (*HotelShark.com*). Provides a composite summary of reviews in a Zagat-like approach.

IgoUgo (*IgoUgo.com*). The site, owned by the same company that operates Travelocity, has 350,000 members; registration required.

LonelyPlanet (*LonelyPlanet.com/thorntree*). The highly regarded British travel book publisher offers opinions and practical information posted by hardcore travelers.

My Travel Guide (*mytravelguide.com*). Launched in 2000, MyTravelGuide draws from more than a million reviews from around the world. Make a big pot of coffee and be prepared to spend a little time reading "about all things travel".

Professional Travel Guide (*ProfessionalTravelGuide.com*). Destination, hotel and cruise reviews filed by several hundred travel journalists.

Travelistic (*travelistic.com*). A compilation of travel videos posted by travelers worldwide. At last count, there were more than 4,000 video posts.

TripAdvisor (*TripAdvisor.com*). Owned by Expedia, TripAdvisor is the most comprehensive listing of professional and amateur reviews of hotels worldwide. In the words of the Wall Street Journal, this site is "a first stop for travel planning". Now in its eighth year, nearly 30 million visitors a month drop by to read what other users have to say about where to stay, eat, and play around the world. Click on the Forums for some of the 10 million user-generated reviews, blogs and videos.

Zoomandgo (*zoomandgo.com*). The site, whose tagline is live it, rate it, shoot it, share it, gathers reviews and video clips of hotels and vacations around the world.

Footnotes

Chapter 1

1. Lydia Bronte, *The Longevity Factor: The New Reality of Long Careers and How It Can Lead to Richer Lives* (1994) p. 317.

Chapter 2

1. Richard P. Johnson, *The New Retirement* (2001) p. 66.
2. Christine Price, Retirement for Women: The Impact of Employment, *Journal of Women and Aging*, 14(3-4) (2002) 41-57.
3. Richard W. Johnson, "Do Spouses Coordinate Their Retirement Decisions?" and Phyllis Moen, Jungmeen Kim and Heather Hofmeister, "*Couples' Work and Psychological Well-Being in Older Adults,*" Social Psychology Quarterly 64 no.1 (2001): 55-71.
4. Phyllis Moen, Jungeem Kim, and Heather Hofmeister, "*Couples' Work/Retirement Transitions, Gender, and Marital Quality,*" Social Psychology Quarterly 64 no.1 (2001): 55-71.
5. Glen Ruffenach, "*Too Much Togetherness?*" The Wall Street Journal, February 14, 2005: sec.R, p. 5
6. *Ibid.* sec. R p.5
7. Ralph Warner, *Get A Life: You don't need a million to retire well* (3rd edition 2001) 112.
8. Thomas Glass, et al. August, 1999. "*Population-Based Study of Social and Productive Activities as Predictors of Survival Among Elderly Americans*", 478-83.
9. Ralph Warner, *Get A Life,* 110-111.
10. Thomas Glass, et al. August, 1999, 478-83.
11. Marc Freedman, *Prime Time: How Baby Boomers Will Revolutionize Retirement and Transform America* (1999) 30.
12. MetLife Foundation / Civic Ventures, *New Face of Work Survey.*
13. Marc Freedman, Prime Time, 30-31.
14. Ibid, 22.

Chapter 3

1. *Can We Talk? The 10 Most Important Questions You and Your Spouse Should Talk About* (Wall Street Journal, Sept. 22, 2007).

Chapter 5

1. Christine Gorman, *"Repairing The Damage,"* Time, February 5, 2001, 56.
2. Ibid, 56.
3. Guy McKhann, M.D. and Marilyn Albert, Ph.D, *Keep Your Brain Young: The Complete Guide to Physical and Emotional Health and Longevity,* (2002), 18.
4. Ibid, 11-12.
5. Ralph Warner, *Get A Life,* 31.
6. Ibid, 30.
7. Archives of Neurology, March 2001; and The Human Brain.
8. Christine Gorman, *"Repairing The Damage,"* 57.
9. Helen Harkness, *Don't Stop the Career Clock,* 57.
10. Andrew Scharlach and Barrie Robinson, *Curriculum Module on The Aging Process,* UC Berkeley, December, 1999, *garnet.berkeley.edu/aging/ModuleProcess.html.*
11. Guy McKhann, M.D. and Marilyn Albert, Ph.D, *Keep Your Brain Young,* 34.
12. Harvard Medical School Special Report, Stress Control, 11.
13. Guy McKhann, M.D. and Marilyn Albert, Ph.D, *Keep Your Brain Young,* 40.

Mike Long, JD/MSW. Private legal practice, 1985 to 1990 in Portland, Oregon. After completing a Masters in Social Work in 1991, Long worked in several mental health settings before joining the Oregon Attorney Assistance Program (OAAP) in 1994. As an attorney-counselor for the OAAP, Long counsels and assists lawyers struggling with a broad spectrum of challenges and concerns. Since 2001, he has been responsible for developing the retirement planning assistance and programming offered by the OAAP.

John Clyde, CFP. A former college and university educator, Clyde became very interested in the field of financial and retirement planning in his early 50's, and retired from education to study for, and to become, a certified financial planner. This career move opened up new vistas, not only as a successful financial consultant, but as a co-developer of retirement workshops for thousands of state employees in Oregon, Idaho, and Washington. This "encore" career has lasted Clyde nearly 20 years, and continues to offer new opportunities, especially in community volunteer activities.

Pat Funk. Raised in the Midwest, Pat has been a saver from day one. But it was while she was in sales and management, at IBM and Data General, that she challenged herself to become financially independent by age 40. And she did, with a few years to spare, by immersing herself in financial planning (including course work for the Certified Financial Planner designation). Thereafter, Pat established several other financial benchmarks—she owned and operated a Colorado bed & breakfast, optimized her real estate investments by becoming a realtor, became a lecturer for a retirement planning firm, and then expanded her financial knowledge base by studying for and passing the Series 7 Investment, Health & Life Insurance, and Investment Advisory licensing tests. Pat now conducts seminars to assist legal professionals to prepare for their own financial transition into retirement.

ACKNOWLEDGMENTS

This book was a collaborative effort in every sense of the word; the product of three authors, all the lawyers who agreed to be interviewed, and all of the lawyers who participated in our retirement workshops whose questions, concerns, and feedback helped us shape this work. We would also like to acknowledge the special contributions of the following individuals who generously took the time to contribute their special expertise and perspectives on subjects essential to this book:

Steve Dotty (on health insurance); Peggy Olson (on Medicare); Mary Osborne (on long-term care insurance), Carol Kanarek (on career counseling), Stephen Gallagher (on the retention of boomer leadership and expertise), Edward Poll (on the purchase and sale of law practices); Mark Bassingthwaighte (on malpractice "tail" coverage); Barbara Fishleder and the Oregon State Bar Professional Liability Fund (for permission to reprint portions of the *Planning Ahead* guide), Mary Silverberg (for her poignant essay in Chapter 8), and to the following individuals for their review and feedback of specific sections: The Silver Oak Advisory Group's Deborah Thomas and Steve Hewitt, (for reviewing *The Financial Planner* and *The Assets and Investments Planner*), and in particular for Steve's input regarding withdrawal strategies, and Kelly Reece and David Avison (for reviewing *The Estate Planner*).

Acknowledgments from Mike Long:

If John Clyde, one of my co-authors, had not enthusiastically agreed to join with me and to contribute his financial and retirement planning expertise and experience, this book simply would not have been written. And to Pat Funk, *presenter extraordinaire* of our lawyer retirement workshops, who was recruited to join a work-in-progress: I appreciate all her efforts to infuse the book with her expertise and passion for investing and financial & retirement planning.

I am also grateful…

…To the Oregon State Bar Professional Liability Fund, with which I've had the good fortune to work for the past 15 years, for their commitment to the work of the Oregon Attorney Assistance Program (OAAP) and their commitment to helping lawyers become more proactive in their planning for retirement and unexpected disability and death;

…To Barbara Fishleder, executive director of the OAAP, for her unwavering professional and personal support these past 15 years.

…To my colleagues at the OAAP, Michael Sweeney, Shari Gregory, Meloney Crawford-Chadwick, and Doug Querin, for holding down the fort when I took time off to write, and for their interest in the book;

…To Liisa Heard, for mediating all the technical disputes that arose between me and my computer, and for even trying her hand at graphic design.

…To my fellow lawyer assistance program directors and staff in this country and Canada for their support and interest for this project;

…To Barbara Harper, director of the Washington State Bar Lawyer Assistance Program, a pioneer in the Lawyer Assistance community for advocating that bar associations and LAPs need to assist lawyers with issues of aging, and in planning for their ultimate transition from practice. I hope she can see some of her vision reflected in this book.

…To my family, Theresa, Sarah, and Becca, with my most sincere appreciation for all their efforts to accept and tolerate all the time and energy this project has absorbed over the past three years. Good news; I will not be writing a sequel.

…To Steve Malm, Ken Hill, and Sue Shellenbarger, for the advice and guidance they shared with me at the beginning of this project.

…Lastly, I would like to dedicate my contributions to this book to my Dad, whose uncompromising work ethic and honesty helped shape my values, and whose career setbacks and disappointments motivated me to chart my own course through the world of work.

Acknowledgments from John Clyde:

Lawyers at Midlife benefits from more than 25 years effort and experience in studying the life transition we commonly call retirement. The concept originated with an established retirement workshop and workbook developed by Bettye Gill and myself for public employees in the Pacific Northwest. Later, when the program was opened to include the Oregon legal community, its content was greatly expanded, modified, and updated by my co-authors, Mike Long, Esq., and retirement planner Pat Funk. But of all the acknowledgments, I particularly wish to thank my wife for her loyal support and constructive thought. As is often the case, two heads are better than one.

NOTES

NOTES

Introducing
www.LawyerAvenue.com

Where legal meets personal

Lawyer Avenue reflects the growing trend between the professional and the personal. And as legal publishers, we want to keep you informed about useful products and services that meet the needs of career, practice AND family.
So, wherever you practice law, this new site is for you…and yours.

Lawyer Avenue has great shopping opportunities for the entire legal community, and is an "information concierge" in the following areas:

Career

A national roster of JD/career consultants.
Where to find career consultants for new law grads.
The latest Job Bank links.
Take My Advice (career essays).
…and more.

Practice

Where to find practice/performance coaches.
Where to find legal marketing support.
Where to find virtual legal assistants.
How and where to outsource legal work.

Self & Family

Where to find the best residential treatment centers.
Where to find the best doctors & hospitals.
Where parents can find college admissions experts.
Where families can find elder care support

Travel

Getting there
Travel planning
Where to eat, where to stay

www.LawyerAvenue.com—Where legal meets personal